Iran's Nuclear Diplomacy

CW01475179

This book examines the dynamics of relations and the substance of the negotiations between the international community and Iran over the latter's nuclear programme.

Iran's nuclear programme and the alleged threat to international peace and security remains one of the most important issues in the United States, as well as in European foreign affairs. In the US, Iran has dominated the political discourse for over three decades and Europe has spent considerable political capital in finding a diplomatic solution to Iran's nuclear ambitions. While relations between both states remain subject to mutual hostility, the EU remains a channel of communication and since 2003 has maintained a multilateral negotiation framework.

By and large, the narrative on nuclear negotiations is dominated by constructivist and realist literature, portraying relations between the US and Iran in ideological terms as a prolonged struggle for regional influence. Embedded within conflict resolution and diplomatic theory, this work attempts to bridge this gap. Drawing upon primary documents and interviews, the text examines negotiation behaviour and strategies and tools of statecraft, as well as analysing technical aspects of initiatives concerning the nuclear programme.

This book will be of much interest to students of nuclear proliferation, international diplomacy, Middle Eastern politics, security studies and IR in general.

Bernd Kaussler is Associate Professor of Political Science at James Madison University, USA. He is also Associate Fellow at the Institute for Iranian Studies at the University of St Andrews, UK.

G5GH7

Routledge New Diplomacy Studies
Series Editors:
Corneliu Bjola
University of Oxford
and
Markus Kornprobst
Diplomatic Academy of Vienna

This new series will publish theoretically challenging and empirically author-itative studies of the traditions, functions, paradigms and institutions of modern diplomacy. Taking a comparative approach, the New Diplomacy Studies series aims to advance research on international diplomacy, publishing innovative accounts of how 'old' and 'new' diplomats help steer international conduct between anarchy and hegemony, handle demands for international stability vs international justice, facilitate transitions between international orders, and address global governance challenges. Dedicated to the exchange of different scholarly perspectives, the series aims to be a forum for inter-paradigm and inter-disciplinary debates, and an opportunity for dialogue between scholars and practitioners.

New Public Diplomacy in the 21st Century
A comparative study of policy and practice
James Pamment

Global Cities, Governance and Diplomacy
The urban link
Michele Acuto

Iran's Nuclear Diplomacy
Power politics and conflict resolution
Bernd Kaussler

Iran's Nuclear Diplomacy

Power politics and conflict resolution

Bernd Kaussler

Routledge
Taylor & Francis Group

LONDON AND NEW YORK

First published 2014
by Routledge
2 Park Square, Milton Park, Abingdon, Oxfordshire OX14 4RN

Simultaneously published in the USA and Canada
by Routledge
711 Third Avenue, New York, NY 10017

First issued in paperback 2014

Routledge is an imprint of the Taylor and Francis Group, an informa business

British Library Cataloguing in Publication Data
A catalogue record for this book is available from the British Library

Library of Congress Cataloging-in-Publication Data
Kaussler, Bernd.
Iran's nuclear diplomacy : power politics and conflict resolution /
Bernd Kaussler.
    pages cm. – (Routledge new diplomacy studies)
    Includes bibliographical references and index.
    1. Nuclear weapons–Iran. 2. Iran–Foreign relations. I. Title.
    U264.5.I7K38 2013
    355.02'170955–dc23   2012050464

ISBN 978-0-415-64385-6 (hbk)
ISBN 978-1-138-90087-5 (pbk)
ISBN 978-0-203-07987-4 (ebk)

Typeset in Times
by Wearset Ltd, Boldon, Tyne and Wear

Thank you Diar, Soraya, Shirin and Dariush for putting up with me.

Contents

Foreword

Few international challenges seem quite as intractable as the continuing dispute between Iran and the international community – represented in this case by the permanent members of the UN Security Council (UNSC) and Germany – over the development and, more importantly, the direction of Iran's nuclear programme. Begun under the late Shah, Iran's civilian nuclear programme was initially intended to provide Iran with both high-end research expertise and a means to diversify its energy sources. At the time nuclear power was regarded as the energy source of the future and a technology no aspiring Great Power could ignore. It was, in sum, always as much a matter of prestige as an economic necessity and European powers in particular competed to satisfy the Shah's yearning for this particular advanced technology. Even so, anxieties persisted as to the Shah's real intentions, and despite the warm relations between Iran and the United States, American governments – both Republican and Democrat – were wary of providing Iran with the technology to enrich uranium, which, many concluded, would provide too great a temptation towards weaponization and proliferation – the Shah had always looked rather warily at developments in South Asia. In this respect, the United States' position has been remarkably consistent. European powers were somewhat more sanguine, partly justifying their growing participation in the programme by arguing that Iran's development of enrichment technology could be delayed but not ultimately prevented.

Ironically, the onset of the Islamic Revolution in 1979 provided an immediate solution to the nuclear conundrum as the programme was shut down on the pretext that it symbolized the Western penetration of Iran and simply served to recycle oil money. Views were soon to change with the traumatic experience of the Iran–Iraq war, the fears of isolation this engendered, as well as anxieties about Iraq's own nuclear programme. The Iranian programme was restarted on the justification that too much money had already been spent; the need for energy diversification was more pressing than ever (especially with the dramatic increase in the Iranian population); and, with the decline in Iran's conventional military power, the attractions of developing a breakout capability were more apparent than ever. Unsurprisingly, other than perhaps to the Iranians themselves, the post-Revolutionary climate was less conducive to Western collaboration and the Iranians were forced to turn to the Pakistanis and North Koreans for technological support. With the fall of the Soviet Union, international attention was more attuned to the threats of proliferation and the costs for Iran became progressively higher, even if this was matched with a greater Iranian skill for surreptitious acquisition. Iranian progress was nonetheless slow and distinctly piecemeal until the sudden and worrying announcement that South Asia had gone nuclear in 1998 encouraged a redoubling of efforts. It was nevertheless the altered geopolitical environment resulting from the tragedy of 9/11 that really focused Western attention on the dangers of proliferation.

Be that as it may, it would be naïve to look at the nuclear impasse between Iran and the international community in isolation from the broader political environment that has shaped Iran's relations with the outside world and the West in particular since 1979. As this excellent study by Dr Kaussler analyses in some detail, at the core of the problem 'lies a fundamental lack of trust and recipro-city'. This has been reinforced by mutually incongruous readings of history, compounded by decades of ideological prejudice and bias, which has cemented views among hardliners on either side of the equation. Even more problematic, however, is the reality that we are not dealing with a bilateral negotiation, but a distinctly multilateral process involving many state actors, as well as non-state actors that populate the political landscapes and often push-and-pull policy in diverse, even occasionally contradictory, directions. The result is a highly complex dynamic that belies the seeming simplicity of the issue at hand and there is little doubt that the *process* of negotiation is both more complicated and complicating, resulting perhaps in the paradox of a highly ideological encounter being ultimately defined in such starkly realist terms.

Ali M. Ansari
University of St Andrews

Introduction

The subject of this book is the Islamic Republic of Iran's nuclear programme and the multilateral efforts which effectively have been seeking to end or at least limit it. This study seeks to examine the nuclear negotiations between the EU, the US government and Iran as well as respective diplomatic strategies and tools of statecraft within the prism of conflict resolution approaches. It is argued that beneath the veneer of over a decade of constructive engagement with Iran to find a diplomatic solution to the nuclear dispute were Western efforts to check Iranian nuclear capabilities, coupled with a range of coercive measures in order to enforce concessions from Iran. Iranian diplomacy was also informed by realist objectives to project power and not to give in to Western demands. The narrative of this book, therefore, describes a intractable conflict scenario, featuring entrenched feelings of mutual fear, mistrust and hostility, causing all main stakeholders to choose tools of power politics over conflict resolution techniques in their interactions with one another.

Iran's nuclear programme and its alleged threat to international peace and security remains one of the most important issues in US as well as the EU's foreign affairs. In the United States, Iran has dominated the political discourse for over three decades. Hostile views of Iran are embraced by both major American political parties and stopping the nuclear programme remains one of President Obama's most pressing foreign policy challenges during his second term in office. In Europe, the so-called EU-3 (Germany, France and Britain) have spent considerable political capital in finding a diplomatic solution to Iran's nuclear ambitions. Tehran's nuclear programme, role and clout in the region, continue to rank high on the West's foreign policy agenda.

While relations between the US and Iran remain subject to mutual hostility, the EU constituted a channel of communication and since 2003 has maintained a multilateral negotiation framework and followed a policy of constructive engagement towards Iran. This book will examine the dynamics of relations and the substance of negotiations between the P5+1 (Permanent Members of the UN Security Council and Germany) and Iran.

There are accounts in the disciplines of international relations and history on US–Iranian relations before and after the 1979 Islamic Revolution. Numerous policy papers in the US and European think-tank community analyse Iranian diplomacy and assess military capabilities and its position towards European and US interests. There is also no shortage of ideologically driven accounts, ranging from Christian eschatological books on Iran (seen as a hostile millenarian construct itself) to neo-conservative literature still advocating regime change, containment and isolation towards Iran. However, there are few scientific monographs on the nature and dynamics of nuclear negotiations and the substance and direction of Iran's nuclear diplomacy.

Embedded within conflict resolution and diplomatic theory, this book intends to approach the period of nuclear negotiations from 2003 to 2012 through a structural negotiation analysis. Drawing on primary documents and research conducted in the US, Europe and Iran, it analyses negotiation behaviour and strategies and respective tools of statecraft. To that end, disclosed diplomatic cables from the US State Department on wikileaks.org and cablegatesearch.net, The Telegraph, The New York Times, The Guardian and other outlets have provided an in-depth insight into multilateral diplomacy and strategic thinking in the US, Europe and Iran. The disclosed classified documents provided extensive information on both determinants and processes of implementing either conflict resolution initiatives or punitive measures by all parties involved.

The main argument forwarded in this book is that EU-3, US and Iranian diplomacy has been informed by realist perceptions of power and control and has used negotiations not as a problem-solving dialogue but as exercises of coercive diplomacy. Disclosed diplomatic cables and intelligence reports from the US State Department and other US government agencies, as well as leaked secret correspondence and consultations between US government officials, the International Atomic Energy Agency (IAEA), EU member states and US regional allies on Iran's nuclear programme and other related issues and leaked proceedings of actual negotiations with the Iranians, confirm that power politics not conflict resolution was the dominant mindset among American, European and Iranian statesmen. Beneath the veneer of Western diplomacy and the professed commitment to engage in a dialogue with Iran were realist motivations at maintaining international order and the balance of power. Engagement with Iran over the nuclear programme, therefore, has essentially been Great Power diplomacy, aiming to check Iranian capabilities rather than pursuing a security and political partnership based on justice and trust.

Theoretically, the book intends to contribute to the literature on conflict resolution dealing with the often-quoted inevitable trade-off between justice and order in international relations. Borrowing Richmond's typology of 'first-generation' conflict management and 'second-generation' conflict resolution approaches, the narrative of dealings between the US, Europe and Iran (and to a lesser extent Russia and China) establishes that diplomatic interactions were firmly rooted as well as operated within a state-centric and self-interested Westphalian international system.[1] Western statesmanship intended to face down Iran rather than sought to find a mutually acceptable agreement. To that end, the US government and EU member states employed the entire range of the diplomatic toolbox. After economic incentives failed to convince Iran to cease its enrichment programme indefinitely, coercive means employed by the US and EU and other states ranged from conventional means of military deterrence, economic sanctions, sabotage and assassinations. Having identified Iran as a so-called 'rogue state', which posed an immediate threat to Middle Eastern and European security, diplomacy oscillated between coercion and reward. European missile defence against Iran's and other alleged rogue ballistic missile threats and extended deterrence in the Persian Gulf, both underwritten by the US, were essentially based on a complete lack of trust of Iranian intentions. Even though US and European intelligence had no definitive proof of a clandestine nuclear weapons programme (the US National Intelligence Estimate in 2007 stated that Iran had given up such programme in 2004), US intelligence continued to assess throughout the entire period of engagement that Iran, at a minimum, was keeping open the option to develop nuclear weapons. Given Iran's fast pace in military procurements, it was believed by US officials, Iran's elite could choose at any time to restart its nuclear weapons programme and eventually arm its conventional missiles with nuclear warheads.[2]

Effectively, power-based diplomacy by all sides not only failed to break the stalemate but in fact created a protracted conflict between Europe, the US and Iran. The Iranian government too never left the realm of power politics and used diplomacy as a means to present positions and project power rather than following a conflict resolution approach. Implementing a strategy of positional bargaining, Iran treated progress in its nuclear programme (the very issue which was identified as a security concern by the UN Security Council) as a bargaining chip vis-à-vis European and American interlocutors. Moreover, by effectively linking Iran's nuclear programme to the very soul of the Iranian nation, seen by its leaders as the vanguard of the Muslim World itself, the Iranian government framed the conflict within a right-based context and therefore gave itself little room for meaningful concessions at the negotiation table. The disclosed documents on Iranian negotiation behaviour, and foreign policy determinants in general, confirm existing conflict resolution literature on the inadequacies of this kind of power-based diplomacy. After the EU's perceived failure to live up to its commitments under the Paris Agreement (2004), Iran resumed enrichment in 2005 and refused to test any subsequent diplomatic initiatives offered by the EU-3 (and later also supported by the US). On the contrary, feeling encircled by violent conflicts in Afghanistan and Iraq and faced with Israel's continuous threats of a military attack, the Iranians maintained power-based diplomacy aimed at balancing against the US and its perceived vassal states in the Persian Gulf.[3] Rather than depoliticizing the actual very technical nature of the nuclear programme, Iranian foreign policy was almost entirely informed by a commitment to conventional and asymmetrical military deterrence. Iran rightly decried Western double standards in its dealings with other nuclear weapon states (India, Pakistan and Israel) without ever addressing its own violations of the Non Proliferation Treaty as well as UN Security Council resolutions. Conscious of Libya's fate and watching with unease the impending fall of Syria, its strongest Arab ally, Iran continued to procure military hardware in order to deter and defend external aggression as well as retaliating by means of its regional non-state proxies. This deterrent posture, coupled with its policy in Iraq, Afghanistan and the Levant, effectively prevented the Iranian government (even like-minded pragmatists) from formulating a conflict resolution approach, which could have de-escalated the conflict, reduced tensions in a meaningful way and allowed the finding of alternative and mutually acceptable solutions.

Essentially, neither side ever left the realm of first-generation conflict management approaches (or power-based status quo diplomacy), and therefore failed to create an environment in which second-generation conflict resolution approaches could have effectively addressed the entire array of areas of mutual concern and interests. Therefore, for over a decade power politics left no room for conflict resolution.

Outline of book

Chapter 1 introduces the concept of constructive engagement within negotiation and conflict resolution literature and examines the diplomatic framework constructed by the EU vis-à-vis Iran. Chapter 2 assesses negotiations leading to the Tehran Declaration in 2003 and Paris Agreement of 2004, in which Iran pledged to sign the Additional Protocol of the Non Proliferation Treaty (NPT). Chapter 3 analyses the offers forwarded by the EU-3 in 2005 and 2006 and Iranian motivations behind resuming enrichment in 2005. Chapter 4 argues that the environment in 2007 and 2008 was marked by Iranian brinkmanship, by starting to posture with its nuclear achievements and link negotiations to areas of Iranian strategic interests. Bellicose rhetoric from the Iranians, who used purported breakthroughs in the nuclear programme as show-case events, was reciprocated by the Bush administration's balance-of-power strategy, which modulated tensions in the region in order to weaken Iran. Chapter 5 analyses the so-called Geneva Deal brokered by the EU-3 and the active participation of the Obama administration as well as initiatives during 2010 to 2012. The failure of the talks maintained a stalemate in which the EU and US have adopted a policy of containment and economic warfare and the Iranian government, defiant of UN Security Council and IAEA Board resolutions, has accelerated the pace of the nuclear programme. Chapter 6 analyses and compares respective foreign policy determinants and diplomatic strategies.

1 Setting the scene

Constructive engagement with Iran

Introduction

On 5 October 2012, three months after the EU imposed an oil embargo against Iran and having just agreed on new tighter trade sanctions, Catherine Ashton, the EU High Representative of the Union for Foreign Affairs and Security Policy, stated that sanctions were 'quite clearly having an effect' and the heightened sanctions were 'to persuade Iran to come to the table'.[1] In December 2011, the US House of Representatives passed HR 1905, The Iran Threat Reduction Act, which limited contacts between US and Iranian officials and imposed a myriad of economic sanctions. HR 1905 effectively wanted to ban diplomacy with Iran. It was signed into law by President Obama in August 2012. In October 2012, President Obama passed Executive Order 120, which implemented certain sanctions set forth in the bill. The American Israel Public Affairs Committee, the very group which drafted most of the legislation, declared that the US imposed the toughest sanctions it 'has ever imposed on any country during peacetime'.[2] In the region, the US government maintained a deterrent posture by continuing to underwrite its Arab allies in the Persian Gulf, most of which secretly pleaded for the US to attack Iran. Both the Bush and the Obama administrations ambiguously kept the military option 'on the table' and stood staunchly by the US's strongest ally, Israel, as it has been threatening Iran with a military attack for the entire period of engagement. Both unilateral sanctions by the EU and US respectively and multilateral sanctions passed by seven UN Security Council resolutions were approved amid targeted assassinations of Iranian nuclear scientists and cyber warfare attacks against Iran's nuclear installations, as well as the so-called proxy war between US forces and militias supported by Iran in Afghanistan and Iraq. After over a decade of a professed commitment to engagement with Iran, the EU along with the US government had transformed engagement into containment. To that end, sanctions have ceased to be a tool of statecraft but have rather become an end in themselves.

The Iranian government initially treated engagement as a means to maintain good relations with Europe and prevent a US-led military campaign, as well as being genuinely committed to finding a mutually acceptable solution to the nuclear question. Between 2003, when the Khatami administration signed the

Additional Protocol of the Non Proliferation Treaty, and early 2005, when the Iranian government resumed enrichment activities owing to the EU's perceived failure to live up to its commitments under the so-called Paris Agreement, engagement was part of the reformist government's foreign policy of détente. However, following the failure to come to a long-term agreement and the subsequent resumption of enrichment activities in early 2005, the Iranian government embraced a negotiation formula which used the continuous progress in the nuclear programme as a bargaining chip and linked it to an entire array of strategic interests to the Islamic Republic.

The central thesis of this book is that engagement with Iran has been a power-based exercise aimed at altering and controlling state behaviour rather than a diplomatic problem-solving strategy.

What is constructive about constructive engagement?

In international relations, constructive engagement is seen a foreign policy strategy intended to seek and maintain dialogue with anathematized or authoritarian regimes.[3] This is important to emphasize since the term itself often tends to remain a source of confusion. In Chinese, the word appears to mean simply the conduct of normal relations, and in German no comparable translation exists.[4] The term itself was first used as a result of the controversial US policy towards South Africa during the terms of Nixon, Carter and then Reagan. Advocating a 'strategy of change' in the face of an internationally growing cacophony for punitive sanctions and the failure of constructive engagement under Carter and Nixon, Ronald Reagan's then Assistant Secretary of State for African Affairs, Chester Crocker, became the architect for a renewed policy of engagement rather than isolation towards South Africa.[5] Accounts on the period of US constructive engagement towards Pretoria describe how this policy – a combination of diplomatic pressure and extension of favourable trade terms as a reward for South African amelioration of apartheid – was intended to catalyse evolutionary change from within the South African polity. Transcending the fallacies of the Carter years and approaches of the Nixon administrations, Crocker suggested during the 1980s a new strategy of constructive engagement which would not only recognize significant changes for which the Botha government had previously received little international credit, but would also reward future developments.[6] While discarding radical and unrealistic demands for a speedy transfer of power, the State Department advocated a 'clear Western readiness to recognize and support positive development and engage credibly in addressing a complex political agenda'.[7] Although US constructive engagement towards South Africa did not succeed in persuading the white government to abandon its apartheid regime, assessments on the policy reveal that it was the bureaucratic failure to implement constructive engagement effectively, rather than the failure of the concept itself, that had led to the decision after 1985 to abandon a dialogue and to re-employ negative sanctions against Pretoria.[8] Essentially, US diplomacy towards South Africa coined the term as well as conceptual mechanism of constructive engagement.

Since constructive engagement still holds a rather elusive status in international relations literature, it is vital to clarify the idea behind it before moving to a conceptual definition. Constructive engagement constitutes a non-coercive strategy and set of diplomatic practices for bringing 'outlaw' or 'rogue' states to conform to what are held by the Great Powers to be legitimate international norms. Using linkage diplomacy as a tactic to encourage changes in another state's policies, George points to its strategic use

> as part of a long-range effort for bringing about fundamental change in the nature of the outlaw state and its leadership, that is, the gradual replacement of its antipathy to the norms and practices of the international system with attitudes and behaviour more supportive of that system.[9]

It is important to emphasize that constructive engagement is distinct from appeasement. While its tactic of conditional reciprocity is different from appeasement, its underlying goal – that is, avoidance of conflict, reduction of tension, re-socialization into international society through non-coercive means – is indeed in line with the general idea behind appeasement.[10] The historical case against appeasement, British diplomacy towards Germany from 1937 to 1939, is well understood and deeply entrenched in the consciousness of generations of policymakers. The traditional view against appeasement, dominated by prominent critics such as L. B. Namier, J. W. Wheeler Bennett, Alan Bullock and Winston Churchill himself, considers it to be a policy of shameful weakness before the challenge of the dictators, which was doomed to fail.[11] It was this traditional negative image of appeasement and the conviction that the Second World War could have been prevented by a policy of timely resistance to German aggression that influenced Western policymakers during the Cold War.[12] Even four decades later this image was still upheld in influential international relations literature. As Hans Morgenthau denounces appeasement as:

> a foreign policy that attempts to meet the threat of imperialism with methods appropriate to a policy of the status quo.... One might say that appeasement is a corrupted policy of compromise, made erroneous by mistaking a policy of imperialism for a policy of the status quo.[13]

Yet the failed attempt of Neville Chamberlain to appease Hitler in the late 1930s and to bring Germany back as a responsible actor into a reconstituted European system may only point to a disastrous historical event rather than discredit the concept altogether. First, the fault of the British government and others during the 1930s was not that they attempted to pursue conciliation in their dealings with Germany. Other policies, such as a consistent policy of deterrence, designed to maintain the Versailles settlement unimpaired, could never have succeeded as long as the most powerful nation in Europe harboured resentment against it. The fault was that Britain and other governments attempted conciliation without sufficient reserves of deterrence as an inducement against alternative courses.[14]

Conceivably, it is true that no degree of armed strength on their part could have convinced Hitler that they really meant business, yet conciliation not underwritten by strength was certain to fail. Hence, drawing on lessons from history, constructive engagement needs to employ both carrots and sticks in such a way that neither of the two options outweighs the other. Effectively, it means that as much as a policy of conciliation without strength is fruitless, so deterrence without conciliation is doomed to ineffectiveness.

Second, the original idea of appeasement (that is, reasonable concessions made from a position of strength) is still a fundamental purpose of diplomacy, 'an essential and sometimes invaluable card in an on-going game which should not be discarded antipathetically because it was once misplayed'. In fact, any charge against appeasement, for the purpose of condemnation, levels against a policy which aims at easing tension and avoiding conflict and therefore misses the mark entirely in a world where such policies are the only means of assuring peaceful coexistence.[15] Nevertheless, appeasement should always be implemented from a position of strength, coupled with the political will to draw on available power capabilities and to use any leverage as incentives for demanded concessions.

Regarding the conditions under which it is viable to employ a policy of appeasement, it is crucial to assess whether there are signs that the object is appeaseable. Essentially, 'appeasement has a rightful place in resolving disputes through negotiated settlement and peaceful change; but it is wholly inappropriate in dealing with force, violence and aggression'. In making concessions the state initiating appeasement towards another country

> should never involve the surrender of fundamental principles upon the preservation of which the claim to loyalty and respect for that government depends. That would constitute betrayal, by the means, of the very ends which they were devised to defend and promote.[16]

In advocating precisely this case for assessing the preconditions to employ a strategy of appeasement or constructive engagement, George attempts to replace the simple generalization so strongly rooted in the post-Munich era, 'if appeasement then World War III', with a more differentiated analysis. He demands to examine historical cases of appeasement in order to identify those conditions under which it is likely to be a viable conflict-avoidance strategy and those in which it is likely to be misguided and contribute to the eventual onset of war.[17]

So, while the British appeasement policy of 1937–1939 is not likely to be easily surpassed as a historic example of how not to conduct policy of détente, Willy Brandt's 1970s *Ostpolitik* towards the Soviet Union and Eastern Europe, on the contrary, proves the success of what today would most probably be referred to as constructive engagement. Brandt had a clear notion not only of the changes that he wished to effect but also of the difficulties that lay in his path, so that his initiative was based on a shrewd assessment of potentials risks and gains and of how to utilize leverage to manoeuvre around obstacles.[18] Though *Ostpolitik* contained the possibility of major concessions to the Soviet Union and the East German regime and thus contained elements of what could be regarded as appeasement, Brandt orchestrated a complex process of détente to ensure that he gained important benefits not only for West Germany but for Europe as a whole. Diplomatic, economic and cultural relations with Eastern European states, which primarily aimed at eliminating distrust and tension, were initiated by Bonn through commercial and credit incentives for these economically depressed governments.[19] Unlike Chamberlain in his dealings with Hitler, Brandt did not rush the détente process in order to move as quickly as possible into appeasement. Making realistic calculations of the complexity and political risks of his course, Brandt knew that Europe could 'approach this goal [an enduring peace order] only step by step, in a long-drawn-out process of détente, that is by means of mutual rapprochement, understanding and cooperation in all areas of interstate relations'. As advocates of constructive engagement would argue today, he also claimed that 'the establishment of diplomatic relations is a means to the attainment of this goal, not an end in itself'.[20] Hence, *Ostpolitik* was a strategy in which diplomatic moves were carefully controlled and timed. Brandt, aware of the two-level game of diplomacy, always aimed at solidifying domestic support before implementing his policy of détente and appeasement. *Ostpolitik* proved that the implementation of détente/appeasement remains potentially viable if employed with due caution and with sensitivity to the greater complexity of the situation and the nature of the risks involved.[21] Indeed, the careful step-by-step process in which Brandt pursued his non-coercive *Ostpolitik* backed by German economic might and NATO deterrence bears important similarities with what today would be regarded as a moral and successful strategy of constructive engagement.

Conflict resolution and power politics

Generally, engagement ought to be informed by a commitment to diplomacy and negotiations. However, the history of international relations presents us with two kinds of diplomacy: first-generation conflict management approaches and second-generation conflict resolution approaches.

First-generation conflict management

Whilst non-coercive in nature, it is argued that engagement can still be a power-based exercise in Westphalian-style diplomacy. Engagement with so-called rogue states is meant to maintain international 'stability', causing states to advance their own interests rather than address issues of justice or fundamental causes of conflict.[22] Embedding the idea within the history of diplomacy, we find that 'great powers are often confronted by ambitious states that are not socialized into the norms of the international system and pose a threat to its orderly workings and stability'.[23] Diplomatic efforts throughout modern international relations history to reform these outlaw states show what significance a 'common concept of legitimacy' and international norms hold for the stability of the international system. Kissinger defined this common concept as an 'international agreement about the nature of workable arrangements and about the permissible aims and methods of foreign policy'. This implies

> the acceptance of the framework of the international order by all major powers, at least to the extent that no state is so dissatisfied that, like Germany after the Treaty of Versailles, it expresses its dissatisfaction in a revolutionary foreign policy.[24]

It is evident that constructive engagement, informed by international security concerns (e.g. non-proliferation, violent conflict, challenges to the balance of power, etc.) as opposed to a human rights dialogue (e.g. the US policy towards Cuba or China), does not seek to resolve underlying roots of conflict or address issues of injustice. Engagement becomes a realist venture rather than a conflict resolution strategy. First-generation conflict management approaches are intended to settle conflicts so as to preserve the international status quo, which has been both engineered and guarded by centuries of Great Power diplomacy. Richmond calls this type 'status quo diplomacy' or 'fine tuning of the balance of power' exemplified in the Cuban Missile Crisis of 1962, Cyprus (1962–today), Dayton (1995), Camp David (1978) as well as more recent mediating efforts by the US in the Palestine–Israel conflict and Western diplomacy towards the Georgia–Russian conflict (2008) and the civil war in Syria (since 2011).[25]

Constructive engagement with Libya provides a particular good case of status quo diplomacy. Constructive engagement with Libya has been credited by European governments and the US as a success in the area of multilateral diplomacy and non-proliferation. When Mohammar Qadaffi announced in December 2003 that he would be dismantling the country's entire biological, nuclear and chemical weapons programme following secret negotiations with British, Russian and US envoys, British Prime Minister Tony Blair credited engagement, saying that '[this] shows that problems of proliferation can, with good will, be tackled through discussion and engagement ... that we can fight this menace through more than purely military means'.[26] The US and British governments were quick to call on Iran to follow the 'Libyan model'. However, notwithstanding its authoritarian character, the Libyan regime soon realized that it had received nothing in return. While trade with the EU increased and foreign relations with Europe and the US improved, the promise of cooperation on nuclear energy never materialized once Libya had handed over its WMD arsenal. In fact, as the US and European allies were enforcing a no-flight zone over Libya in 2011, which would eventually help to overthrow the regime, Pentagon officials said that the '2003 deal removed Colonel Qaddafi's biggest trump card: the threat of using a nuclear weapon, or even just selling nuclear material or technology, if he believed it was the only way to save his 42-year rule'.[27] The Libyan regime's realization that neither Iran nor North Korea were likely to follow their example was already evident during a private meeting between a US Senator and Qadaffi in Libya in 2006:

[The U.S.] Senator noted the dramatic shift in US–Libyan relations from the 1980s to now and asked if there was a model that could be applied to the US–Iran relationship. Qadhafi said that Libya urged both North Korea and Iran to give up their WMD programmes, but that it had not convinced them because, 'if you want Libya to be a model, Libya should get a reward.' When the Senator pressed for more specifics, Qadhafi claimed 'the US promised the US and Britain would provide peaceful nuclear energy and Libya would be the Japan of North Africa through technical transfers. But nothing happened. Supposedly the US, EU and China were going to build us nuclear power stations, this is the reward we were hoping for.'[28]

Engagement with Libya solely served to dismantle the WMD programme, to control Libyan behaviour and, therefore, to reorganize the balance of power rather than fully reciprocate the regime's offer of détente.

Advocates of the realist tradition would see engagement solely as a power-based exercise in diplomacy to maintain 'stability'. States advance their own interests rather than address issues of justice or fundamental causes of conflict.[29] Although the inviolability of agreements figures greatly in Western diplomatic theory, realists value deceit and coercion as legitimate methods of conducting diplomacy since all states have a 'propensity for competitiveness'.[30] In the most classic of all realist accounts on diplomacy, Machiavelli argued that the central role of the state is to prepare for war or to prevent it. Deception, according to Machiavelli, gives states engaged in negotiations added chances of success even at the expense of credibility.[31] British diplomat and theorist Harold Nicholson has equated such negotiations to a 'military campaign ... to out-flank your opponent and to occupy strategic positions which are at once consolidated before any further advance is made'.[32] Henry Kissinger similarly holds that the manipulation of political and military factors is the essence of statecraft.[33] Many contemporary realists treat Thucydides' *History of the Peloponnesian War* as an affirmation of the concept of power in negotiations between states. In particular, the substance of the 'Melian Dialogue' is that 'morality is subordinate to considerations of necessity and power, and that justice is contingent on a balance of power between states'. As the Athenians put it, 'justice is what is decided when equal forces are opposed, while possibilities are what superiors impose and the weak acquiesce to'. Realists contend that the lack of security in the international environment compels states to seek power, not social justice.[34] Since first-generation conflict management approaches intend to control or even manipulate state behaviour in order to compel a state to negotiate or make concessions, sanctions have become the tool of choice for such kinds of diplomacy.[35] The efficacy of sanctions has been subject to extensive debate; in which scholars seek to find an answer to the question of whether economic sanctions actually work in respect to stated policy goals. In the most extensive study of sanctions, Hufbauer, Schott and Elliott measured success in terms of achieving stated policy goals. After examining 115 cases in which sanctions were used, Hufbauer concluded that sanctions were successful 35 per cent of the time.[36] A more recent study by Cliff Morgan, Navin Bapat and Valentin Krustev analyses 888 cases of threatened and imposed sanctions during the period 1971 to 2000 and puts the success of multilateral sanctions rate at 54.8 per cent and that of unilateral sanctions at 39.5 per cent.[37]

Hufbauer's findings have shown that although sanctions which had the most profound economic impact on a country were the ones most likely to achieve their goals, economic pain does not have to lead to political gain.[38] The 'rally around the flag' effect, and especially the human suffering[39] associated with a sanction regime, lends support to the claim that constructive engagement together with a sanction regime, specifically aimed at the government's ability to manoeuvre (e.g. military adventures, control of financial flows), could produce the expected outcome at less cost to a country's population.

First-generation conflict management employs forms of manipulative persuasion, various forms of coercion and even the threat or use of force. The reference to 'carrots and sticks' presumes that a strategy based on punitive measures combined with incentives is effective at altering state behaviour or restoring the balance of power. Essentially, it is status quo diplomacy informed by power politics.

Second-generation conflict resolution

The US government's rationale that led to the war against Iraq was largely a product of the neo-conservative movement, which advocated an American internationalism to bring 'change from a position of strength' to the world as a whole and to the Middle East in particular. Contrary to this coercive expression of US foreign policy stands the EU's Common Foreign and Security Policy (CFSP). EU diplomacy is thought to be based on Europe's 'ability to persuade' with non-coercive means as opposed to the 'ability to compel' through coercive means. Neo-conservatives may well argue that the EU's projection of soft power in its engagement with third countries is a sign of weakness rather than strength.[40] The question, however, is whether Europe's soft-power approach is actually working. Put simply, it seems that the EU does not change countries' behaviour and extract concessions by threatening to invade them, but rather with the incentive of contractual relations or the prospect of membership. For countries like Bosnia, Ukraine or Turkey, the only thing worse than having to deal with the Brussels bureaucracy is being unable to deal with it at all. EU membership and contractual relations with the Union are such powerful lures that countries are willing to change economic, judicial, legal and political structures just to join or enter such agreements.[41] In fact the Euro-Mediterranean partnership, also known as the Barcelona Process, was created to turn the Mediterranean–Middle East region into a region of dialogue, exchange and cooperation, with the objective of establishing peace, stability and prosperity. While the prospect of belonging to a free-trade area is being held out to countries such as Jordan; Syria; Lebanon; Algeria and Morocco as the economic incentive, the ultimate goal is to bring political concerns such as democracy, good governance, the rule of law and human rights in these Middle Eastern states into harmony with EU standards. This transformative power, which the EU is wielding or attempting to hold over the Middle East, is what Nye refers to as 'soft power': that is, the attraction of one's ideas or the ability to set the political agenda in a way that shapes the preferences of others.[42] Nye argues that Europe also derives soft power from its foreign policies: it not only gains 'credibility from its position on global climate change, international law, and human rights treaties' but, as Jack Straw claims, also has 'experience in the subtle art of soft power' and 'tends to exerts its influence overseas via the promotion of democracy and development through trade and aid'.[43] In a disclosed US diplomatic cable on EU scepticism on the efficacy of sanctions and US strategic outreach efforts to convince EU member states of their importance as a foreign policy tool, the US Embassy in Brussels noted:

> The Commission is primarily designed to deploy the power of attraction (the proverbial carrot) in the EU's regional expansion and engagement with third countries. Rather than responding to problematic situations by restricting participation in community life, the EU prefers to offer explicit incentives in exchange for desired behavorial change.[44]

Advocates of second-generation conflict resolution strategies would put the EU's stated commitment to constructive engagement in its foreign affairs within the context of liberal institutionalism. The concept of international regime theory in the context of constructive engagement is vital because it helps to explain both: (1) the short-term mechanism for cooperation and/or rapprochement and (2) the long-term mechanism to control the target state's behaviour.

Keohane and Axelrod's approaches to cooperation and the entire literature on international regimes represent a successful attempt to bridge the realist–liberal gap by being neither as broad as international structure analysis nor as narrow as the study of formal organizations. Borrowing from behavioural science, scholars of international regime theory argue that states under controlled conditions may reciprocate the cooperative acts of their opponents in a reciprocal pattern while international laws and norms shape states' preferences for such cooperation.[45] Hence, any attempt to explain constructive engagement as a second-generation conflict resolution strategy has to be embedded within regime theory which essentially, as John Ruggie put it, claims that 'international behaviour is institutionalised'.[46] More specifically, Ruggie defined regimes as 'a set of mutual expectations, rules and regulations, plans and organizational energies and financial commitments'.[47] Diplomacy here is a process of negotiation by rational communication, advocating a solution which is to be found with and not against the other party.[48]

Negotiators are aiming for what scholars in conflict resolution theory refer to as a 'win–win solution'. Such an outcome, also called 'positive-sum' is a mutually agreeable negotiating outcome in which the interests of both parties are satisfied, and which is often the result of joint problem-solving. Such outcomes are likely when the future relationship between the conflict parties matters to both, when the interests of the parties are interdependent and when the parties are prepared to cooperate in joint problem-solving: that is, if the conflict parties manage to reconcile their respective interests rather than positions.[49] As Richmond defines it:

> The aim of negotiation is to reorganize the balance of power in a manner that is acceptable to both sides, so creating stability in their relationship. While a change in the perception of the conflict as zero-sum would be the optimum outcome, it is more likely that the two sides will be increasingly motivated by the need to alter the balance of power in their own favour, in the process changing the stakes into items that can be used to benefit both parties.[50]

The formidable challenge of a problem-solving orientation on negotiation, which covers the phase of pre-negotiation and actual negotiation, is to reflect on the causes of conflict to arrive at a common definition and joint solutions that satisfy the basic needs of all sides. A problem-solving orientation focused on information exchange, therefore, seeks to eliminate undermining factors such as mistrust among the parties, selective and distorted perceptions, negative attitudes and images, poor communication and a competitive win–lose orientation that attempts to force or extract capitulation from the adversary.[51] There are two fundamental parts of the problem-solving process most applicable to constructive engagement:

1   Diagnosing the conflicting demand or concern (figuring out what the cause of the 'stickiness' is, or identifying the problem).
2   Developing alternative solutions to the problem through a joint effort acceptable to both parties.[52]

The shift towards a cooperative win–win orientation begins by allowing representatives of the parties

> to talk freely to one another, to exchange information about their interests and priorities and to work together to identify the issues dividing, brainstorm in search of alternatives that bridge their opposing interests, and collectively evaluate those alternatives from the viewpoint of their mutual welfare.[53]

An important way of approaching negotiations is what Fischer and Ury call 'principled negotiation', which suggests that one looks for mutual gains wherever possible, and that where your interests conflict you should insist that the result be 'based on same fair standards independent of the will of either side'.[54] Claiming that 'principled negotiation' is a technique designed to produce wise outcomes efficiently and amicably which can be used under almost every circumstance, in particular when dealing with another culture, Fischer and Ury list four basic points to follow:

People: Separate the people from the problem.
Interests: Focus on interests, not on positions.
Options: Generate a variety of possibilities before deciding what to do.
Criteria: Insist that the result be based on some objective standard.[55]

In sum, problem-solving workshops during pre-negotiation can provide states with an opportunity to demonstrate the feasibility of more formal negotiations and determine the basis for future joint activity. These workshops provide unique forums for low-risk exchange.[56]

If pre-negotiations are successfully concluded, the next task for both states would be to move into 'around the table mode'. For constructive engagement this means that the negotiators try to agree on basic principles of a settlement: 'the formula stage'.[57] Once this important point has been reached – that is, the perception by each side that the other is serious about finding a negotiated solution – each side must now decide how to present the case in the most convincing and tactically advantageous light. While most scholars on negotiation assume a universal diplomatic culture,[58] negotiators, however, maintain that culture and language were formative in the choice of approaching the formula. Hence, two basic styles of persuasion can be identified. The first is the 'factual–inductive', which draws conclusions on the basis of factual evidence: eschewing a grand philosophical debate, it plunges straight into discussion of concrete detail, building an agreement primarily through mutual compromise of exchanged concessions. This style is the Anglo-Saxon pragmatic tradition of the common law on which most Western diplomats rely and which is also consistent with the legal training that most public officials have received.[59] The second approach is the 'axiomatic–deductive' style, which first establishes the principles, or formula, governing the issues susceptible of a solution and then works out the implementing details. Zartman argues that the deductive approach based on a formula is both present and desirable in successful negotiations[60] and is therefore viable for constructive engagement. This approach is particularly useful for cross-cultural negotiations, reconciling a high-context[61] approach of first agreeing on axioms and philosophical principles with a low-context[62] pragmatic approach of concession and compromise.[63]

Constructive engagement with Iran

Unlike appeasement, constructive engagement should be perceived as a non-coercive strategy to bring about meaningful change in a state's behaviour. The EU's policy of constructive engagement created the diplomatic environment in which negotiations between outside powers and Iran have been conducted. At the beginning engagement aimed to 'reintegrate' Iran back into the international community. The then EU Commissioner for External Relations, Chris Patten, gave a speech at the Iranian Foreign Ministry, during the height of engagement in 2003, entitled 'The Iranian choice – an opportunity to embrace the family of nations', during which he reminded the Iranian government that 'no nation state, however mighty, is sufficient unto itself. Cooperation with our partners – cooperation between the EU and Iran – is a requirement, not an ideal.'[64] Reiterating that such cooperation was conditional on human rights improvements, Patten's vision was one of which:

> I am convinced that there is a vital role that Iran, if it really wants to, can play on this international stage, among the Family of Nations. You may seize that role tomorrow, or in twenty years from now – the choice lies with you. Rome was not built in one day, nor was a democratic Europe or even the European Union created overnight. But the challenge – the imperative of working with others – is one that every modern society has to face.[65]

The Critical Dialogue: 1992–1997

The policy of constructive engagement pursued by the EU towards Iran from 1992 until 2000 was a common foreign and security policy (CFSP) aimed at maintaining contact with Iran in order to influence its regime on certain areas of concern for Europe. This policy was coined 'Critical Dialogue' and was endorsed by the European Council at the European Union summit in Edinburgh on 11–12 December 1992. The Critical Dialogue was adopted to pursue a range of goals which were all officially articulated by the European Council of Ministers:

> Given Iran's importance in the region, the European Council reaffirms its beliefs that a dialogue should be maintained with the Iranian Government. This should be a critical dialogue, which reflects concern about Iranian behaviour and calls for improvement in a number of areas, particularly human rights, the death sentence pronounced by a Fatwa against the author Salman Rushdie, which is contrary to international law, and terrorism. Improvements in these areas will be important in determining the extent to which closer relations and confidence can be developed.[66]

The conclusion further stated that the Council 'accepts the right of countries to acquire the means to defend themselves, but is concerned that Iran's arms procurement should not pose a threat to regional stability'. Within the context of the Israel–Palestine peace process the Council 'expressed the wish that Iran will take a constructive approach here'.[67] Contrary to the European proposal, the US rejected any engagement and pursued a policy of 'active containment'[68] against Iran. From 1995 onwards, Washington implemented increasingly severe sanctions aiming to 'isolate' Iran until it halted its alleged plans to acquire nuclear weapons, obstruction of the Middle East peace process and support of international terrorism.[69] The EU's refusal to support the sanctions led to transatlantic tensions in particular with respect to the Iran Libya Sanctions Act (ILSA) and the 1997 conflict over its extraterritorial aspect.[70] Thus, the first European CFSP was a genuine constructive engagement approach, refusing to employ negative sanctions but actually seeking a dialogue with Tehran to improve Iranian behaviour and, in the long run, to reintegrate it into the international system. In fact, based on the geopolitical significance of Iran in the region, the EU dismissed any policy of isolation and containment, stating that 'security and stability cannot be achieved without Iran or even against it'. European governments were convinced that the only way to approach Iran about their demands and to make it observe international norms was through direct contact and dialogue.[71] Europe's stake in Iran's economy and the prospect of deepening commercial relations with the election of Rafsanjani certainly was the significant determinant leading the EU to engagement.

When on 10 April 1997 a German court found the highest Iranian authorities – including the Supreme Leader – responsible for killing members of the Kurdish opposition in Berlin, the Critical Dialogue was suspended.[72] It was only the election of President Khatami and the promise of a new moderate rhetoric in Iran's foreign policy with the call for 'dialogue between civilizations' that persuaded Europe to restore relations with Iran and to enter into what henceforth was called a 'Comprehensive Dialogue'. Convinced that the election of Khatami and new developments in Iran vindicated a policy of active influence, the Comprehensive Dialogue reaffirmed previous demands and concerns but offered incentives for cooperation more publicly. Having agreed that renewed contacts with Iran should be 'comprehensive, leading to a dialogue on both the areas of concern … and on issues of mutual interest',[73] specific enticements on financial and technical cooperation regarding the areas of energy, drugs, refugees and trade and investment were made should Iran show progress on the issues of human rights, its intention to develop WMD, the *fatwa* against Salman Rushdie and its support for radical groups as well as greater domestic economic reform.[74]

The Critical and Comprehensive Dialogues were a policy of constructive engagement with the aim of reintegrating a revisionist state back into the international community, while it was the first ever Common Security and Foreign Policy endorsed by the European Union and at times lacked coordination and coherence and was subject to asymmetries in EU–Iran interdependence.[75]

The main stated objective was to induce changes in Iranian behaviour to move this 'important country towards responsible and constructive cooperation'.[76] This policy was based on two closely related assumptions. First, European diplomacy should engage with different political forces in Iran aiming at persuading moderates in Iran that a change in policy was in Iran's basic self-interest. Convinced that a policy of 'isolation and speechlessness'[77] would prove ineffective, supporters of Critical Dialogue argued that keeping open lines of communication would force the Iranian political elite to face the issues of greatest concern for Europe.[78] Second, critical engagement has rested upon the assumption that Iranian behaviour can be influenced through communication and incentives within an approach which Peter Rudolf characterized as 'diffuse linkage'. While it was stated that further improvement of European Iranian relations is linked with Tehran's living up to European demands, linkage may be termed diffuse because before the adoption of the Comprehensive Dialogue incentives had not been publicly explained or tied to specific changes in Iranian behaviour. While it was presumed that Iran would fulfil as many expectations as possible before progress was offered, the time frame for Iranian concessions remained open.[79]

The Comprehensive Dialogue: 1998–2003

In 2000, the EU forwarded a Trade and Cooperation Agreement (TCA) to Iran as an incentive to deepen economic and diplomatic relations but linked to progress in four areas: human rights, non-proliferation, terrorism and the Middle East peace process. Tying Iran closer to the EU politically and economically, it was believed, would ultimately allow Europe to extract significant concessions from the Iranian government.[80] Reciprocating newly elected President Khatami's détente, which largely helped to restore relations with Britain to the ambassadorial level after ten years over the *fatwa* against Salman Rushdie, the rationale was that the EU would eventually assist the reformist agenda by tilting the balance of interests and would encourage moderate policies and the process of democratization in the country.[81]

In a communiqué sent to the Council, the EU Commission recognized the changes that were taking place, noting the momentum reformists had gained in 2000 as well as the impediments posed by conservatives, stating that 'despite the mixed picture ... the prospects for positive and gradual political evolution are better than they have been since 1979'.[82] Reflecting a commitment to engage, the Council adopted its recommendation on the Iran policy based on following approach:

- Encouragement of political and economic reform through
- more frequent official and unofficial bilateral contracts;
  - development of exchange/cooperation in areas of mutual interest and concern (such as drugs, rule of law, refugees, etc.);
  - readiness to engage in dialogue on human rights;
  - strengthening the CFSP dialogue by deepening the dialogue in areas such as regional security, weapons of mass destruction, nuclear proliferation;
  - seeking appropriate ways of developing people-to-people contacts.
- Promotion of bilateral economic relations through
  - negotiation of a Trade and Cooperation Agreement;
  - continuation of Commission–Iran working groups on energy, trade and investment.[83]

The irony of the Comprehensive Dialogue was that while the human rights dialogue bore progress in legislation and policy as well as supporting stakeholders of human rights and democracy through the various multi-track roundtables organized by the EU, by 2004 Germany, Britain and France had largely shifted their priorities to non-proliferation. Europe's soft-power approach towards Iran empowered like-minded Iranian activists, intellectuals and politicians. Moreover, it depoliticized the promotion of human rights discourse by enabling Iranian civil society through approaching it from within a *Shi'a* discourse, thus highlighting existing constitutional provisions of human rights and uncovering the very secular realities of human rights violations in the Islamic Republic.[84] Reformists largely interpreted the priority shift from human to conventional security concerns as betrayal of their cause. As Shirin Ebadi noted again following the 2009 elections: 'the West cares more about its own security than human rights. I think they're wrong. … Undemocratic countries are more dangerous than a nuclear bomb. It's undemocratic countries that jeopardize international peace.'[85] Turning a blind eye towards the gradual usurpation of reformists by conservatives which culminated in the Guardian Council's barring of over 3,500 reformist candidates for the elections of the seventh *Majlis* in February 2004, thus securing a hardliner majority, the EU-3 completely shifted its priority towards nuclear diplomacy. By the end of 2005, various EU governments had become disillusioned at the efficacy of the human rights dialogue, causing the Dutch Presidency to review the dialogue altogether. In a private meeting between EU members, the British EU Presidency Representative said that

> a human rights dialogue was still valuable because it was a way to register concerns; it was worth pursuing if both sides were committed. [and that] the EU would not give Iran the satisfaction of saying that it was the EU that walked away and emphasized that direct aid contributions from Western countries should complement, not replace, human rights dialogues.

However, it was also noted by an official from the British Foreign and Commonwealth Office (FCO) that the deterioration of the nuclear track might call further engagement into question.[86] With mounting pressure from the Bush administration and a lack of progress with regard to human rights and rule law, the human rights dialogue was eventually decoupled from engagement and the EU focused solely on nuclear diplomacy.[87]

Nuclear diplomacy (2003–2012): power politics and conflict resolution

This book provides an assessment of nuclear negotiations between the EU/US and Iran since 2003. The main argument forwarded is that the EU created a diplomatic architecture and may have ultimately prevented a US-led or sanctioned military campaign against Iran, but ultimately failed to implement an effective problem-solving strategy. Rather, it is argued that the objective of engagement during this period was for Iran to accept the security framework laid out by the EU-3 and the US government. Engagement had ceased to be an exercise in problem-solving and had morphed into coercive diplomacy by all parties involved.

To Iran, engagement served to check US pressure and maintain good relations with Europe, as well as to use Europe's professed commitment to diplomacy as a means to project power and link EU demands to a myriad of Iranian interests.

EU/US and Iranian diplomacy has effectively been informed by realist perceptions of power and control. It is argued that the stalemate over the nuclear programme is a direct result of these mutually opposed objectives. For the Europeans, Iran's nuclear programme constitutes a serious security concern, and as long as the IAEA cannot rule out a military dimension the Europeans will insist that the mastery of nuclear technology under the NPT is qualified. As conservative governments in Germany, Britain and France have witnessed a deterioration of respective bilateral relations with Iran since 2005 and professed an eagerness to recalibrate transatlantic relations after the fallout over Iraq in 2003, the EU-3 ceased to serve as an honest broker in the US–EU–Iran triangle.

On the contrary, it is argued, EU diplomacy sought to check Iranian nuclear ambitions and capabilities and continues to employ a dual-track approach of carrots and sticks, largely in tandem with Washington. Likewise, the Iranian government, while insisting on its right to enrichment, has failed to propose or implement any sustainable and meaningful confidence-building measures towards the European Union. As the Iranian regime justified itself in terms of nationalism and populism towards its domestic constituents, its interlocutor never translated its genuine security needs into workable diplomatic initiatives. Rather, diplomacy remained underwritten by deterrence and an intransigent anti-Western propaganda.

The Bush and Obama administrations too were guided by a Cold War mindset, seeking tactical advantage over Iran and favouring sanctions and other forms of coercive diplomacy over genuine constructive engagement.[88] By the end of 2012, the US had passed the most stringent sets of sanctions since the Islamic Revolution of 1979. Diplomacy turned into economic warfare, aiming both at forcing the government to compromise and polarizing its population to rise up against the Iranian government.

None of the three main actors (EU-3, US and Iran) have employed a problem-solving approach during negotiations. Far from looking for mutually acceptable solutions, constructive engagement has morphed into containment, while Iran has used negotiation as a power-based exercise in statecraft.

2 Old Europe's diplomacy
The 2004 Paris Agreement

Introduction

Negotiations between the EU and Iran led to the so-called Tehran Declaration in 2003, which set the foundation for the Islamic Republic to sign the Additional Protocol in December 2003, thus subjecting itself to an IAEA inspection regime. Tehran's motivation behind this commitment was largely to avoid being brought before the UN Security Council, whereas for the EU-3 the subsequent Paris Accord in November 2004 was a means to establish a framework of negotiations. Given the mutually exclusive interpretations of the agreement (suspension as a temporary confidence-building gesture vs suspension seen by the EU as the first step towards complete cessation of enrichment), and the IAEA's disclosure of previous violations of safeguard agreements and Iran's covert uranium enrichment programme, Iran insisted on the promised rewards, while the EU felt unable to carry out the commitments of the Paris Agreement.

Engagement amid war

The US-led invasions of Afghanistan in 2001 and Iraq in 2003 reinforced a strategic stalemate for all parties. Those policymakers in the US administration who were guided by neo-conservative visions of a new Middle East, and were seemingly emboldened by the initial military success, anticipated that occupied Iraq and Afghanistan would translate into leverage against Iran. The nuclear programme was largely seen through this prism. US intelligence indicated a weapons programme and key figures within the US administration advocated a coercive stance against Iran. EU policy was considered too benign, lacking the resolve and urgency to contain Iran's perceived nuclear threat. Iran's offer of détente in 2003 was, therefore, rejected by hardliners within the administration. On the other hand, to the EU-3, particularly France and Germany, engagement was still the policy of choice, but needed to show tangible results. To Paris and Berlin, it was a diplomatic exercise, intending Iran to subject itself to an intrusive IAEA inspections regime, but also served as a showcase event to prove to US hardliners that 'Old' Europe's diplomacy could still yield results.[1] Iran's signing of the Additional Protocol in December and the Paris Accord in

November 2004 was intended to build a sustainable negotiation architecture with the aim of permanent suspension. Finally, the reformist Iranian government interpreted the tectonic shifts in the region since 2001 and Europe's offer of engagement as opportunities to both seek détente with the US and deepen economic and political relations with the Europeans. To that end, the nuclear programme served as leverage and certainly was not an agenda item to be negotiated away.

By 2002, two years into their policy of Comprehensive Dialogue towards Iran, the Europeans remained committed to the principle of engagement. Still hopeful regarding the changes which were taking place in Iranian politics, it was believed that engagement would ultimately empower the reformists and thus allow the younger generation to push for genuine democracy.[2] The economic incentives of offering a Trade and Cooperation Agreement (TCA) with the EU and Iran's accession to the WTO were considered by European governments as effective carrots. Calling US efforts to block the WTO linkage in nuclear negotiations a 'misguided policy', an Italian official privately told US officials at a WTO General Council Meeting in May 2002 about the value of linking economic cooperation to Iran's political conduct with the West:

> Italy supports everyone for WTO accession. The WTO's most compelling aspect is its inclusiveness. 'When Israelis speak, for example, the Arabs don't walk out.' The US, he insisted, was asking the wrong question: ... the question isn't whether Iran's political conduct warrants WTO membership but whether the world is better off with Iran, notwithstanding its politics, subject to international trade rules. He believes Iran's eventual WTO membership would help stabilize the world trading system.[3]

Not realizing that the Iranians would never give up on a major strategic objective like the nuclear programme in exchange for improved economic relations with the EU or WTO membership, many EU member states considered linkage to these economic regimes to be the cornerstone of the Comprehensive Dialogue.

Parallel to EU–Iranian roundtables, Russian technicians began the construction of a heavy water facility in the Bushehr reactor. The Bush administration considered Putin's increased technical and inherently political support for Iran's nuclear programme as threatening to derail US–Russian relations and pushed the Russian government to deny Iran a functioning reactor, which, it was believed by hardliners, would ultimately be used for illegitimate purposes. In an August 2002 meeting with senior Italian Foreign Ministry officials, Prime Minister Berlusconi was pushed to 'express in the strongest terms our shared fear that Iran has the capability of using the technology Russia plans to sell to Iran to advance its program of weapons of mass destruction'.[4]

Despite US efforts, President Khatami, still trying to push through his reformist agenda domestically, continued to insist on Iran's right to enrich uranium and the peaceful nature of the programme.[5] As the Supreme Leader publicly proclaimed that Iran would not make any concessions towards the US on the nuclear issue,[6] pragmatists in the Iranian Foreign Ministry were working on diplomatic initiatives which could have ended in détente between both countries. The so-called 'Grand Bargain' initiative was rooted in initial meetings between Iranian and American officials during the Bonn negotiations to set up Afghanistan's post-Taliban government. Between November 2001 and May 2003, several meetings were held between US Deputy Assistant Secretary of State for Near Eastern Affairs Ryan Crocker, Special Envoy for Afghanistan James Dobbins and Iranian FM officials, including Deputy Iranian Foreign Minister Javad Zarif.[7] Notwithstanding President Bush's 2002 State of the Union Address, in which he called Iran a part of an 'Axis of Evil', the Iranian government also participated at the 2002 Tokyo conference for international financial support for the Karzai government, pledging $560 million in aid over five years.[8] Likewise, before the March 2003 invasion of Iraq, the Iranian Foreign Ministry privately indicated that it would not oppose the removal of Saddam Hussein but warned that the MKO in Iraq could not be allowed to exploit the situation. According to the Iranian Ambassador to Italy, the Iranian government was approached by the Iraqi Foreign Minister to ally itself with Baghdad and resist US aggression in exchange for shutting down 'Camp Ashraf' in Iraq, but turned down the offer.[9] In an April 2003 meeting between Iranian Foreign Minister Sayad Mohammad Sadr and King Hussein of Jordan, this position was reinforced and conveyed to the US Embassy in Amman.[10] While underscoring the Iranian President's 'strong concerns with unilateral action against Saddam' and the need for the UN, President Khatami's brother conveyed to Prime Minister Berlusconi that the Iranian government would be supporting post-conflict reconstruction efforts.[11] As the US wanted to secure Iranian cooperation in Afghanistan and Iraq, Iranian motivations were primarily of a strategic nature. As the US had removed two of Iran's major foes, the Iranian leadership saw US military presence along its borders less as a threat but more as an opportunity to seek engagement with the US on its own terms. Seeing Iranian influence in Iraq and progress in its nuclear programme as political capital, the offer forwarded to the Bush administration in May 2003 was done from a perception of leverage. It contained following tracks of cooperation:

1   The proposal offered 'Iranian influence for activity supporting political stabilisation and the establishment of democratic institutions and a non-religious government'.[12]
2   Catering to US security objectives, it also offered cooperation with regard to releasing information on al-Qaeda leaders, who had been detained and interrogated by Iranian intelligence after fleeing from Afghanistan.[13]
3   The offer also pledged Iranian support in the Middle East peace process and pledged cessation of 'any material support to Palestinian opposition groups (Hamas, Jihad, etc.) from Iranian territory, pressure on these organizations to stop violent action against civilians within borders of 1967'. The letter also promised Iranian support to turn Hizbollah into 'a mere political

organization within Lebanon' and accepted the 'Arab League Beirut declaration (Saudi initiative, two-states-approach)'.[14]

4   Most importantly, the letter contained a nuclear track. Aware of the Bush administration's heightened concerns over the progress in its nuclear programme, the Iranian government offered 'full transparency for security that there are no Iranian endeavours to develop or possess WMD, full cooperation with IAEA based on Iranian adoption of all relevant instruments (93 + 2 and all further IAEA protocols)'.[15]

While forwarding Iranian aims (which included 'halt of US hostile behavior and rectification of status of Iran in the US', the end of sanctions, recognition of Iranian security interests and full access to peaceful nuclear technology), the offer outlined three parallel working groups to negotiate a roadmap towards re-establishing relations. They addressed the three main areas of mutual concern/interest: (1) the nuclear programme, (2) terrorism and regional security, (3) economic cooperation. Despite Iran offering much tighter controls of its nuclear facilities by the IAEA in exchange for recognition of its strategic interests and access to nuclear energy, the offer was discarded by the Bush administration.[16]

Far from pursuing the offer of détente, the US government focused on the findings of the IAEA June 2003 report, which did not cite any NPT violations but merely noted Iran's failure to declare the import of natural uranium in 1991, the activities involving the subsequent processing at the Natanz uranium enrichment facility and the heavy water production plant at Arak.[17] Neo-conservative policymakers interpreted the report as further confirmation that the nuclear file ought to be brought before the UN Security Council and that the EU's engagement was not going anywhere.[18]

The 2003 Tehran Declaration

As the US government lobbied allies to move the nuclear case to the UN Security Council, the Iranian Foreign Minister focused on the fact that it had not violated its safeguards obligation. Foreign Ministry officials insisted that the heavy water enrichment facility had not been declared any sooner as they did not want to come under increased scrutiny. In a meeting with Canadian Foreign Minister Graham, Iranian Foreign Minister Kharrazi said that his government 'was being as transparent as possible and would have no problem "in principle" in signing the additional protocol, but that the additional protocol was controversial in Tehran'. The internal debate over the expediency of signing the Additional Protocol, according to Kharrazi, was the expectation among Iranian officials that it was unlikely to satisfy the US and would not relieve international pressure.[19] Iranian suspicions proved correct as the US government, while publicly calling Iran to sign it, told its regional allies that it regarded the Additional Protocol (AP) as important but not sufficient.[20] Pressure on Iran increased substantially after IAEA inspectors found more undeclared enriched uranium. The subsequent IAEA resolution on 12 September 2003 stated:

(h) Noting with concern:
  • that the Agency environmental sampling at Natanz has revealed the presence of two types of high enriched uranium, which requires additional work to enable the Agency to arrive at a conclusion;
  • that IAEA inspectors found considerable modifications had been made to the premises at the Kalaye Electric Company prior to inspections that may impact on the accuracy of the environmental sampling;
  • that some of Iran's statements to the IAEA have undergone significant and material changes, and that the number of outstanding issues has increased since the report;
  • that despite the Board's statement in June 2003 encouraging Iran, as a confidence-building measure, not to introduce nuclear material into its pilot centrifuge enrichment cascade at Natanz, Iran has introduced such material;

(i) Expressing grave concern that, more than one year after initial IAEA inquiries to Iran about undeclared activities, Iran has still not enabled the IAEA to provide the assurances required by Member States that all nuclear material in Iran is declared and submitted to Agency safeguards and that there are no undeclared nuclear activities in Iran,[21]

The IAEA gave Iran until the end of October to ensure verification of compliance with the NPT's safeguards agreements.[22] The highest decision-making body of the EU also emphasized the importance of this deadline. Congratulating Shirin Ebadi on her award of the Nobel Peace Prize, the Council of the European Union charged Iran 'promptly and unconditionally to sign, to ratify and to implement the IAEA Additional Protocol on Safeguards and to act immediately in accordance with it'. For the first time, the Council also called on Iran to suspend all enrichment activities.[23] Notwithstanding US demands for another non-compliance resolution by the IAEA board, the Europeans opted for quiet diplomacy in order to keep the Iranians at the negotiation table. A senior official at the Dutch Ministry of Foreign Affairs told US officials in confidence 'that pushing for a resolution in the present climate may cause Iran to become less cooperative with IAEA, possibly giving them an excuse to withdraw from the NPT altogether'. According to the official's view, a

> two-pronged approach [was] necessary in dealing with Iran: obtaining Iranian accession to an Additional Protocol and providing full cooperation with the IAEA, and also international efforts to move Iran away from those elements of its program that will lead it to a breakout capability.[24]

The Dutch appreciated that the Iranians were working in a highly volatile domestic arena and that any more pressure was unlikely to produce results.[25] The IAEA's ultimatum caused a heated debate between reformists in the government and conservatives close to the Supreme Leader. Conscious of the looming referral of the nuclear case to the UN Security Council, reformists lobbied for the signing of the Additional Protocol and saw engagement with the EU as a means of avoiding punitive measures against Iran. To that end, the head of the Atomic Energy Organization of Iran (AEOI), Gholam-Reza Azadegan, called on the EU to 'depoliticize the nuclear negotiations in order to allow the IAEA to conduct [inspections] without propaganda'.[26] For the Iranians to invite the Foreign Ministers of the EU-3 and eventually agree to European demands was largely meant to avoid referral to the UN Security Council and presented a departure from Khatami's previous rights-based position. Positioning their argument within international law, Iranian negotiators argued that Iran could not be deprived of the rights it enjoyed under NPT Article IV, which granted the right to 'develop research, production and use of nuclear energy for peaceful purposes without discrimination'.[27] Following consultations with the Director General of the IAEA, Mohamed El Baradei, and after submitting required documentations to the agency, the Iranian government hosted the Foreign Ministers of Germany, France and Britain on 21 October 2003. In the concluding declaration, the Iranian government reaffirmed that its intentions were for peaceful purposes and committed itself to fully cooperate with the IAEA, declared its intention to sign the Additional Protocol, as well as agreeing to voluntarily suspend enrichment activities.[28] In exchange – and contingent on satisfactory assurances – the EU-3 promised long-term cooperation and access to modern technology.[29] The Khatami government and the Secretary of the Supreme National Security Council, Hassan Rowhani, treated the declaration as a demonstration of good faith. Far from surrendering Iranian rights under the NPT, the Iranian government demonstrated full transparency and thus wanted to prove that the programme was solely peaceful.[30] Purportedly, the decision to lift suspension was made in a meeting which included all members of the political elite, including former Prime Minister Mousavi.[31] The US National Intelligence Estimate of 2007 concluded that it was during this period that the Iranian leadership ordered a halt to weaponization work because of international pressure.[32] While the Iranians denied the finding of the National Intelligence Estimate (NIE) of 2007 that it had been working on a weapons programme, the leadership certainly wanted to avoid referral to the UN Security Council. The declaration to sign the Additional Protocol caused much public objection among hardliners, accusing the government of treason.[33] Defending the decision as one informed by national interest, Foreign Ministry officials were quick to highlight that Europe too must honour its commitments in the declaration.[34] The EU High Representative for CFSP, Javier Solana, called the Tehran Declaration a first step towards enrichment suspension as well as a long-term agreement and promised that negotiations on a Trade and Cooperation Agreement would be resumed as soon as suspension was verified.[35] However, subsequent reports by the IAEA, which disclosed more previously unknown details about the programme (most of which were disclosed through communications from the Iranian government), caused the Europeans to focus on Iranian assurances rather than fulfilling their own promises. Even though the November 2003 report by the IAEA concluded that there was no evidence that the previously undeclared nuclear material and activities were part of a nuclear weapons programme, Iran's 'past pattern of concealment' called for more time to verify the programme's exclusive peaceful nature.[36] Overall, Iran's own disclosure and visits by IAEA officials showed that Iran had completed 'the front end of a nuclear fuel cycle, including uranium mining and milling, conversion, enrichment, fuel fabrication, heavy water production, a light water reactor, a heavy water research reactor and associated research and development facilities'.[37] Even though the Iranian government formally signed the Additional Protocol on 18 December 2003, EU governments and particularly the United States focused on Iranian breaches rather than these confidence-building measures. El Baradei cautioned: 'proceed slowly and cautiously with Iran, so Iran does not feel threatened and turn into another North Korea'. As Qaddafi had just decided to dismantle Libya's entire WMD programme under the auspices of the Chemical Weapons Convention,[38] El Baradei reminded the Spanish Foreign Minister, Ana de Palacio:

> that where Libya has 'locked up' and made available for inspection its nuclear program equipment, Iran has only suspended its enrichment activities. Iran's nuclear program is far more developed than Libya's and could be restarted at any moment. It will be important, said El Baradei, not to provoke Iran, but rather to coax it into cooperating with the international community and eventually abandoning its program.[39]

The Italian Foreign Ministry described the 'mood at the IAEA after receiving El Baradei's February 24 report on Iran [as] business as usual and that Tehran is singing the same old song'.[40] To the Italian officials in particular two breaches stood out as very 'disturbing': Iran's omission of P-2 centrifuges (advanced centrifuges) from its November declaration and its production of polonium.[41] Dutch and Spanish officials also expressed concerns about the alleged military aspects of the nuclear programme but – in line with the EU-3 tone – did not favour a referral to the UN Security Council, rather believing that the carrot of the TCA with the EU would be most effective. To that end, it was made clear to the Iranian government that negotiations towards the TCA would not resume until the EU received 'a clear bill of health', which according to Senior Dutch Ministry of Foreign Affairs officials was unlikely to happen.[42] The Foreign Affairs Select Committee of the British parliament also interpreted El Baradei's report as one showing Iran as 'guilty of either careless inefficiency or of deliberate deceit'.[43] According to Seyed Hossein Mousavian's autobiography, not even the Iranian negotiation team knew that Iran had obtained drawings from Pakistan for the P-2s, along with less sophisticated technology. Mousavian writes:

> Once again, Iran was acknowledging facts after they had been discovered by others ... I more than once heard important news for the first time from IAEA officials or the foreign media and then had to work on reformulating plans to manage the crises that the news gave rise to.[44]

Overall, EU governments wanted Iran to comply with IAEA commitments, which also meant that it had to allow immediate resumption of inspections of all nuclear sites. Crediting the EU's multilateral initiative as one, which managed to sway Iran to modify its policies, EU officials felt vindicated at the efficacy of engagement. To that end, Europeans continued to resist US calls for UNSC referral but rather intrusive monitoring and verification measures under IAEA auspices.[45] As Europeans called for continued vigilance by means of multilateral diplomacy and IAEA inspections, the Iranian Foreign Minister communicated to the Italian Foreign Ministry that it even though it had 'complied with almost all EU-3 demands [it] had received no recognition for its efforts [and failure on part of the EU to deliver] would soon become a major internal problem in Iran'.[46] The Iranians rightly felt that they had disclosed previously unknown information about the nuclear programme as well as meeting European demands by signing the Additional Protocol, but far from receiving the promised rewards had only earned more criticism. The Iranian Embassy's Second Secretary, communicated to FCO officials as well as to his French counterpart in London that the way Iran was being treated by the international community over the nuclear programme, in particular the 'hard line represented by the US and most recent IAEA BoG [Board of Governors] report was playing into the hands of the fundamentalists in Tehran'. Reiterating the civilian nature of the programme, he told the FCO that Iran wanted to 'move closer to the West and wants European business, especially in the energy sector, to invest'. While thanking coalition forces for removing Saddam Hussein for the sake of regional security, the Iranian Embassy in London conveyed its concerns over the US government's ulterior motives regarding the future of Iraq and the region, as well as Iran. Fearing an 'Iraq style armed intervention' stemming out of the increased vilification of Iran, the Iranian Embassy warned that more of the coercive diplomacy employed against Iran might cause his government to go down the same path as North Korea rather than towards 'Westernization'.[47]

The 2004 Paris Agreement

EU officials conducting the negotiations appreciated the Iranian government's frustration. To make matters worse for the reformist government, nuclear negotiations ran parallel to the EU's human rights roundtables with Iran (Roundtable on Discrimination and Torture in December 2002; Roundtable on the Rule of Law in March 2003; Roundtable on Freedom of Expression in October 2003; Roundtable on Administration of Justice in June 2004) in order to bring 'concrete improvements in the respect of human rights and fundamental freedoms'.[48] However, the EU-3 and EU Commission dealt exclusively on nuclear affairs with Hassan Rowhani, Khamenei's appointed chair of the Supreme National Security Council. By almost completely sidestepping the elected government, EU officials appreciated that they had effectively undermined Khatami's legitimacy.[49] Having received no rewards and feeling essentially humiliated before its domestic constituency, the Iranian government eventually threatened to withdraw from the Comprehensive Dialogue. It is against this background that one has to understand the EU's rather benign reaction to the so-called election coup d'état in January 2004, when over 3,500 reformist candidates were disqualified by the Guardian Council, thus effectively paving the way for conservatives to win a landslide victory in the Iranian parliament.[50] EU officials were conscious of forces at play in Iranian politics. Hardliners were eager to start purging reformists from the political arena (a campaign which purportedly reached its climax in the 2009 presidential elections) and clearly felt that the Europeans would not reprimand them, rather wanting to keep them at the negotiation table. Effectively a series of initiatives by the EU to sway Iran on the nuclear issue made the government irrelevant and strengthened the unelected elements in the Iranian political system. Therefore, following the January parliamentary elections, a priority for the EU was to keep Iranians at the negotiation table as well as create a new climate of trust.[51] Essentially, this meant turning a blind eye to the human rights violations. Prince Charles's humanitarian visit following the earthquake in Bam – the first royal visit since 1978 – was seen by many in Iran as a conferral upon the coup.[52]

Following the Tehran Declaration, the EU-3 with its High Representative for CFSP, Javier Solana, and other officials in the EU Commission started to pursue a highly coordinated initiative to bring the negotiations towards a meaningful agreement. As far as the then still nascent CFSP was concerned, by 2004 all EU policies towards Iran were being coordinated by the EU-3 and Solana, with his Council Secretariat playing a central role as clearing-house and main policy driver.[53] By October 2004, these efforts were informed by a sense of urgency among EU officials and the EU-3 as Iran had just announced its successful conversion of thirty-seven tons of yellowcake into uranium hexafluoride and seemed to have mastered the complex centrifuge technology related to uranium enrichment. Both represented 'chokepoints' for US and EU officials, which, according to their estimates, moved Iran closer to the breakout capability.[54] Even though EU officials quietly acknowledged that engagement with Iran had failed, the US Embassy in Brussels noted that 'their only prescription was more engagement'.[55] To the EU, major incentives were needed in order to sway Iran. This ultimately also meant that the US needed to extend 'significant carrots', which to EU officials had to include some kind of security guarantees.[56] To the EU, referral to the UN Security Council would shift the issue to 'an almost inevitable path toward conflict', fearing that Iran would be likely to withdraw from the NPT altogether and accelerate its enrichment activities without any multilateral inspections regime. Europeans wanted to prevent Iran from withdrawing and pursuing nuclear weapons outside the NPT. US State Department officials questioned this European premise, seeing Iran pursuing nuclear weapons within the NPT as even worse. To the US government, referral to the UN Security Council primarily served as 'legal basis for requiring Iran to suspend enrichment, and also put Iran's programme in a broader context than its narrower NPT obligations'. As Iran was not violating the NPT and the IAEA could only 'call on' Iran to suspect enrichment activities, referral to the UNSC was seen as vital by the Bush administration in compelling Iran to do so.[57] During consultations in October 2004, a Senior EU official, told Canadian and US diplomats:

> The US seems concerned that Iran would respond to a G8 proposal (and thus postpone referral to the UNSC). I'm concerned they won't respond at all. If Iran does respond to a G8 initiative, even on the eve of the November Board meeting, EU member states are not likely to support referral to the UNSC.[58]

Underneath the veneer of US–EU coordinated diplomacy towards Iran were substantial disagreements, not only about the substance and direction of diplomatic initiatives on the nuclear programme, but about the engagement with the wider region as a whole. As the Bush administration had just announced its Greater Middle East (GME) Initiative (to be launched at the G8 Meeting in Georgia in June 2004) to help transform the region towards democracy, the EU embraced the 'Barcelona Process' and the 'European Neighbourhood Policy' as effective regimes to promote economic, political and security cooperation with the region. US officials appreciated that the Barcelona Process was an initiative which the EU wanted to keep separate from US regional efforts.[59] At a time when US credibility in the region was low and when Arab countries (led by Egypt and Saudi Arabia) rejected the GME as an attempt to impose Western views on the Arab World,[60] EU governments saw little expediency in being associated with the Bush administration's democratization efforts. What this meant for diplomacy towards Iran was that, essentially, Europeans were not on board with the GME whereas the US administration did not want to link a G8 initiative to nuclear diplomacy without simultaneously referring Iran to the UNSC. On these grounds, the Bush administration rejected European demands to throw in US incentives and security guarantees. This US reluctance to support a G8-backed initiative was summarized by the US Embassy in Brussels:

> There are several implications for transatlantic relations in the EU's approach. First, the EU is not at present prepared to support pursuing a G8 package in parallel with referral to the UNSC. In their eyes, these are mutually exclusive approaches, and US insistence on referral in November will be viewed as explicitly undermining chances for successful G8 initiative. Failure of a G8 initiative – either due to the G8's inability to agree on a package, or due to Iran's rejection of an agreed package – could also be laid at the US's door if the US is viewed as having prevented agreement on a package, or is viewed as being unwilling to offer a carrot sufficiently enticing to bring Iran around. The last place the EU will look to place blame will be Tehran, absent an outright Iranian rejection of a G8 package the EU judges to be 'sufficient'. We thus risk a break with the EU over (a) the composition of a G8 package – specifically, what US incentives are included, and (b) how the G8 initiative is linked to referral to the UNSC – specifically, whether the

US would agree not to seek referral if Iran responds positively to a G8 initiative. A break with the EU over either issue could complicate our efforts in the IAEA Board to refer Iran to the UNSC or, once in the UNSC, our ability to secure the votes needed to take any action.[61]

In addition to EU–US disagreements on how best to elicit Iranian cooperation (which one US official at the Embassy in Brussels described as another potential 'transatlantic train wreck')[62] was the position of Russia, which agreed to hold the US$1 billion project at the Bushehr nuclear facility but had made it clear that it was seeking a substantial stake in Iran's economy. On 6 May 2004, the US House of Representatives passed Resolution 398 in an almost unanimous vote, calling on the US government 'to use all appropriate means to deter, dissuade, and prevent Iran from acquiring nuclear weapons' and requiring Europe, Japan and Russia to cut commercial and energy ties with Iran. It also demanded that Russia 'suspend its nuclear cooperation with Iran and refrain from making an agreement on the supply of nuclear fuel to the reactor in Bushehr' until Iran halted all activities which might be associated with a nuclear weapons programme.[63]

So, when the EU-3 and the High Representative for CFS met the Iranian delegation in Paris in November 2004 for another round of talks, the offer forwarded to the Iranians was neither underwritten by a G8-wide initiative nor supported by the US government.

In the so-called Paris Accord, the Iranians committed themselves to voluntarily extend uranium enrichment and reprocessing activities, which included the manufacturing and import of gas centrifuges, plutonium separation and tests or production of uranium conversion installation.[64] The language used in the final communiqué was important as, contrary to the US position, EU officials moved away from insisting on enrichment cessation but rather emphasized 'objective guarantees' in a long-term agreement. Without this clause, the Iranians would have not signed off to the document. Therefore, the most important part in the Paris Agreement read:

> Sustaining the suspension, while negotiations on a long-term agreement are under way, will be essential for the continuation of the overall process. In the context of this suspension, the E3/EU and Iran have agreed to begin negotiations, with a view to reaching a mutually acceptable agreement on long term arrangements. The agreement will provide objective guarantees that Iran's nuclear programme is exclusively for peaceful purposes. It will equally provide firm guarantees on nuclear, technological and economic cooperation and firm commitments on security issues.[65]

The IAEA report, which was made public on the same day, commended Iran for having made good progress in correcting previous breaches, but the IAEA still needed assurance that there were no undeclared enrichment activities on two issues: 'the origin of LEU and HEU particle contamination found at various locations in Iran; and the extent of Iran's efforts to import, manufacture and use centrifuges of both the P-1 and P-2 designs'.[66]

Immediately following the Paris deal, the EU Commission renewed negotiations with Iran on the Trade and Cooperation Agreement as well as wanting to reopen its dialogues on human rights and terrorism. Most importantly, talks on a long-term agreement started in December.[67] According to a senior EU official, neither the 13 December ministerial meeting nor the 17 December Nuclear Working Group were substantive. While they served as 'ice-breakers' with Cyrus Naseri, Iran's new representative to the IAEA, in a closed meeting with US officials, the official questioned whether the EU-3 could achieve its goals without eventual US involvement.[68] During negotiations, it became evident that neither the EU-3 nor the Iranian government were willing to shift their red lines. To the EU-3 the demand for permanent cessation remained non-negotiable and 'no other objective-guarantee' would suffice. By the same token, Iranian interlocutors did 'not even hint at the possibility of giving up the sacred right to develop and maintain a nuclear fuel cycle'. Iranians spent much time posturing and, according to the EU official, 'always sought to maintain a façade of equality, as though they should be treated with the same trust and respect as any other 'responsible' state. Talks also revealed Iranian mistrust of the Russians and wanted 'a more reliable source of fuel that would not squeeze them for extra profit or political gain'.[69] Essentially, to the EU, the talks were used by the Iranians to buy time and the official doubted that Iran would ever 'make a strategic decision to come clean until the US was somehow involved'.[70] The list presented by the Iranian delegation wanted the working groups to be divided into a nuclear group, a political and security group and a group for technology and economic development. The EU official shared this list with US diplomats in Brussels:

Nuclear Group:
1   objective guarantees
2   peaceful applications, including:
     a   nuclear fuel supplies ('can't rely on tricky Russians')
     b   joint projects (not defined).

Political and Security Group:
1   sustained partnership on regional issues
2   cooperation on counter-terrorism
3   security assurances (Note: we took this as code for US engagement)
4   nuclear weapons free zone in the Middle East
5   export controls
6   defense relations, including:
     a   counter-narcotics
     b   counter-terrorism
     c   conventional defense cooperation.

Technology and Economic Development:
1   easing EU export restrictions
2   technical assistance
3   financial assistance
4   energy
5   trade liberalization.[71]

According to the senior EU official, the EU-3 did not respond to this list nor did they want to discuss Iranian demands to ease European exports or allow an Iranian delegation to tour European energy facilities; rather, they questioned Iran's need for a 6,000 megawatt nuclear energy capacity by 2020.[72] Talks in January 2005 were also characterized by intransigence on both sides. In the political/security group, Iranians wanted to limit talks to al-Qaeda and the MEK while Europe wanted to expand to Iranian proxies. In the technology group, Iranians asked for much-needed spare parts for their ageing civilian aircraft fleet but this was deferred by EU officials on the grounds that it was linked to US sanctions. In the nuclear group, the Iranian delegation, according to a senior French Foreign Ministry official, was not ready to make any concessions to EU demands of indefinite suspension.[73] Iranian interlocutors were operating in a highly charged political environment back in Iran. As a senior official in the French Foreign Ministry, remarked to US officials in Washington: 'the internal dynamics in Iran are very important – not everyone in Iran is looking for a successful outcome ... those doing the negotiations have to demonstrate that they haven't given in to the interests of the West'.[74] Following the Paris Agreement, conservatives in the Iranian parliament and outlets close to the Supreme Leader called on the Iranian government to resume enrichment should the EU fail to meet its commitments.[75] There were also critical voices over the IAEA Board of Governors resolution, which was drafted by the EU-3 and presented on 29 November. *Majlis* Speaker Gholam-Ali Haddad-Adel warned that the resolution ought to reflect EU commitments, saying that

> we are waiting to see what decision the IAEA will make in the meeting. We will see if it will be a decision on legal grounds or a political one under US pressure that will have the effect of fanning their strategy of creating hegemony and chaos.[76]

The spokesman of the Iranian delegation to the IAEA, Seyed Hossein Mousavian, called the resolution the 'most positive draft resolution issued on Iran's nuclear programme ever since the crisis on Iran's nuclear activities started'. However, Mousavian and numerous top officials considered the resolution as proof that Iran had carried out its commitments and had, therefore, been taken out from the Board of Governors' agenda altogether. Rather, it was now up to Europe to meet its commitments on the basis of the Paris Agreement.[77] President Khatami too treated the resolution as a step forward towards cooperation, saying, 'Iran is following up cooperation with the IAEA and the European

Union in good faith and will be victorious in building confidence with the international community.'[78] Faced with domestic dissent over selling out to the Europeans, the Khatami government needed the EU's promised rewards to materialize.

However, the Bush administration's position eventually hardened. Having obtained information from the dissident group MEK (which was listed as a terrorist group by the US Department of State) which allegedly contained Iranian designs for a nuclear warhead, US Secretary of State Colin Powell accused Iran of secretly working on technology to fit a nuclear warhead on a missile. In early 2005, the Bush administration then presented the data, which alleged to show Iran having tested detailed high explosives and a nuclear-capable missile warhead. The Iranian government dismissed the 'alleged studies' as forgeries by hostile intelligence services. Then, on 22 December, Iran's intelligence minister announced the arrest of more than ten people on spying charges, accusing them of passing sensitive information on Iran's nuclear programme to the Israeli Mossad and the CIA.[79] In late 2011, these alleged studies would be eventually handed over to the IAEA by the US government.

Because of the deteriorating tone of US diplomacy (the EU publicly criticized the US government after it had rejected Iran's application to join the WTO for the twentieth time[80]), the EU-3 had few options to settle the impasse in negotiations. As such, the EU-3 continued to apply pressure on the Iranians to implement the Board of Governors resolution and respect its commitments for suspension.[81] Notwithstanding conciliatory remarks by Rowhani in Kuwait in June, which said that if the US were 'to change its language of threats and end sanctions they imposed on Iranian interests ... I believe new conditions will prevail in relations between Iran and America',[82] the Bush administration continued to refuse to participate in talks but rather emphasized Iran's threat to regional security.[83] With the Iranian parliament and government officials announcing resumption of uranium enrichment, the Paris Agreement had effectively failed.

Conclusion

The EU-3 brokered agreements in Tehran in 2003 and Paris in 2004 for several reasons. First, the EU-3 and the Bush administration insisted on full enrichment cessation and dismantling of Iran's fissile material production efforts. Diplomatic communication between European governments and the US Department of State indicates that there was no trust towards Iran. Even though Iran had disclosed its previous breaches to the IAEA and signed the Additional Protocol, neither the EU-3 nor the US government considered the NPT as a sufficient regime to monitor Iran. Essentially, the Iranians were told that the rights under the NPT did not apply to them. Much of Iranian diplomacy was, therefore, used to emphasize that enrichment was an unqualified right. Second, after the Bush administration rejected the proposal of détente by the Iranians in 2003 on the grounds that it must have been insincere, the US government remained absent from nuclear talks. Even though the Europeans quietly acknowledged to the US State Department that the US constituted an important variable without which the nuclear issue was unlikely to be resolved, the Bush administration refused to take part in negotiations. In the absence of a major US policy shift towards Iran, the perception of the Khatami administration and conservatives alike was that they had made concessions but were given no rewards in exchange. The Iranians had suspended enrichment but gained nothing in return. Finally, there were considerable ideological differences between the US and European powers, which made coordinated engagement almost impossible. The Bush administration was frustrated with European insistence on 'effective multilateralism' and 'assertive, full spectrum engagement'.[84] Even though there was a transatlantic consensus that a nuclear Iran was unacceptable, the US favoured pressure and isolation over engagement.[85] To the US, engagement was ultimately a sign of weakness. With the EU lacking a military capability, US officials perceived that there was no other viable alternative available to European governments. Between 2003 and 2004, EU engagement towards Iran was seen by the US Embassy in Brussels as rewarding Iran for complying with commitments it had made and breached.[86]

> Unfortunately, the ESS [European Security Strategy] fails to address adequately the question of what the EU should do if multilateral efforts fail. The Europeans still find it difficult to answer the question of how to deal with states or non-state actors that defy the international community, or seek to circumvent accepted rules of behavior. As we saw in their approach in Iraq, and are seeing again in Iran, the Europeans advocate carrot-and-stick diplomacy that is heavy on the carrot but are extremely reluctant to use the stick.[87]

Officials in the Bush administration perceived Iran to be negotiating in bad faith and were waiting for the Europeans to take on a more coercive stance, thus effectively negotiating in bad faith themselves. To that end, a senior official at the US Mission to the European Union wrote to Washington that

> our best ally in changing the EU view over time will probably to be Iran's own duplicity. Sharing information that indicates Iran's response to the EU-3 is a tactical ploy, and not a strategic decision to forego pursuit of nuclear weapons, can help the EU draw its own conclusions about the ineffectiveness of engagement.[88]

Eventually, with the British government taking over the EU Presidency in July 2005 and the Iranian government's announcement that it would resume enrichment, EU member states' positions towards Iran hardened, advocating referral to the UN Security Council.[89]

3   The arc of extremism

Ahmadinejad, the EU-3 and the Bush administration (2005–2007)

Introduction

The perceived failure on the part of the EU to live up to the commitments of the Paris Agreement and the June 2005 election of Mahmoud Ahmadinejad, who was driven by a new form of Iranian nationalism fundamentally tied to the nuclear programme, caused the Iranian government to resume enrichment in Isfahan. The EU-3 offer in August 2005 was largely informed by an objective to maintain a framework of negotiations on a package that would be acceptable to the Iranians as well as the Bush administration, which still largely considered engagement as too conciliatory. The EU's reaffirmation of unilateral security guarantees, international fuel assurances and the offer of long-term cooperation in the civil nuclear field between Iran and Russia was largely irrelevant to Iranian policymakers, who only too well appreciated the fact the US was not on board. Throughout 2006 and 2007, the EU negotiators were largely caught in the middle, mediating between Iran, which was not interested in a compromise but rather felt emboldened regarding its rising clout in a new Middle East (particular after the perceived Hezbollah victory against Israel in the June 2006 conflict), and the US, which saw the referral to the UN Security Council as the means to legitimize containment of Iran. Essentially, the EU-3 was unable to mediate with Washington and Tehran and thus effectively negotiated in bad faith. This chapter argues that Tehran viewed the 2005 offer as too intrusive, considering inspections to be beyond the Safeguards Agreement or the Additional Protocol. On this basis, enrichment activities resumed.

'The cow is out of the barn'

EU negotiators still viewed negotiations for the TCA and parallel Political Agreement with Iran as an effective means to control Iranian behaviour in the long term. EU Council Secretariat officials were confident in January 2005 that talks could be upheld and would ultimately serve confidence-building purposes. It was still believed that these agreements provided Iran with a sufficient incentive to maintain enrichment suspension until mid-2005. However, it was recognized by senior EU officials that 'locking in a long-term agreement' required 'a positive signal from the US'. A senior EU Council official told US diplomats that the success of EU political and economic initiatives was ultimately contingent on US policy, cautioning that

> should the talks reach the point where a small step by the US could keep the enrichment suspension in place, it would be difficult for the EU to blame Iran if the US proved unwilling to make a gesture toward Tehran.[1]

Notwithstanding EU optimism, the actual negotiations in the three EU–Iran working groups (political and security; economic cooperation and technology; nuclear) were dominated by Iranian demands that they should be presented with 'concrete, meaningful packages'[2] and insistence by EU officials for Iran to give 'objective guarantees' for non-military diversion. The Iranian government interpreted as progress the fact that the IAEA's March 2005 Board Meeting did not have Iran on the agenda for the first time in almost two years, and were eager to flesh out the particulars of a strategic relationship with the EU.[3] On the other hand, the EU-3, in particular the French government, feared that negotiations were being moved from the technical to the political level. In a meeting between French President Jacques Chirac and Hassan Rowhani in February, Chirac's Middle East adviser described the Iranian Chief Negotiator's visit to Paris, London and Berlin as an attempt to politicize the talks by 'taking them to the highest political echelon' in order 'to maximize the chances of an outcome most favourable to them'. In the meeting, Chirac reiterated EU demands for 'objective guarantees' and 'permanent measures' and told Rowhani that Iran needed to 'join up with the new realities in the region'.[4] In an interview with *Le Monde*, Rowhani then accused the EU of being 'incapable of keeping promises', and complained that nothing had been done to help Iran acquire much-needed civil Airbus aircraft or gain entry into the WTO. Frustrated at the slow pace of talks, he described the principal problem as one of interpretation of the term 'objective guarantees'.[5] Iranian diplomats appreciated that the key concern for Europeans was the permanence of an Iranian commitment of non-diversion. Guarantees for non-diversion needed to be honoured by successive Iranian governments and, as such, must not be subject to change as political conditions changed in Iran.[6] Likewise, EU envoys continued to emphasize that Iran need not produce uranium for the Tehran Research Reactor (TRR) and Bushehr but rather could obtain it from the international market. Therefore, the best way to reassure the Europeans and the US about non-diversion, it was believed by EU officials, was to abandon the entire enrichment process altogether. To Mousavian, Iran's position was informed by 'the experience of Western countries breaching their contracts with Iran after the 1979 Islamic Revolution', which caused the Iranian government not to

> trust promises from the international community to provide the fuel it needed in the long term. Furthermore, the rights to enrichment were inalienable under the NPT, regardless of whether depriving a country of those rights would be an expedient means of guaranteeing non-diversion.[7]

The Iranians presented two proposals to the EU-3/Iran Political and Security Working Group on 17 January and 23 March 2005. Both proposals maintained that existing international regimes (the NPT, the Safeguards Agreement, the Additional Protocol and cooperation with the IAEA)[8] were the most reliable 'objective guarantees'. Reflecting this mindset, the March proposal envisioned following a performance-based 'General Framework for Objective Guarantees, Firm Guarantees, and Firm Commitments':

A.1 Actions by Iran in Phase 1 (April–July 2005)
- Approval of the Additional Protocol in the cabinet
- Policy declaration on Iran's open fuel cycle (non-reprocessing)
- Presentation of legislation on peaceful use of nuclear technology, including permanent ban on production, Stockpiling and use of nuclear weapons to the Majlis
- Resumption of the work of the uranium conversion facility (UCF)
- Storage of UF6 [uranium hexafluoride] under Agency surveillance.

A.2 Actions by EU-3/EU in Phase 1
- Declaration of EU policy to guarantee Iran's access to EU markets and financial and public and private investment resources
- Declaration of EU recognition of Iran as a major source of energy supply for Europe
- Launching of feasibility studies for building of new nuclear power plants in Iran by EU-3/EU members.

B.1 Actions by Iran in Phase 2
- Presentation of the Additional Protocol to the Majlis for Ratification
- Strengthening of Legal Export Control Mechanisms
- Policy declaration on the ceiling of enrichment at LEU level
- Policy declaration on conversion of all enriched uranium to fuel rods
- Assembly, installation and testing of 3,000 centrifuges in Natanz.

B.2 Actions by EU-3/EU in Phase 2
- Declaration of EU policy to guarantee Iran's access to advancer and nuclear technology
- Declaration of EU readiness to participate in building new nuclear power plants in Iran
- Signing of contracts for construction of nuclear power plants in Iran by EU-3/EU members.

C.1 Actions by Iran in Phase 3
- Employing all appropriate measures for adoption of the legislation on peaceful use of nuclear technology, including permanent ban on production, stockpiling and use of nuclear weapons by the Majlis

- Allowing continuous on-site presence of IAEA inspectors, which can include EU-3/EU nationals at the UCF and Natanz
- Commissioning of the above centrifuges in Natanz
- Immediate conversion of the total product of the above to fuel rods
- Incremental manufacturing, assembly and installation of centrifuge components up to the numbers envisaged for Natanz

C.2 Actions by EU-3/EU in Phase 3
- Normalizing Iran's status under G8 export control regulations
- Firm guarantees on the supply of fuel necessary for Iranian nuclear power reactors to complement Iran's domestic production
- Presentation and active follow-up of an EU initiative to establish a zone free of weapons of mass destruction in the Middle East.

D.1 Actions by Iran in Phase 4
- Employing all appropriate measures for ratification of the Additional Protocol by the Majlis
- Commencement of phased commissioning of Natanz
- Immediate conversion of the total product of the above to fuel rods.

D.2 Actions by the EU-3/EU in Phase 4
- Conclusion of contracts for defence items
- Beginning of construction of new nuclear power plants in Iran by EU-3/EU members.[9]

The proposal coincided with a conference in Tehran on 'Nuclear Technology and Sustainable Development', sponsored by the Iranian Centre for Strategic Research, the Foreign Ministry, the Atomic Energy Organization of Iran and the Ministry of Science Research and Technology. The French Foreign Ministry's Director for Policy Planning, who was the only EU official to attend the conference, perceived the purpose of the conference as being to reinforce the official position about the irrevocability of the nuclear programme. The French official noted that one Iranian conference participant referred to the Iranian government's red line against cessation of enrichment as 'the cow is out of the barn'.[10] However, El Baradei interpreted Rowhani's March proposal as one informed by diplomatic manoeuvring between the Iranian government, which wanted to see progress 'in the form of concrete deliverables', and the EU. According to El Baradei's own understanding, the Iranians wanted to complete a small conversion plant and a small pilot enrichment facility but freeze the industrial-scale enrichment plant at Natanz for a number of years. Thus, the March proposal was meant to signal to the Europeans that Iran was willing to reduce the scale of enrichment yet simultaneously communicate to the Iranian public that the country's enrichment programme was on-going.[11]

Notwithstanding the Bush administration's decision to drop its opposition to Iran's application to the WTO and to consider 'on a case-by-case basis' the export licensing of spare parts for Iran's civilian aircraft,[12] the EU-3/Iran Steering Committee meeting in April 2005 showed that neither side was able to deliver. According to Mousavian, the Iranian negotiators reminded their European counterparts of the domestic pressures they were facing, saying that they were accused of 'having been tricked into accepting suspension and getting nothing in return'.[13] The Iranian parliament had just passed a resolution opposing what it perceived to be US efforts to overthrow the Islamic Republic. In April 2005, pursuant to a US$3 million Congressional appropriation, the US State Department solicited initiatives from various 'educational institutions, humanitarian groups, nongovernmental organizations, and individuals inside Iran to support the advancement of democracy and human rights'. Iranian Ambassador to the UN Mohammad Javad Zarif denounced this initiative as a violation of the Algiers Accords.[14] Against this backdrop, hardliners continued to exert pressure on Khatami's government. When the Iranian negotiation team met with the EU-3 in London on 29 April, Rowhani warned EU diplomats that he had been given the order by the Supreme Leader to restart uranium conversion activities at the plant in Isfahan.[15] The proposal presented during the Steering Committee meeting in London centred on short-term confidence-building measures. The most important elements were:

- Iran's adoption of the IAEA Additional Protocol
- A policy declaration of no reprocessing by Iran
- Continued enrichment suspension for six months
- Establishment of joint task forces on counter-terrorism and export control
- An EU declaration recognizing Iran as a major source of energy for Europe.[16]

Unable to come to agreement on the Iranian proposal owing to US opposition to any agreement which would have granted Iran's right to enrichment, the March proposal failed to produce any breakthrough.[17] Following a meeting between the EU-3 Ambassadors to the IAEA and El Baradei in Vienna, Rowhani was presented with a letter on 11 May, which according to the IAEA chief was too threatening and offered no carrots. It communicated that

> Iran should be in no doubt that any such change to the suspension would be a clear breach of the Paris Agreement and of the IAEA resolutions. It would bring the negotiating process to an end. The consequences beyond could only be negative for Iran.

According to the French Foreign Ministry's Political Director, Iran

> had missed an opportunity to take advantage of previous EU offers for cooperation, e.g. on civilian nuclear programmes, but had chosen instead to block such offers. He said 'we have proof' that Iranian enrichment had nothing to do with civilian programs.[18]

To the EU-3, Iran's intent to restart conversion activities was seen as a 'grey area' as the issue of conversion had not been covered in the 2003 IAEA defini- tion of enrichment activity, and it was only after the EU-3/Iran meetings in Brus- sels and Paris in February and November 2004 that the EU-3 incorporated the definition to include the process of conversion. The French Foreign Ministry cautioned the US Embassy in Paris that 'some could consider that conversion did not amount to enrichment, and the Iranians were fully aware of this gray area. It was for this reason, a senior French official said, that the EU-3 letter referred to the Paris agreement.'[19] To the EU-3 as well as other EU member states, the resumption of conversion at Isfahan was regarded as a test of Euro- pean resolve and warranted IAEA Board and UNSC referral.[20] What the Iranian government considered as leverage towards the EU-3 and a sign of strength vis- à-vis a domestic audience was treated as a trigger to end negotiations.

The 2005 presidential elections and the EU August proposal

Officials in the EU and the US government anticipated that the 17 June presiden- tial elections in Iran would bring former President and Expediency Council Chairman Hashemi Rafsanjani back into the President's Office. Seeing him as a president who stood 'above factions' and as having a track record of 'decreasing tensions and building confidence internationally', many political stalwarts in Iran too were convinced that Rafsanjani alone could 'engineer any negotiations with honour and authority'. Former Commander of Iran's Law Enforcement Forces and former air force pilot Mohamad Baqer Qalibaf was seen by many as the only viable contender among all candidates.[21] Therefore, when former mayor of Tehran Mahmoud Ahmadinejad won the elections, responses ranged from disbe- lief to the EU governments and the Bush administration altogether questioning the legitimacy of the elections. During a visit to Kuwait, US Principal Deputy Assistant Secretary of State Elizabeth L. Cheney called the elections not free and described Iran's democracy as 'backward'.[22] German Foreign Minister Joshka Fischer privately noted to a visiting American delegation that 'no one expected Ahmadinejad's victory', 'least of all Iranian negotiators on the nuclear issue who … were in shock after the election results came in'.[23] Even though EU officials indicated to the US government that EU policy towards Iran would not change regardless of the new president and personnel changes within the new Iranian administration (most notably the resignation of Hassan Rowhani in August), the arrival of President Ahmadinejad proved to be a destabilizing factor for EU–Iran negotiations.[24] On 18 July, Hassan Rowhani wrote a letter to the EU-3 caution- ing President Chirac and Chancellor Schroeder in particular not to use the outcome of the presidential elections as a pretext to withhold a mutually agree- able proposal. Rowhani also reminded the EU-3 that the new Iranian govern- ment and all successive administrations would continue to honour past agreements. The letter reiterated commencement of low-capacity enrichment at the Isfahan plant under full scope monitoring, and repeated the offer to negotiate a mutually acceptable monitoring mechanism for Natanz and arrangements to import materials needed for uranium conversion and the export of UF6.[25] During private meetings between Mousavian and his counterparts in Paris, London and Berlin respectively, he proposed a 'fifth and last package as contingency', given the EU-3's unwillingness to agree to the terms of the previous proposal. Mousavian proposed following roadmap:

- As a first step, Iran would resume uranium conversion at the Isfahan plant and would export its product to an agreed-upon country in exchange for yellowcake.
- As a second step, Iran would begin enrichment at Natanz in a limited pilot plant with some 3,000 centrifuges, but would export all enriched uranium to an agreed-upon country.
- Negotiations would continue for a maximum of one year to reach a final compromise on 'objective guarantees' of non-diversion and 'firm guarantees' for comprehensive relations.
- The timetable for the industrial-level production of fuel would be agreed upon, based on Iran's fuel requirements.[26]

According to Mousavian's memoirs, the German representative, Michael Schaefer, received his proposal positively and encouraged him to discuss it with the French and British officials. However, the French Foreign Ministry's Political Director, Stanislas Lefebvre de Laboulaye, and the FCO's Director-General for Political Affairs, John Sawers, considered the proposal unworkable, citing the US government's objection to any enrichment activities.[27] Disclosed US State Department cables indicate that both the French and British governments in particular viewed negotiations as a means to maintain the status quo of enrichment cessation rather than as venues for effective problem-solving. With the election of Ahmadinejad, the FCO told US diplomats that 'Iran had entered a tricky phase following the elections. It could no longer be said there was a range of views within Iran's ruling elite – all institutions are now in the hands of the hard-line/radical camp.'[28] Neither the French nor British were working towards reaching a deal with the new Iranian administration but rather were in the process of preparing EU-3 diplomacy towards adopting a more coercive stance. In a meeting with US Embassy staff in Paris in July 2005, the French 'expected the Iranian dossier to reach a crisis point' within the following few months, predicting that the current Iranian government would seek to break off negotiations with the EU. According to Foreign Ministry officials, the EU-3 was planning to provide a new proposal following the inauguration of Ahmadinejad. However, the French official told US diplomats that 'the EU proposal will be unattractive from the Iranian perspective'. Likewise, at a high-level meeting between EU Troika representatives and US State Department officials, The FCO assured the US government of the EU's red line that 'Iran not be permitted to develop any fuel cycle', outlining EU strategy as one in which the EU 'sticks by its commitments to the Iranians, so that any violations will be clearly the fault of the Iranians'. Both the British and French Foreign Ministries expected Iranian rejection of the forthcoming proposal and a subsequent end of suspension of reprocessing, which would ultimately bring the nuclear dossier before the UN Security Council.[29] When the EU-3 presented the Iranian government with its proposal on 8 August 2005, seals at the Isfahan conversion plant had already been removed by Iranian authorities but conversion activities had not yet started.[30] Three days later, the Iranian government rejected the proposal as 'an insult to the Iranian nation, for which the EU-3 must apologize' and began to resume conversion activities at Isfahan. It was communicated to the Iranians that the resumption of conversion work undermined the Paris Agreement and that negotiations would be terminated.[31] Iran's actions warranted a resolution by the IAEA's Board of Directors which urged Iran to 're-establish full suspension of all enrichment-related activities including the production of feed material, including through tests or production at the Uranium Conversion Facility'.[32] The proposal by the EU-3 was entitled 'Framework for a Long-Term Agreement between the Islamic Republic of Iran and France, Germany and the United Kingdom, With the Support of the High Representative of the European Union'. It contained following main elements:

- Arrangements for the assured supply of low-enriched uranium [LEU] for any light water reactors constructed in Iran
- Establishing a buffer store of nuclear fuel located in a third country
- A commitment by Iran not to pursue fuel cycle technologies, reviewable after ten years
- A legally binding commitment by Iran not to withdraw from the NPT and Iran's adoption of the Additional Protocol.
- Arrangements for Iran to return spent nuclear fuel to supplier countries
- EU recognition of Iran as a long-term source of fossil fuel energy
- EU–Iran cooperation in a variety of political–security areas, including Iraq and Afghanistan, terrorism and drug trafficking.[33]

As a French Foreign Ministry official privately noted prior to offering the package, it proved highly undesirable to the Iranians as it largely catered to the Bush administration's red line of not tolerating any enrichment and provided no meaningful incentives to the Iranians. In his memoirs, El Baradei described the tone of the proposal as 'patronizing, bordering on arrogant'.[34] During a visit by members of the Foreign Select Committee of the House of Commons to Tehran in 2007, Iranian interlocutors complained that the EU-3/EU appeared complacent about securing a deal during the period of suspension because they had already temporarily stopped Iran's programme.[35] In August 2005, at an emergency meeting of the IAEA Board of Governors, the Iranian representative reminded the EU-3 that Iran's voluntary suspension and flexibility regarding coming to an agreement had been met by intransigence and lack of political will on the part of the EU-3. Reminding IAEA member states that the installation, erection and commissioning of the Isfahan UCF had been made in accordance with Iran's safeguard obligations, Salehi said that twenty months of voluntary restraint had neither produced an agreement nor reaped any benefits for Iran. As such, Salehi demonstrated resolve before the Board of Governors and reminded member states of the legal framework as perceived by the Iranian government:

- Will Iran resume safeguarded operations at UCF? Absolutely, it is within our rights. We will restart UCF under agency monitoring at a date of our choice.
- Will Iran give up its civilian uranium enrichment capability? Absolutely not. Our suspension was voluntary and non-legally binding and can be terminated at any time of our choosing. However, for the present, we will maintain suspension at Natanz.
- Is the E3/EU proposal for a framework agreement satisfactory? As we have said, the E3/EU proposal is wholly inadequate and runs counter to the letter and spirit of the Paris Agreement.
- Is Iran threatening to leave the NPT or agency safeguards? Never. We have repeatedly stated our firm commitment to remain a member of the NPT and of agency safeguards in good standing.
- If Iran resumes operations at UCF, the E3/EU say that they will support the US to refer Iran to the Security Council for its past failures or for resumption of enrichment-related activities. As we have said, first, Iran's suspension of its enrichment-related activities in conformity with the NPT is purely on a voluntary and non-legally binding basis; second, the agency's original definition of enrichment did not include conversion activities. The statute stipulates referral to the Security Council, not on the grounds of failures, but only if and when diversion to prohibited purposes has been established. No evidence has been found of any diversion through intrusive and sustained inspections as the director-general has reported; hence no legal basis for referral.[36]

In its 2007 report, the Foreign Select Committee of the House of Commons itself concluded that the August 2005 package presented to Iran was asking too much from the Iranians, saying that 'the E3/EU was too slow to build on Iran's suspension of enrichment activities. By failing to present a compelling offer to Tehran before the ascendancy of President Ahmadinejad, the E3/EU made reaching an agreement a much more challenging task.'[37] To the Iranians, the August proposal warranted an end to negotiations and enrichment suspension. For months, Iranian officials communicated this to EU-3 interlocutors that uranium conversion at Isfahan might be resumed, as was not covered by the Paris Agreement. Moreover, the uranium hexafluoride (UF6) produced was to be exported. Mousavian reiterated that the only acceptable formula for the Iranian government was resumption of work at Isfahan as well as a pilot programme at Natanz. As Mousavian notes,

But the EU-3 did not accept the honest and realistic suggestions of the Iranian negotiators, and consequently Iran resumed the Isfahan uranium-conversion project as soon as it received the EU-3's July 2005 proposal, which insisted again on the permanent cessation of Iran's enrichment activities.[38]

Between January and February 2006, the Iranian government started removing IAEA safeguard seals on the P-1 type gas centrifuges in the presence of IAEA inspectors at Natanz, as well as at the Pars Trash and Farayand Technique sites. On 11 January, enrichment tests were started in Natanz by feeding a single P-1 type machine with UF6 gas.[39] On 5 February 2006, President Ahmadinejad sent a letter to the IAEA in which he required implementation of the law passed by the *Majlis* on 3 November 2005. In this letter he ordered the IAEA to remove seals on uranium enrichment equipment and material at Natanz and other facilities and to undertake research and development related to uranium enrichment.[40] President Ahmadinejad's order to cease all voluntary cooperation with the IAEA under the Additional Protocol of the NPT came the day after the IAEA referred Iran's nuclear file to the UN Security Council.[41]

No tricks from Russia and China

The Russian government proposed another initiative in October 2005 for a joint Russian–Iranian enrichment programme in Russia. Putin's diplomacy towards Iran was informed by the need to confirm Russian's status as a world power. The Beslan massacre in 2004 had indicated the on-going crisis in Chechnya and the pro-Western 'Orange Revolution' in the Ukraine witnessed the loss of one of Russia's closest allies in 2005.[42] As the US focused on President Ahmadinejad's hostile rhetoric towards Israel, the Russian initiative aimed at keeping negotiations with the EU-3 going. Even though Russian officials privately indicated to the US that Russia would be unwilling to support sanctions against Iran, as Russian interests proved too vulnerable to Iranian retaliatory measures, it was made clear by the Russian government to Iran that it could not prevent a referral to the UN Security Council by the IAEA.[43] The Russian proposal, which was supported by the US, EU-3 and China, confirmed an assured supply of nuclear fuel from Russia as well as a joint Russian–Iranian enrichment programme in Russia. In a private meeting between the Russian Security Council Secretary and Ali Larijani in January 2006, the Iranians were told that the removal of the seals at Natanz was not consistent with Russia's understanding of the Paris Agreement, which according to Ivanov was that during negotiations there could be no enrichment activities, and that this included research and development on enrichment.[44] The Russian government made it clear that it was imperative for the Iranians to restore the moratorium and return to negotiations. During the meeting Larijani was also informed that no Iranian scientists would have access to the technical side of fuel production of the proposed joint Russian–Iranian enrichment programme and that this bilateral regime would be of indefinite duration until Iran re-established its credibility with the IAEA.[45] The most important reason that the proposal did not gain any traction despite months of negotiations between Russian and Iranian delegations was Iran's insistence that the joint enterprise be implemented while Iran continued enrichment work in Iran.

The most important aspect of the January 2006 meeting was that the Russian government reiterated the fact that Russia had no veto power at the IAEA and could therefore not prevent a referral to the UN Security Council, telling Larijani that

> Iran should have no illusions about the situation it was in, and should expect no tricks from Russia or China to prevent a referral. If it wanted to avoid that outcome, it would need to reinstate its moratorium and resume negotiations with the EU-3.[46]

Larijani threaten that referral to the UN Security Council would warrant curtailment of Iran's cooperation with the IAEA and that it would start producing enrichment on an industrial scale.[47]

Overall, the Russian proposal failed for two reasons: First, by demanding continued enrichment simultaneous to the joint venture, Iran continued to insist on unfettered development of the entire fuel cycle. Second, even though Russia maintained a tough stance on Iran's departure from its moratorium and reiterated that it could not prevent Iran being reported to the UN Security Council by the IAEA, Putin's Iran policy was ambiguous. In November 2005, the Russian government announced that Russia and Iran had signed a contract to deliver thirty short-range Tor-M1 surface-to-air missile systems in the next two years. The system, intended to protect Iran's nuclear facilities against US or Israeli air strikes, was part of a major arms deal between both countries, estimated at US$1 billion and signed in December 2005.[48] While the contract would be broken by the Russian government in 2010, largely because of US opposition, Russia's provision of good offices during that period was perceived by the Iranian government as an effective buffer against the West.[49] In fact, in his memoirs Rowhani criticized Larijani for relying on a Chinese–Russian axis and thinking that there was no further need to continue negotiations with the Europeans. Rowhani writes that Ahmadinejad's

> new nuclear team did not take seriously enough the 'very dangerous' September 2005 resolution of the International Atomic Energy Association's (IAEA) board of governors.... It was after September 2005 that the new nuclear team realized the [limited] weight of the East! And then they went looking for the West, which was of course already too late.[50]

Likewise, as much as Iran underestimated the EU-3's resolve, the Europeans too thought that the threat of UN Security Council referral alone would be an effective stick. As the then British Foreign Secretary, Jack Straw, testified before the House of Commons Foreign Select Committee in 2006:

> The question I ask is, if the Security Council means nothing at all, why did the Iranian Government go to huge lengths, astonishing lengths, to lobby

every single member of the Board of Governors they could find against this resolution? Why did they imply to many of these states that they would lose contracts in terms of oil? There were all sorts of insinuations made in order that this matter could not get before the Security Council. My answer to that is they are worried about being isolated and being before the court of world opinion.[51]

To the US government, the September 2005 non-compliance resolutions had set an important precedent, perceiving that it had broken the need for consensus among IAEA BoG members. Likewise, at a November 2006 coordination meeting between representatives from the EU Commission, the US State Department and the Canadian Foreign Ministry, a senior Canadian official, said that the September IAEA resolutions 'made a pitch for continued close collaboration, strategizing and working on the NAM and the "weak-kneed" in the IAEA'.[52] As the EU-3 moved to open a new diplomatic phase and were in the process of crafting a resolution at the UN Security Council, EU members were privately assured that this did not mean immediately seeking a Chapter VII action but rather confirming the IAEA's authority in the matter.[53] In Iran, President Ahmadinejad and his cabinet moved carefully, catering to both domestic constituents, which for months had been rallied up against Western pressure, as well as to the EU-3 and the US government. As one US State Department official described in February 2006:

> Iran's reaction to pressure typically mixes bravado with pragmatism. Ahmedinejad is trying to play it both ways, claiming he has 'no choice' but to end compliance with the Additional Protocol, out of 'respect' for the law that parliament passed last year, while at the same time pointedly avoiding closing the door to further diplomatic negotiations in the run-up to March, when Iran's case is due to come up for further debate.[54]

The P5+1 package and UN Security Council Resolutions 1696 and 1737

By ceasing to apply the obligations under the Additional Protocol, Iran's nuclear programme made significant advancements between March and 31 July 2006, when the UN Security Council adopted its first resolution against Iran (UNSC RES 1696). The most important milestone was obtaining enrichment levels at 5 per cent U235 and starting research and development of the advanced P-2 type centrifuges.[55] Following weeks of negotiations between the EU-3 and Iran, a new package was presented to the Iranian government in June 2006. The significance of the package was the fact that it was backed by all permanent members of the UN Security Council. For the Bush administration to have underwritten the package of incentives was largely informed by Secretary of State Condoleezza Rice's quiet diplomatic outreach towards Iran. Frustrated by the State Department's failure to have an effective pool of Persian speakers and experts on Iran, Rice set up several 'Iran Watch' stations in US embassies and consulates in the Middle East, Central Asia and Europe. John Limbert, who was responsible for the Iran Watch stations during his tenure as Deputy Assistant Secretary of State for Iran in 2009–2010, called the posts 'useful in providing a reality check for US policymakers in the form of unvarnished information about Iranian political developments'.[56] With Rice having surrounded herself with pragmatists within the State Department, most notably Nicholas Burns and Robert Zoellick, the conditional offer forwarded to Iran, which sought direct dialogue, constituted a significant shift in the US position towards the Islamic Republic.[57] However, the offer to join the talks with the EU-3 was contingent on responding positively to the IAEA's call for the suspension of enrichment-related and reprocessing activities as a confidence-building measure. The Bush administration's leap of pragmatism towards the Iranians was lauded by Europeans, regional allies and El Baradei himself.[58] The package, entitled 'Elements of a Proposal to Iran', demanded suspension of enrichment and reprocessing activities and offered significant political and economic incentives. It offered 'legally binding multi-layered fuel assurances to Iran, based on a participation as a partner in an international facility in Russia to provide enrichment'. Most importantly, the offer contained a clause that the moratorium would be reviewed.[59] Ali Larijani conveyed to El Baradei that the proposal contained some positive aspects but also ambiguities that needed resolving. With Iran reluctant to discuss these areas of concern with the EU-3 and emboldened by a sense of its own rising power in the region, El Baradei's June report to the Board of Governors indicated continuation of conversion and enrichment activities and construction of the heavy water research reactor. On 31 July, backed by China and Russia, the UN Security Council, acting under Article 40 of Chapter VII, passed Resolution 1696. This made the suspension of enrichment-related and reprocessing activities, including research and development, mandatory. For the first time, Iran was obliged under international law to cease enrichment. The resolution referred to the P5 + 1 offer as a channel to negotiate but also made it clear that non-compliance by 31 August would warrant the UN Security Council to 'adopt appropriate measures under Article 41 of Chapter VII of the Charter of the United Nations'.[60] Iran's counter-proposal, delivered 22 August, was largely devoted to highlighting ambiguities of the EU-3's June proposal without referring to past Iranian failures to comply with its obligations. Far from fleshing out particulars of moving towards a negotiated solution, the twenty-one-page proposal berated the June offer for being 'vague on nuclear cooperation, transfer of nuclear technology, construction of nuclear power plants in Iran and guaranteed supply of required fuel'. The letter rejected 'the use of the Security Council as a pressure tool to push forward the P5 + 1 proposal' and demanded not only the cessation of the UN Security Council's involvement but also the normalization of Iran's file at the IAEA, which meant altogether dropping discussion of the nuclear programme before the Board of Governors. While Larijani's letter expressed Iran's readiness to provide legal guarantees that it would never abandon its membership of the NPT and IAEA, this was contingent on the nuclear case being removed from the UN Security Council. On the most important issue of enrichment cessation, the Iranians indicated that they would consider cessation only during negotiations and not before.[61] During a closed meeting between IAEA's 'like-minded countries' in Vienna, the French representative to the IAEA considered Larijani's letter a rejection of the EU-3+3 approach as it refused the now mandatory cessation of enrichment and all R&D activities. As noted by the French representative:

> In sum, the reply is along the lines of previous Iranian statements in that it typically neither accepts nor rejects outright the E3 plus 3 proposals. By offering various carrots, like the hint that Iran is prepared to resume the suspension or resume Additional Protocol Co-operation (if a series of very difficult to meet conditions is fulfilled) the Iranian goal obviously is to split the international community and draw us into a process of talks about talks, on Iranian terms, while making no commitments of its own while continuing with its enrichment program.[62]

Officials at the Permanent Mission of the United States to the IAEA also considered an Iranian counter-offer without suspension as a means 'to buy more time and limit support for a UNSC sanctions resolutions'.[63] By 31 August, the deadline set by the UN Security Council, El Baradei had reported that uranium enrichment activities had not been suspended. Iranian authorities had also not halted construction of the heavy water research reactor at Arak, failed to provide the transparency required to confirm the peaceful nature of its nuclear programme and denied IAEA inspectors access to enrichment facilities at Natanz.[64] El Baradei cautioned for a 'slow, diplomatic approach' with Iran in order to allow 'moderates the space to negotiate', warning that sanctions would ultimately play into the hands of conservatives and would make a negotiated settlement impossible.[65] Seeing El Baradei's efforts as too conciliatory in the face of Iran's defiance of UNSC RES 1696, the US government and the so-called group of 'like-minded' countries at the IAEA (EU-3, Canada, Australia, New Zealand, Japan, Korea, Argentina and Norway) concurred that the resolution made 'suspension a legally binding requirement, as opposed to a voluntary confidence measure'.[66] It was decided that El Baradei's report served the group's 'interest in highlighting Iran's defiance of UNSC 1696'.[67]

'In Javier we trust'

Following an initiative by El Baradei to maintain a dialogue with Iran, the EU-3 agreed to appoint Javier Solana to meet with Ali Larijani to discuss a 'freeze-for-freeze' formula. El Baradei's framework was based on four principles: (1) Iran would suspend enrichment during the talks; (2) the US and the EU would reciprocate and suspend UN Security Council sanctions during this period; (3) the Europeans and Americans would affirm Iran's right to peaceful nuclear energy and reiterate that the suspension would not be permanent; (4) a statement had to be issued which reiterated Iran's political independence and sovereignty.[68] According to the Head of the Unit for European Common Foreign and Security Policy for the Finnish Foreign Ministry (Finland had the EU Presidency at the time), even though the mantra within the EU remained 'in Javier we trust', initial meetings between Solana and Larijani produced little optimism within the EU. It was made clear to Larijani that the meetings were 'clarifications' rather than 'negotiations'.[69] It was precisely Solana's lack of authority which proved difficult in allowing the meetings to gain much traction. As the Russian Security Council Secretary noted himself during a briefing with the US Ambassador in Moscow concerning his meeting with Larijani in Spain: 'One factor contributing to Larijani's wavering in the negotiations ... was his lack of understanding over who Solana represented and the extent of his mandate.'[70] Overall, following the bloody conflict between Hezbollah and Israel in July 2006 and Iran's alleged active support of the Lebanese militia, neither Solana nor El Baradei was in a position to deliver US-backed security assurances to the Iranians. At the same time, Larijani was unable to accept enrichment suspension as a precondition to entering talks. In the end, Larijani was dismissed by the US State Department for wielding no power at the negotiation table. As the Under Secretary of State told the Japanese government in November 2006: 'Diplomacy alone has failed, US told Nishida. Iran's nuclear negotiator Ali Larijani never showed up for his appointments in New York, possibly due to having lost influence relative to President Mahmoud Ahmadinejad.'[71]

On that basis, Iran's 22 August proposal was formally rejected by the Permanent Members of the UN Security Council on 4 October 2006. By then, the EU-3 and the US government had already started working towards punitive measures at the UN Security Council. Having secured Chinese and Russian support for sanctions against Iran (Russia demanded that activity at Bushehr and arms sales should be outside any sanctions regime),[72] the UN Security Council passed Resolution 1737 under Article 41 of Chapter VII of the UN Charter. It demanded that Iran suspend 'proliferation sensitive nuclear activities', banned the supply of nuclear-related technology and materials to Iran, froze the assets of key entities and individuals engaged in the nuclear programme and issued travel bans on key stakeholders of the programme.[73] It was the first time, that UN Security Council sanctions were imposed against Iran. Iran's parliament retaliated by passing a bill which required the government to expedite the nuclear programme and revise its cooperation with the IAEA on 27 December.[74] Two days prior to this, President Ahmadinejad boasted that 'Iran is now a nuclear power'. Concerted efforts by the Iranian government to create realities on the ground together with the bill had set the foundation for accelerated instalment of over 3,000 centrifuges at the facility in Natanz in January 2007 and had made negotiations increasingly a zero-sum environment.[75] To the Iranian government, enrichment and other related research and development activities had become a *faît accompli* to be used a bargaining tool.[76] To the EU-3, the referral to the UN Security Council and the sanctions passed by the second resolution in particular served to uphold the integrity of the IAEA and the non-proliferation regime. More than that, Iran's scorn for the IAEA in the face of EU-3 diplomatic efforts had become an issue critical to the transatlantic relationship and EU credibility itself. By the end of 2006, stakes on both sides had become substantially higher than when EU and Iranian envoys first met in 2003.[77]

The arc of extremism: Ahmadinejad, the EU-3 and the Bush administration

On 1 August 2005, British Prime Minister Tony Blair gave a foreign policy speech at the Los Angeles World Affairs Council in which he outlined a foreign policy strategy to overcome the challenges in the Middle East. Calling the conflicts in the region a 'struggle between … reactionary Islam and moderate, mainstream Islam', the Prime Minister stated:

> From now on, we need a whole strategy for the Middle East. If we are faced with an arc of extremism, we need a corresponding arc of moderation and reconciliation. Each part is linked. Progress between Israel and Palestine affects Iraq. Progress in Iraq affects democracy in the region. Progress for Moderate, Mainstream Islam anywhere puts Reactionary Islam on the defensive everywhere. But none of it happens unless in each individual part the necessary energy and commitment is displayed not fitfully, but continuously…. My argument to you today is this: we will not win the battle against this global extremism unless we win it at the level of values as much as force, unless we show we are even-handed, fair and just in our application of those values to the world.[78]

In the speech, Blair gave Iran and Syria a choice:

> come in to the international community and play by the same rules as the rest of us; or be confronted. Their support of terrorism, their deliberate export of instability, their desire to see wrecked the democratic prospect in Iraq, is utterly unjustifiable, dangerous and wrong. If they keep raising the stakes, they will find they have miscalculated.[79]

Blair's use of hegemonic and value-laden rhetoric was indicative of international relations during this period. The EU-3 had altogether shifted towards a more coercive course regarding Iran. Convinced that popular support for restarting enrichment activities as well as fear of government reprisals had prevented like-minded Iranian officials from being able to negotiate with the West and conscious of the political upsurge of the Iranian Revolutionary Guard Corps (IRGC),[80] the EU-3 had started to adopt the same power-based strategy towards Iran as the US government. Iran's access to nuclear energy was qualified and depended on Iranian compliance with its non-proliferation commitments. Therefore, the EU-3 demanded that Iran move back to the pre-2003 environment. By the same token, Iran's foreign policy and its negotiation strategy on the nuclear programme was not geared towards problem-solving but rather intended to expedite mastering of the entire nuclear fuel cycle in order to create a point of no return.

International relations during the 2006 initiatives proved highly volatile. The conflict between Israel and Hezbollah in July and North Korea's first test of a nuclear device in October 2006 reinforced the respective positions of the EU-3 and the Bush administration that Iran's nuclear ambitions had to be curtailed. Notwithstanding pleas by the Lebanese government for an immediate ceasefire and humanitarian support in the face of Israel's military campaign against southern Lebanon, the conflict, which had started 12 July 2006, only ended with a UN-brokered ceasefire on 14 August 2006. The US government, as well as the German and British governments, was unwilling to call for an immediate ceasefire but rather upheld Israel's right to self-defence. As the Bush administration and the Israeli government upheld the narrative that Iran was using Hezbollah to project its power in the region, a military defeat of the *Shi'a* militia, it was hoped, would ultimately cause the decline of Iran's standing within both Lebanese politics and the region at large.[81] Iranian anti-Israel and anti-US propaganda during the conflict aimed at bolstering its image as leader of the Islamic resistance and directly threatened Israel and the US with retaliation.[82] Notwithstanding the provisions contained in UN Security Council Resolution 1710, which provided for a beefed-up UN presence in southern Lebanon to implement the ceasefire, Israel's deterrent capabilities had suffered and its military weakness towards an asymmetric enemy had been exposed.[83] Having swiftly rearmed its *Shi'a* ally, Iran emerged out of the conflict feeling emboldened about its rising clout in a new Middle East. In doing so, it only reinforced, in the eyes of US and European policymakers its status as international pariah. In his memoirs, El Baradei writes that both he and UN General Secretary Kofi Anan noted the blatant double standards as Iran's nuclear programme continued to be a threat to international security while at the same time the US and Europe resisted calls for a ceasefire.[84]

Following UN Security Council Resolution 1737 in December, containment of Iran, in the eyes of the Bush administration, had become sanctioned by multilateral consensus. To that end military means were used to project power against Iran. President Bush issued an order to undertake a broad military offensive against Iranian operatives in Iraq, which led to a raid of the Iranian Consulate in Erbil in January 2007 and the detention of five Iranian diplomats by US forces.[85] Publicly and in private conversations with Iraqi officials, the US government insisted that the raid, together with previous arrests of alleged IRGC officers in Baghdad in December 2006, was targeting Quds operatives. To US authorities, Quds Force activities in Iraq were unacceptable and posed a threat to US and Iraqi interests by facilitating anti-ISF (Iraqi Security Forces) and anti-coalition networks and operations.[86] On 4 February, Jalal Sharafi, who was Second Secretary at the Iranian Embassy in Baghdad, was kidnapped by men wearing Iraqi uniforms.[87] After the release of the five diplomats arrested at the Consulate on

9 July 2009, a senior US official claimed that US authorities were aware they had diplomatic credentials and had not been involved in anti-coalition activities but were in effect hostages, taken to try to persuade Iran to reduce its support for anti-US violence in Iraq.[88] On 20 February, a second US aircraft carrier, USS *John C. Stenis*, arrived in the Persian Gulf, backed by 6,500 sailors and Marines and minesweeping ships.[89] It was against this backdrop of Cold War-like diplomacy that eight British Royal Navy sailors and seven Royal Marines were seized by Iranian forces close to the mouth of the Shatt al-Arab waterway on 23 March. The Iranian government claimed that the sailors had confessed to entering Iranian waters illegally. Iranian authorities threatened to put them on trial and broadcast forced confession on state television.[90] Following numerous diplomatic initiatives by the FCO and coinciding with the release of Jalal Sharafi on 3 April and assurances given to the Iranian Foreign Ministry to grant consular access to the five detained Iranian diplomats, President Ahmadinejad announced that he would free the sailors as 'a gift' to Britain.[91] Allegedly the decision to proceed with the release was made by the Supreme Leader, over the objection of President Ahmadinejad and hardliners in the government.[92] What in the eyes of members of the reformist opposition was merely a 'political stunt' to divert attention from the third UN Security Council resolution (Resolution 1747, passed on 24 March 2007), which had elicited public criticism of the government's handling on the nuclear issue, was genuinely seen by hardliners in the government as effective leverage to secure concessions from the British and Americans.[93] The crisis, which was effectively handled by the FCO through what the Foreign Affairs Committee lauded as 'quiet diplomacy', caused a significant deterioration in British–Iranian relations.

Iranian brinkmanship did not provide any strategic depth. In March, Mohammad Saidi announced that it had been decided to move towards installing 3,000 centrifuges by May and declared that the demands made by the UN Security Council lacked any legal foundation. Following these developments, the board of IAEA governors stated that it was 'unable to verify the absence of undeclared nuclear material and activities' and demanded to address outstanding verification issues through the implementation of the Additional Protocol.[94] At the UN Security Council, Foreign Minister Manouchehr Mottaki blamed the Council for failing to intervene in the Israel–Hezbollah conflict and criticized its permanent members for decades of anti-Iranian actions. Calling 1747 'unlawful', Mottaki ended his speech by saying that 'suspension was not an option'.[95] Resolution 1747 further tightened the previous sanctions regime and extended an arms embargo, demanded the cessation of any financial assistance (except humanitarian) either bilaterally or through international financial institutions, and added a new list of entities and persons banned from international travel, imposing financial controls on them. The resolution maintained the structure of 1737, most notably the mandatory requirement for Iran to suspend enrichment-related and reprocessing activities and work on heavy water-related projects.[96] To the Iranian government, nuclear diplomacy had been reduced to a test of strength, leaving it more isolated internationally.

In this volatile environment, trilateral talks were held between the US, Iraq and Iran over the security situation in May, June and August of 2007. While the Baghdad talks had no impact on bilateral relations and led to no agreement, pressure from the US government and Iraqi *Shi'a* leaders eventually underscored US and Iraqi resolve in countering Iranian-backed insurgency activities. The meetings were largely used to confront the Iranian delegation with evidence of Iranian involvement.[97] The British Ambassador to Iran believed that the trilateral talks were approved by the Supreme Leader, possibly as a conciliatory gesture towards those groups inside the country who advocated an opening with the US and to test the waters. The Iranians themselves were disappointed with the talks as they lacked any substance. Still viewing the US as its most fundamental external threat, Iran's main strategy in Iraq, according to the Ambassador, was to use its support for political violence in the country as a tool to counteract the US threat.[98] Regionally, Larijani's message at the Arab Strategy Forum in Dubai for an Iranian–Gulf alliance, presenting Iran as a more attractive ally than the US, failed to resonate with its intended audience.[99] On the contrary, Gulf Cooperation Council (GCC) leaders emphasized their loyalty to their alliance with the US while the Bush administration reaffirmed its security commitments to the region as a way to counter Iranian hegemony.[100] The Gulf states' perception of Iran as a strategic threat only reinforced the Bush administration's strategy of containment and deterrence against Iran. To that end, a meeting between officials from the US Embassy in Kuwait and the Advisor to the GCC Secretary General in October 2006 discussed GCC perceptions of Iran. Reflecting on a two-day conference on the nuclear programme sponsored by the Expediency Council, during which he visited the nuclear facility in Isfahan, the GCC official told US diplomats:

> Now, there is an increasing awareness that something must be done – 'politically, strategically, economically, or militarily' – to contain Iran regionally, or, as he put it, to 'clip the claws of the lion'. According to [the official], this awareness had been growing since the beginning of the year, but crystallized with the conflict in Lebanon. Kuwait became more fully aware of the threat from Iran during Ahmadinejad's visit in February, he said. The Kuwaiti leadership wanted to know if Ahmadinejad was really serious and were convinced in their meetings with him that he was 'seriously crazy', [the official] claimed. He noted that the afternoon Ahmadinejad left Kuwait, the Amir instructed Kuwait's emergency services agencies to begin emergency/disaster planning preparations.[101]

Conclusion

Overall, Blair's 'arc of extremism' had manifested itself during the period 2006–2007. Not in the Manichean form of moderate Islam vs reactionary Islam, which he envisioned, but very much embodied by a return to Cold War diplomacy of all parties involved. Diplomatic overtures by the US were limited and contingent on suspension of enrichment activities. The Bush administration perceived the referral to the UN Security Council as a means to legitimize multilateral containment of Iran. The EU-3 failed to mediate between Iran and the US and felt compelled, in order to maintain credibility, to recalibrate its strategy to a more punitive approach. The Iranian government, under the leadership of President Ahmadinejad, treated progress in the nuclear programme as a means of changing the nature of nuclear talks. Informed as much by Iranian nationalism as by Islamism, the Iranian President used nuclear summitry to seek Western acceptance of Iran as an equal power. With the rise of the IRGC in leadership positions, Iranian politics and foreign policy alike had become increasingly militarized, which in turn only reinforced the region's security dilemma. Domestically, however, the government's intransigence had increasingly contributed to domestic dissenters criticizing the president as the cause of Iran's increased international isolation.

4 'Bigger sticks and bigger carrots'

The 2008 proposal

Introduction

The years 2007 to 2008 marked the period when Europe started to focus on the punitive part of its so-called 'dual track' approach to Iran. Conscious that failure to achieve Iranian compliance would send the wrong signals and might set a precedent prompting other countries to proliferate,[1] EU governments started to align themselves with the US position that Iranian compliance with the NPT had to be enforced rather than solely negotiated. While the dialogue was to be maintained and, in fact, led to another proposal in June 2008, sanctions were meant to check Iran's perceived proliferation activities. Even though UN Security Council Resolution 1747 had afforded punitive measures against Iran's financial sector and its overall conventional procurement efforts, some EU member states (most notably Germany and France) demanded more concrete evidence on Iranian wrong-doing. This was needed to frame the public narrative for new EU measures as well as to avoid legal challenges through national courts as well as the European Court of Justice. The British and French governments were working towards the implementation of these measures along with the Bush administration. The proxy-war between the US and Iran in Iraq and Afghanistan continued, coupled with concerted efforts by the British and US governments to isolate Iran economically, and had largely determined the international environment leading up to the EU/US-sponsored 'carrot and stick proposal' in June 2008. The most important variable informing Iran's diplomatic posture was the Bush administration's backing of the proposal which ultimately reflected the decision by the US government to test European engagement temporarily. Rather than reciprocating these modest diplomatic overtures, heralded by US Secretary of State Condoleezza Rice, hardliners in Iran interpreted these signals as a tactical victory for Iran. Ultimately, pre-negotiations between the US/EU and Iran broke down owing to the irreconcilability of US and Iranian positions. As the US government was insisting on uranium cessation as precondition for talks, the Iranians insisted on it as a fundamental right under the NPT.

Managing the 2007 National Intelligence Estimate

In diplomatic terms, the fallout of the 2007 National Intelligence Estimate (NIE)[2] continued to complicate French, British and US efforts to maintain a multilateral front against Iran. During a closed meeting with US officials, the French Presidency strategic affairs adviser called for joint efforts to counter the negative effects of the estimate and to work towards a third sanctions resolution at the UN Security Council. In his opinion the NIE had changed the entire multilateral framework of nuclear diplomacy, undermining Russian and Chinese support and EU efforts at maintaining the momentum against Iran:

> too many people have only absorbed the key judgments related to Iran's apparent suspension of its nuclear weapons program in 2003 and ignored the others about worrisome aspects of Iran's ongoing program. This is especially true within the EU, where those governments resisting tougher sanctions – Austria and Italy – are weakening whatever EU resolve there was to move forward or even to issue a tough statement at the upcoming GAERC [General Affairs and External Relations Council]. China and Russia ... were using the NIE to support their arguments to slow down or not proceed to the third sanctions resolution. They were using others, ignorance of the overall situation to throw up roadblocks. The Arabs, in the meantime, were interpreting the NIE's release as likely to hasten a military operation to deal with Iran's program. This was partly based on the presumption that reservations predicated on some governments' reading of the NIE would prevent diplomatic progress within the UNSC and lead the US and Israel to decide that military action was the only viable alternative to ensure Iran did not develop nuclear weapons.[3]

To the Foreign and Commonwealth Office's Iran Coordinator, 'presentation' of the key findings of the 2007 NIE was of 'critical importance' to the British government, citing concerns that 'the public and Western partners must not allow the NIE to be seen as distracting in any way from current international diplomatic efforts on Iran, as any diplomatic momentum lost would be very hard to recover'. To the FCO, the issue had to be framed so as to make a distinction between 'Iran's ultimate intentions on its nuclear program, to which [the official] argued the report does not speak, and Iran's technical capabilities, especially as to weaponization, which he said was the main focus of the NIE'.[4] Of particular concern to the British and Americans were El Baradei's efforts during his trips to Iran, and they took particular exception to his public remark that the NIE had 'vindicated' Iran.[5] As far as French officials were concerned, no further delays from Iran were acceptable and the focus now had to be put on verifying the key finding of the NIE (i.e. that the weapons programme no longer existed) and actually press the IAEA to uncover the pre-2003 weapons programme.[6] To that end, the US and British representatives to the IAEA expected an admission of guilt from Iran:

The [UK Ambassador] did not expect a confession from Iran, and EU diplomats in Tehran also did not believe the regime was ready to negotiate.... For the [US Ambassador] what mattered was a confession at the 'macro-level' and an unequivocal decision not to pursue a weapons program. Such a decision, like that made by the DPRK or Libya, was more difficult now, he opined. The Iranians were not convinced, were not ready to come clean, and were inclined to keep their options open; in this context, it made sense to keep the pressure on.[7]

Notwithstanding the subsequent public diplomacy campaign that was implemented by the British, Israeli and US governments, President Ahmadinejad called the NIE a 'victory for the Iranian nation against the world powers' and a '*coup de grâce* for those people who chanted slogans based on fabrications and the pretext of proliferation'.[8] Likewise, the head of the *Majlis* National Security Council committee, Ala'eddin Borujerdi, interpreted the NIE as a 'testament to the fact that Iran has been earnest in its claims that its nuclear activities are peaceful'.[9]

By January 2008, British diplomats started a concerted campaign for EU member states to support additional measures against Iranian financial institutions. The FCO communicated to the US State Department that no new EU measures against Iran would happen before the General Affairs and External Relations Council (GAERC) in March 2008. Conscious of legal and political justification afforded by a third UN Security Council resolution, the FCO was confident that the EU would designate Bank Melli at the GAERC but that the governments of Spain, Italy, Germany, the Netherlands, Denmark, France and Belgium would be reluctant to support any other 'autonomous measures' against Iran. The FCO identified the German government as 'the keystone of next steps ... within the EU' to push unilateral measures forward'. While the UNSC draft resolution had been agreed on 22 January in Berlin, the FCO intended to lobby UN Security Council members Libya, South Africa, Vietnam and Indonesia to support a third resolution against Iran.[10]

Power politics vs El Baradei

The FCO's concern over Iranian non-compliance with UNSC resolutions and EU-3 démarches was confirmed by IAEA head Mohammed El Baradei's briefing with British Foreign Secretary David Miliband. According to El Baradei, during his January visit to Tehran, 'Iranian officials appeared very relaxed and seemed to be feeling no pressure on the nuclear file'. Based on his conversations, the IAEA head estimated that there were no chances for enrichment suspension and only a rather slim possibility of getting the Iranians to agree to a freeze on enrichment. El Baradei was also told that the Iranians were in the process of installing 'twelve new research centrifuges in Natanz in due course with the object of increasing centrifuge efficiency'. With regard to the issue of contamination by uranium particles at a university laboratory, El Baradei concluded that Iran's explanation and supporting documentation were plausible and, as stated in the IAEA report in February, considered this question as 'no longer outstanding at this stage'. Iran also informed the IAEA about the installation of a new sub-critical centrifuge (IR-2) at the Natanz Pilot Fuel Enrichment Plant (NPFEP). The Agency confirmed that a single IR-2 test machine and a ten-machine IR-2 test cascade had been installed at the PFEP.[11] Three days after the IAEA report, IAEA Deputy Director General Olli Heinonen briefed member states, including the Iranian delegation, on outstanding questions about the scope and direction of Iran's alleged nuclear weaponization studies. The briefing was based on intelligence obtained by member states and included documents on interconnected projects, overseen by the Iranian Ministry of Defence, Armed Forces and Logistics (MODAFL), for converting UO2 to UF4 (Green Salt Project), for testing high-power explosives and for designing a missile re-entry vehicle. In the briefing, the IAEA noted that the altitude described in the obtained documents excluded the possibility that the warhead was designed to accommodate conventional explosives or chemical and biological charges.[12]

To the Iranian Foreign Minister, the meeting with El Baradei in Tehran and the subsequent IAEA report in February reaffirmed Iranian compliance. To Mottaki, previous resolutions adopted against Iran by the UN Security Council lacked any technical or legal justification but rather were the product of Western *realpolitik*. The Iranian Ambassador to the IAEA, too, considered Heinonen's briefing as a joint British and US effort to discredit the report.[13] Mottaki warned that that continuation of this process would further discredit the Security Council and undermine the IAEA status as an international body.[14] This mindset was reflected across the entire Iranian political spectrum.[15]

It is important to note that El Baradei's mediating role and his fact-finding missions to Tehran were not appreciated as an effective backchannel by the British and US governments. Far from it: the FCO and State Department questioned the Director General's neutrality in the nuclear negotiations. As the US Embassy in London wrote in February 2008:

> HMG [Her Majesty's Government] had a skeptical view of El Baradei's pro-IRI inclinations before he left for Iran. The above readout suggests that the skepticism was well-founded: the IAEA chief, in gauging for P5+1 governments the prospects of obtaining Iranian cooperation on suspension and transparency, may have come near to accepting his Tehran interlocutor's confident demeanor, and dispositive statements, at face value.[16]

Sharing these prejudices, Israeli Defence Intelligence communicated to the US Embassy in Tel Aviv in December 2007 that El Baradei saw himself 'as playing a peacemaking role, and has surrounded himself with staff who do not wish to challenge him'. US diplomats were advised to marginalize El Baradei within the international community and 'shake his confidence by working through his interlocutors, like the Egyptian and Austrian foreign ministers'. US diplomats were urged by the Israelis to 'take measures to chip away at the staff bolstering his supreme confidence'. During the same meeting, a senior US State Department official concurred with the Israelis, asserting that the US government had previously engaged with the IAEA's Secretariat but thought that more work was still needed with Heinonen and other staff members in order to influence El Baradei.[17] Frustrated by El Baradei's insistence that there was no proof that the Iranian government had decided to run a nuclear weapons programme and that the international community must continue to work with Iranian chief negotiator Ali Larijani, the US government wanted to increase the pressure on the IAEA: 'we should try to hold El Baradei to his statement that there must be a "confession", that Iran must come clean on its P-1 and P-2 programs in November, and must address concerns about its military programs'.[18]

By not considering the IAEA head as an honest broker with regard to Iran's nuclear file, both US and Israeli diplomacy dedicated significant diplomatic resources in framing the narrative as one of proliferation and weaponization rather than allowing the IAEA and the EU-3 to engage in meaningful problem-solving diplomacy. The objective was not to test Iran on previous P5 + 1 demands, but rather to further tighten the international consensus on a mechanism to prevent Iran from further developing nuclear capacities and procuring weapons systems internationally.

To that end, the diplomatic campaign by the Bush administration was underwritten by coercive measures and informed by its commitment to extended deterrence in the Persian Gulf. To many observers in the region, President Bush's Middle East tour in January 2008 served to advance US geopolitical goals and to demonize Iran rather than seeking peace in the Middle East or constructively reaching out to Iran.[19] In what the White House billed as a major foreign policy address in Abu Dhabi, President Bush maintained a bellicose rhetoric towards Iran, stating 'one cause of instability in the Middle East is the extremists supported and embodied by the regime that sits in Tehran. Iran is today the world's leading state sponsor of terror.' Bush further rallied Arab states and 'friends around the world to confront this danger before it is too late'.[20] The backdrop of the speech was an encounter between IRGC patrol boats and US Navy warships. What the US government considered an increasing aggressive assertion of Iran's control over the Persian Gulf referred to an alleged harassment of US vessels by IRGC patrol boats in January. While the Navy later admitted that the video footages produced and recorded radio threats threatening to blow up the US vessels were inaccurate, both states treated the incident as a test of strength and accused each other of escalating tensions.[21] To many observers in Iran, the naval incident and Bush's recent trip to the region served to remind Iran that regardless of the 2007 NIE, the Iranian government was expected to meet UN Security Council demands and the Bush administration retained the political resolve and means to enforce its position through military force.[22]

Tightening financial measures against Iran

The passing of UN Security Council Resolution 1803 on 3 March 2008 was intended to further tighten the economic embargo against Iran.[23] Resolution 1803 contained the following main statements and clauses:

- Iran has not established full and sustained suspension of all enrichment-related and reprocessing activities and heavy water-related projects as set out in Resolution 1696 (2006), 1737 (2006), and 1747 (2007), nor resumed its cooperation with the IAEA under the Additional Protocol, nor taken the other steps required by the IAEA Board of Governors, nor complied with the provisions of Security Council Resolution 1696 (2006), 1737 (2006) and 1747 (2007) and which are essential to build confidence, and *deploring* Iran's refusal to take these steps.

- *Reaffirms* that Iran shall without further delay take the steps required by the IAEA Board of Governors in its Resolution GOV/2006/14, which are essential to build confidence in the exclusively peaceful purpose of its nuclear programme and to resolve outstanding questions, and, in this context, *affirms* its decision that Iran shall without delay take the steps required in paragraph 2 of Resolution 1737 (2006), and *underlines* that the IAEA has sought confirmation that Iran will apply Code 3.1 modified.

- *Calls upon* all States to exercise vigilance and restraint regarding the entry into or transit through their territories of individuals who are engaged in, directly associated with or providing support for Iran's proliferation sensitive nuclear activities or for the development of nuclear weapon delivery systems.

- *Decides* that all States shall take the necessary measures to prevent the entry into or transit through their territories of individuals designated in Annex II to this resolution.

- *Calls upon* all States to exercise vigilance in entering into new commitments for public provided financial support for trade with Iran, including the granting of export credits, guarantees or insurance, to their nationals or entities involved in such trade, in order to avoid such financial support contributing to the proliferation sensitive nuclear activities.

- *Calls upon* all States to exercise vigilance over the activities of financial institutions in their territories with all banks domiciled in Iran, in particular with Bank Melli and Bank Saderat, and their branches and subsidiaries abroad, in order to avoid such activities contributing to the proliferation sensitive nuclear activities.[24]

The US government considered the freezing of assets of persons and entities and the additional travel ban on persons associated with the nuclear programme and proliferation activities, coupled with additional trade and financial restrictions, as an effective means to sway Iranian behaviour. On 10 March, in a meeting between Conservative Leader David Cameron and US Deputy Secretary of the Treasury, the US envoy expressed his confidence that 1803 would have a major impact on Iran's banking sector:

> The word is out that any financial institution that engages in Iranian-related transactions risks its reputation … the EU-3 are solid on building barriers to illicit Iranian financial transactions, but as a result the Iranians are moving their banking and commercial transactions to the south.[25]

As observed by the US Treasury, large state-owned companies, most notably the National Iranian Oil Company (NIOC) and Pars Oil and Gas Company (POGC) started shifting their attention to Russia, China and other Asian countries. While Iran still managed to secure some European investments in its oil and gas sector in late 2007,[26] the decision by Shell and Total, respectively, not to re-enter into new stages of the development of Iran's South Pars gas field (the largest in the world), citing 'political risks', constituted a serious economic setback for Iran.[27] Evidently, Iranian efforts to increase Chinese and Russian stakes in the economy reflected political calculations to undermine future UN Security Council resolutions as well as to cater to both countries' growing domestic energy needs.[28] While the US$16 billion memorandum of understanding between China's National Offshore Oil Corp. (CNOOC) and Iran's Pars Oil and Gas Company[29] was largely seen by Iranian officials as successfully driving a wedge between the US, the EU and China, the financial and technical capabilities of Iran's new Russian and Chinese partners were, however, limited and proved unsustainable in the long-term downstream process of oil and gas exploitation. Most of the memoranda with Russian and Chinese firms failed to materialize. In fact, far from translating into immediate diplomatic capital, Iranian oil and gas authorities largely considered Moscow as an unreliable trading partner and thus only reluctantly substituted Russian for European firms.[30] Moreover, from a technological aspect, Russian and Chinese firms lacked Western state-of the art equipment, particularly liquefied natural gas (LNG) technology.

To policymakers in Europe and the US, sanctions started to have the desired effect. By mid-2008, the measures in place had deprived Iran of much-needed financial and technical capabilities in the gas and oil sector, and essentially postponed implementations of various projects and forced national companies to work with limited domestic capacities.[31] Since 2007, Iranian importers and exporters had found it increasingly hard to obtain Letters of Credit. According to US intelligence at the time, Iranian trade suffered worldwide (including with Southeast Asia and China) and across all sectors. As Iranian traders linked increasing problems with commercial transactions to the pressures which the US government had put on the international banking sector rather than to UNSC sanctions, officials in the Bush administration felt particularly vindicated at the efficacy of unilateral sanctions[32]

Tehran's 'Iran–Pakistan–India' project, supplying Pakistan and India, also reflected Iran's stepped-up strategy of expending political capital in pursuit of gas exports to its immediate neighbours in the Gulf and Asia. Even though Delhi, as a result of US pressure, had put the US$7.5 billion deal on ice by October of 2008, Iranian officials continued to insist throughout 2008 that a bilateral agreement with Islamabad could be reached even without India's participation in the large-scale project.[33] Looking west, Tehran also attempted to consolidate a strategic footing in the European market by bidding to become a stakeholder in the Nabucco Pipeline instead of merely a gas supplier to the project. The Nabucco Pipeline has an expected annual capacity of 37 bcm and will reportedly carry Iran's gas to Turkey, Greece, Italy, Switzerland, Germany and Turkey. The international consortium, which had originally been backed by the EU as a means to move away from reliance on Russia by gaining access to central Asian gas, had increasingly been capitalized by Tehran in order to deepen EU–Iran interdependence. However, given the slow pace of actually bringing gas projects on stream, conservative projections at the time estimated that Iran would lack sufficient gas for such large-scale export schemes until 2015.[34] The Iranian government's energy offensive proved an effective bargaining chip, which at the time was seen with great unease by the Israeli and US governments.[35] However, given Iran's lack of domestic technical expertise and the complex legal and highly politicized environment for international firms, these economic diplomatic initiatives provided little strategic depth towards the EU and the United Sates.

In fact, concerted efforts by the Iranian government to focus its attention to Middle Eastern, Asian and Russian firms,[36] rather than addressing demands stipulated by the UN Security Council resolutions and EU communications, had many directing their criticism against the handling of the nuclear issue by the President, as was revealed by an open letter by sixty prominent economists (the third of its kind at the time). It blamed the president's confrontational foreign policies for the poor performance of the economy:

> Unfortunately, despite the constant efforts of the officials, due to the kind of thinking behind those policies and due to the weakness in having a comprehensive understanding of the problems and difficulties, instead of making use of all legal and lawful capacities and strengthening the existing institutions, the policies that have been adopted [by the government] have resulted in destroying the existing structures.[37]

At the time of the new sanctions, political rivals, particularly reformists and pragmatists, were preparing to centre most of their 2009 presidential campaigns on economic issues and foreign policy. Most notably, political heavyweight Akbar Hashemi Rafsanjani repeatedly criticized Ahmadinejad's continuous economic failures, claiming his government had 'turned into a great employer' which, far from tackling the structural problems of the Islamic Republic, had only increased Iran's oil dependency.[38] Economic indicators were working against the President. At the time, more than fourteen million Iranians (a fifth of the population) were living below the poverty line[39] and felt alienated by a government that, in the eyes of many Iranians, seem to rebuke rather than follow scientific counsel. Public outrage against the President manifested itself on all levels, prompting Grand Ayatollah Abol-Karim Mousavi-Ardebili to complain about rising inflation and the rising price of even basic consumer products, such as bread, despite US$3.2 billion in flour subsidies per year.[40] Former nuclear negotiator Hassan Rowhani stressed the need for a 'positive foreign policy' and openly questioned the substance and direction of Ahmadinejad's nuclear diplomacy. Calling for moderation in foreign policy and a commitment to engagement, Rowhani stressed that diplomacy is not an exercise in power but is rather underwritten by a commitment to compromise. Reminding his listeners that the Prophet himself negotiated with enemies and entered into agreements with them for the sake of peace, the former chair of the National Security Council demanded a return to pragmatism in Iranian foreign policy.[41]

Conscious of these critical voices in Iran's political landscape, the EU and the US government manoeuvred carefully in rhetoric following the outcome of parliamentary elections in Iran on 14 March. Witnessing the rise of technocratic MPs in the eighth *Majlis*, who largely ran on a platform of prioritizing pragmatism over ideology, it was believed that the government would have to adopt a more conciliatory foreign policy tone. The technocrats and moderate conservatives were represented by following key figures: then Tehran Mayor Mohammad Bagher Qualibaf; Mohsen Rezai, Secretary of the Expediency Council, who continued to criticize the government for inflammatory foreign policy; and the incoming Speaker, Ali Larijani, who had resigned as chief negotiator over disputes with Ahmadinejad and who was believed to be pushing for more moderation with the West.[42] It was decided that a statement criticizing the lack of free and fair election procedures and the barring of reformist candidates would be made via the Slovenian EU Presidency rather than the General Council in Brussels. It was believed that this would 'enable ... supportive EU governments, such as UK, Holland, and France, to avoid likely opposition by some EU members to making any statement at all on Iran's elections'.[43]

'Bigger sticks and bigger carrots': the 14 June 2008 proposal

The international environment leading up to the EU-3 package in June was marked by a determination by all sides to enter negotiations from a position of strength. To that end, the British and US governments continued to consolidate economic pressure on Iran as well as framing the narrative as one of suspected weaponization and Iran's rogue behaviour in Afghanistan and Iraq. The EU-3, championed by Germany and France, emphasized the EU's commitment to engagement and recognition of Iranian strategic interest but made it contingent on transparency and trust. Iranian diplomacy followed a two-track approach and was underwritten by confrontational posturing vis-à-vis the West while simultaneously selling the idea of renewed negotiations to domestic constituents. To that end, missile tests and volatile rhetoric served to save face as Saeed Jalili was re-entering talks with Javier Solana, despite the fact that the Iranian government had stated – following the sanctions – that it would from now on solely deal with the IAEA.

In the months leading up to the new proposal, the British FCO prioritized the coordination of EU-wide implementation of sanctions and new financial tools against Iran. In May 2008, Foreign Secretary Miliband perceived the UK to be 'at the forefront of international financial efforts against Iran' and reiterated the British government's commitment 'to push its EU partners on Iran as hard as possible'. Moreover, the Sanctions Officer for the FCO communicated to the US Embassy in London that the Financial Service Authority would 'push the legal envelope to limit Iranian banking activity by both Iranian and UK financial institutions in London and UK diplomats in Brussels will lead the charge for a very tough language in the EU Common Position on Iran'.[44] While FCO efforts dedicated considerable diplomatic resources to coordinating EU measures, the financial gravity of London as a global banking centre presented numerous legal and economic challenges for the British government. As much as the FCO and Prime Minister backed a strong stance against Iran, HM Treasury found itself protecting the capital's financial position and legal framework. Conscious of charges that the FSA had politicized its investigations against Iranian banks in London, the agency insisted on a 'proportionate approach (i.e. the punishment should fit the crime)'. After the British Ambassador to Iran had been summoned by the Iranian Foreign Ministry concerning the 'political abuse of the FSA against Iranian banks', the British government expressed concern that if it went 'too far under UK law it will run the risk of losing and having to pay compensation to the Iranian banks'.[45] To British financial authorities, the mere existence of the UNSC resolution was not sufficient legal justification to revoke Bank Sepah and Bank Melli's licences in the UK. Moreover, British intelligence had found no evidence that Bank Melli's branch in London had participated in any proliferation activities, but rather was concerned with its parent in Iran, over which it had evidently no legal or regulatory lever.[46] Communications between the British and US government indicate the Bush administration's frustration over the EU's complex political and legal hurdles at implementing punitive measures against Iran.

To the British and US governments, financial restrictions against Iranian banks were an effective means of curtailing proliferation efforts and bringing the Iranians back to the negotiation table. In a meeting one week prior to offering Iran another package, the FCO's Political Director noted that the current policy 'is not working but hasn't yet failed either. The West needed bigger sticks and bigger carrots.' Overall, it was believed that engagement on the nuclear issue would ultimately stimulate a debate in Iran and help turn the people against the regime.[47]

The British government described the EU sanctions track as a three-step process: (1) listings of Iranian financial institutions, (2) gold-plating UN Security Council Resolution 1803 and (3) wider measures that include the sanctions on energy and investment and withdrawing defence attachés. According to the FCO's Political Director, the 'EU had not pulled the trigger' on these measures but would do so as soon the Iranians rejected the incentive package, offered by Solana.[48] Aware that taking any aggressive action before Iran was given the P5 + 1 package 'would appear disingenuous to the rest of the world and complicate efforts to gain support', it was decided to make these measures public at the EU meeting hosted by France in July.[49]

Along with efforts to further consolidate Iran's economic isolation in the region and Asia,[50] the Bush administration escalated its rhetoric towards Iran and largely attributed instability in Iraq to Iranian support for insurgents and other *Shi'a* groups. The 11 April testimonies given to the US Congress by General

David Petraeus and Ryan Crocker portrayed the *Shi'a* insurgency as largely being underwritten by the Revolutionary Guards, seeking to turn Iraqi Special Groups into a Hezbollah-like force to serve its interests and fight a proxy war against the Iraqi government and coalition forces in Iraq.[51]

It was against this background that Javier Solana, accompanied by representatives from the P5 + 1 (excluding US diplomats), presented Iranian Foreign Minister Manouchehr Mottaki with the latest offer.

The significance of the package was that it not only offered extensive support in nuclear, economic (including civil aviation) and political cooperation, but also expressed US and EU-backed commitments to regional security. The most important aspects of the letter, which reconfirmed the 2006 offer and which was also signed by the US Secretary of State, Condoleezza Rice, were:

Possible areas of cooperation with Iran

In order to seek a comprehensive, long-term and proper solution of the Iranian nuclear issue consistent with relevant UN Security Council resolutions and building further upon the proposal presented to Iran in June 2006, which remains on the table, the elements below are proposed as topics for negotiations between China, France, Germany, Iran, Russia, the United Kingdom, and the United States, joined by the High Representative of the European Union, as long as Iran verifiably suspends its enrichment-related and reprocessing activities, pursuant to OP 15 and OP 19(a) of UNSCR 1803 ...

Nuclear energy

- Provision of technological and financial assistance necessary for Iran's peaceful use of nuclear energy, support for the resumption of technical cooperation projects in Iran by the IAEA.
- Support for construction of LWR based on state-of-the-art technology.
- Support for R&D in nuclear energy as international confidence is gradually restored.
- Provision of legally binding nuclear fuel supply guarantees.
- Cooperation with regard to management of spent fuel and radioactive waste.

Political

- Improving the six countries' and the EU's relations with Iran and building up mutual trust ...
- Promotion of dialogue and cooperation on non-proliferation, regional security and stabilization issues.
- Work with Iran and others in the region to encourage confidence-building measures and regional security. Establishment of appropriate consultation and cooperation mechanisms.
- Support for a conference on regional security issues.
- Reaffirmation that a solution to the Iranian nuclear issue would

contribute to non-proliferation efforts and to realizing the objective of a Middle East free of weapons of mass destruction, including their means of delivery.

- Cooperation on Afghanistan, including on intensified cooperation in the fight against drug trafficking, support for programmes on the return of Afghan refugees to Afghanistan
- Cooperation on reconstruction of Afghanistan; cooperation on guarding the Iran–Afghan border.

Economic

- Steps towards the normalization of trade and economic relations, such as improving Iran's access to the international economy, markets and capital through practical support for full integration into international structures, including the World Trade Organization, and to create the framework for increased direct investment in Iran and trade with Iran.

Energy partnership

- Steps towards the normalization of cooperation with Iran in the area of energy: establishment of a long-term and wide-ranging strategic energy partnership between Iran and the European Union and other willing partners, with concrete and practical applications/measures ...

Civil aviation

- Civil aviation cooperation, including the possible removal of restrictions on manufacturers exporting aircraft to Iran.
- Enabling Iran to renew its civil aviation fleet; assisting Iran to ensure that Iranian aircraft meet international safety standards.

Economic, social and human development/humanitarian issues

- Provide, as necessary, assistance to Iran's economic and social development and humanitarian need.
- Cooperation/technical support in education in areas of benefit to Iran:
  - Supporting Iranians to take courses, placements or degrees in areas such as civil engineering, agriculture and environmental studies.
  - Supporting partnerships between Higher Education Institutions, e.g. public health, rural livelihoods, joint scientific projects, public administration, history and philosophy.
- Cooperation in the field of development of effective emergency response capabilities (e.g. seismology, earth quake research, disaster control, etc.).

Implementation mechanism

- Constitution of joint monitoring groups for the implementation of a future agreement.[52]

Recognizing Iran's right to peaceful nuclear activities and extending a substantial offer of technology transfer to Iran and economic cooperation, Javier Solana considered the package as 'generous'.[53] However, contrary to German and French recommendations to drop the suspension clause prior to negotiations, the dual freeze (i.e. no new sanctions in exchange for uranium enrichment cessation) only referred to the pre-negotiation phase. Formal negotiations at the UN were again subject to Iran suspending all of its enrichment activities.[54] During the meeting between Solana and the Iranians, Mottaki insisted on linking Iran's response to the inventive package with a response from the P5 + 1 to Iran's May proposal, saying that Iran could not consider the offer until they responded. Solana rejected this linkage, saying that the proposal contained nothing new and that negotiations could only proceed if Iran suspended enrichment activities.[55] Back in 2007, German Chancellor Angela Merkel had proposed to the US government that it ought to give up the precondition of immediate suspension of enrichment and offer to talk about a range of strategic interests of concern to Iran and the United States.[56] Even the Foreign and Select Committee of the House of Commons had asked for a major change in British and collective Western policy on Iran's nuclear programme in February 2008 and quietly urged the US to engage directly and drop the suspension requirement before entering talks with Tehran. FCO officials, however, dismissed these recommendations and reiterated the British government's support for the 'two-track' strategy of sanctions and EU measures.[57]

Jalili contended that the package was similar to Iran's May 2008 offer,[58] and agreed that it was now up to the Iranian government to respond. To that end, Jalili said they would 'study [the offer] carefully'.[59] The FCO interpreted the tone in Iranian media during the talks as revealing a softening in the official Iranian position.[60] Parallel to the June proposal, the British government anticipated Iran would not respond in a 'useful fashion' and therefore considered a forthcoming UN Security Council resolution on Iran as necessary. FCO officials argued that 'whether a fourth resolution contains any new sanctions will be relatively unimportant, but such a measure would have important symbolic value, and impress Iran, and should therefore be pursued, despite the likely reluctance of China.'[61] According to the FCO's Multilateral Team Leader:

> the Iranians, because of their national pride and dislike for any appearance of international isolation, are more susceptible to international opprobrium than Western policy makers often appreciate … the special Iranian need to be seen internationally in a positive light, is a vulnerability Western policy makers should not overlook; the psychological dimension of Iran's relationship with the outside world, in HMG's view, gives multilateral measures, especially in the Security Council, a special status and impact.[62]

For the FCO to anticipate Tehran's rejection of the proposal again reveals that British foreign policy towards the region, and Iran in particular, was not merely being implemented in tandem with the US government but was essentially informed by a similar mindset. Diplomatic communications between Foggy Bottom and Whitehall confirm that engagement was seen as an opportunity for projecting power and political resolve rather than as an exercise in conflict resolution.[63] In advance of EU sanctions, the British government was the first member state to freeze the assets of Bank Melli in London four days before the P5 + 1 offer.[64]

The talks that followed up on the proposal were held in Geneva on 19 July. The US government decided to send Under Secretary of State William Burns to participate. Talks coincided with Condoleezza Rice forwarding the idea of opening a US interest section inside the Swiss Embassy in Tehran. While the State Department and the Iranian Foreign Ministry both highlighted the need for a consular presence rather than re-establishing full diplomatic relations, the prospect of pushing for a thaw in relations gained considerable traction among US senators as well as being initially reciprocated by the Iranian government. International media treated the prospect of an interest section as an 'incentive' for Tehran to agree to the proposal.[65] Though the US State Department never formally forwarded a request to the Iranian Foreign Ministry, the prospect soon became subject to intense debate among key decision-makers in Iran. Ali Larijani, the Speaker of the Parliament, not only was vehemently opposed to the prospect but also considered the Geneva talks as detrimental to Iranian interests.[66] Dismissing it as an American ploy to initiate acts of sabotage and subversion of Iran's youth, he saw the prospect of détente with the US government as, therefore, not linked to the negotiations in Geneva.[67] Overall, there was a sense that Iran found itself in a position of strength, seeing US initiatives and the very presence of William Burns not as opportunity for détente but rather as a sign of American weakness and a vindication of Iran's policies.

At the 19 July meeting at the UN offices in Geneva, the Iranian delegation issued a non-paper to the P5 + 1, proposing a three-stage framework for negotiations. Preliminary talks between Jalili and Solana would agree on an agenda and modalities governing subsequent negotiations. The second stage foresaw a 'minimum of four meetings' between the Foreign Ministers of the P5 + 1 and the Iranian delegation, but was contingent on parties abstaining 'from referring to, or discussing, divergent issues that can potentially hinder the progress of negotiations'. The P5 + 1 would also refrain from taking any multilateral or unilateral measures against Iran.[68] In this pre-negotiation phase, it was suggested by the non-paper that parties would agree on an agenda, which would outline and finalize agreements on comprehensive cooperation. The third stage would start with the P5 + 1 'discontinuing sanctions and existing UNSC resolutions' and Iran would in turn complete the 'agreed action' (without explaining what this would actually entail).[69] The final agreement to be negotiated during this stage related to 'collective obligations on economic, political, regional, international, nuclear, energy, security and defense cooperation'. With completion of this agreement, Iran's nuclear case had to be concluded in the UN Security Council as well as taken out of the Board of Governors' agenda. The implementation of safeguards had to be returned to normal in Iran.[70] The non-paper coincided with a missile test by Iranian forces in the Persian Gulf. Revolutionary Guards Commander Hossein Salami described the testing of a new version of the Shahab-3 missile as proof that 'Iran is prepared to defend the integrity of the nation' and managed to draw sharp criticism from the US government. At the same time, United States and British warships were conducting naval manoeuvres in the Persian Gulf, purportedly within range of the launching site of the missiles.[71] The tests served two purposes: they catered to a domestic audience and were meant to sell the idea of negotiations as well as projecting power towards the West and thus giving the impression that Iran was entering talks from a position of strength.[72] Far from this translating into any diplomatic capital, Western powers felt vindicated concerning Iranian intransigence. Bellicose rhetoric coupled with a non-paper which contained virtually no meaningful substance led to the July talks failing to produce any agreement. According to Javier Solana, pre-negotiations failed because the Iranians failed to provide 'an answer to the moist important question' regarding Iran's willingness to suspend its fuel cycle activities.[73] Ultimately, pre-negotiations broke down because of the irreconcilability of US and Iranian positions, with the former demanding enrichment cessation as a precondition for talks and the latter insisting on it as a fundamental right under the NPT. Moreover, hardliners in Iran interpreted the initiatives forwarded by the US government as a victory for Iranian diplomacy rather than as an opportunity for engagement, and thus failed to reciprocate the Bush administration's diplomatic overtures.[74] Initiatives by the US Congress to start inter-parliamentary relations with the *Majlis* were also met with suspicion by Ali Larijani and became subject to partisan politics. Meetings between three members of the *Majlis* Economic Commission and members of Congress during the IMF/World Bank meeting in Washington in October failed to initiate any engagement. According to the three *Majlis* Deputies (both reformist Mohammad-Reza Tabesh and conservative Gholam-Reza Mesbahi-Moghaddam and Kazem Delkhosh), the government decided to deny any one faction the triumph of resuming relations with the United States.[75]

Iranian diplomacy

Iranian diplomacy before and after the June proposal was largely informed by a perceived position of strength. The nuclear programme was no longer an issue to be negotiated away with outside powers but was the very bargaining chip that could be relied upon to link to an entire array of Iranian strategic interests. The IAEA confirmed the non-diversion of declared nuclear material in Iran in its 15 September report, but stated 'that the alleged studies have remained a matter of serious concern to an assessment of a possible military dimension to Iran's nuclear program'.[76] On 27 September, the UN Security Council then passed Resolution 1835, which called on Iran to cease enrichment activities but did not mandate new sanctions wanted by the United States and the EU.

Far from demanding a change in the course of diplomacy, the reception of both resolutions in Iran reflected a mindset prevailing among key decision-makers. In a speech in September, the Supreme Leader stressed the value of patience in Islamic culture, reiterating that officials must show patience in confronting the adversaries of the Islamic Republic, while cautioning that 'rationality and moderation is not tantamount to compromise with the usurpers'.[77] The mindset was clear: Iran would ultimately achieve its goals and would not back down from the standoff as outside powers, it was expected, would ultimately give up.[78] Scientific achievements and nuclear progress in particular had become a means of political enfranchisement in international relations and ultimately reflected Iran's emerging status as a global power.[79] By November, the Atomic Energy Organization of Iran confirmed that 5,000 centrifuges were running at the Natanz power plant and that the Russian-backed Bushehr plant was in the final stages of being set up.[80] More significantly, the Iranian government refused to allow the IAEA a scheduled visit to the Arak heavy water reactor as well as failing to address outstanding questions by the IAEA concerning weaponization.[81]

With the nation seeing itself as a vanguard of the Muslim World, neither of the resolutions caused Iran to surrender at the negotiating table. On the contrary, dismissing Resolution 1835 for having not imposed any new sanctions, President Ahmadinejad reiterated that his government was seeking a non-permanent seat in the UN Security Council in order 'to make sure that the UN is the organization of all nations and not the organization of some powers and lobbies'.[82] The Secretary of Iran's National Security Council criticized the resolutions as lacking content and not being constructive, only fuelling further mistrust of Iranians. Likewise, Iran's Permanent Representative to the UN said:

> The Iranian nation is determined to pursue its definitive right to the peaceful use of nuclear technology irrespective of the illegal decision of the Security Council.... The instigators of the resolution should be seeking to gain Iran's trust through constructive cooperation.[83]

To that end, Saeed Jalili sent a letter to Javier Solana in which he criticized the West's 'unreasonable behavior' in nuclear talks with Iran as well as asking for clarifications of some items in the official proposal. To the Iranians, Western powers and particular the United States were negotiating in bad faith:[84]

> It is interesting for the international community to see that in the course of talks when a rational question is raised, the other party to the talks resorts to levers of pressure instead of offering answers to questions and trying to remove ambiguities. In the judgment of the world community, this unreasonable behavior is an indication of the lack of a clear response to the principled questions of the Islamic Republic of Iran. It also reinforces the doubt that some powers look at talks as merely a tactical tool. The absence of civilized tradition of dialogue among certain powers that prefer to use levers of pressure instead of reasoning is not a matter that is unknown to the world community.[85]

Despite the fact that the Iranian delegation communicated its interest in further negotiations, the P5+1 neither reciprocated this initiative nor provided an official response to the clarification request by Jalili.[86] On the contrary, participation at a nuclear conference hosted by the Iranian government in November was actively discouraged by the British government, as it feared that attendance would 'give credibility to Iran's claims about its nuclear activities'.[87] At the conference, Gholamreza Aghazadeh, the head of Iran's Atomic Energy Organization, proposed the forming of a consortium of regional states for building light-water nuclear power plants in the Persian Gulf.[88] Six days prior to the conference, British Foreign Minister David Miliband gave a speech in Abu Dhabi warning Arab states about Iranian influence in the region and rallying Gulf monarchies in preventing Iran from acquiring nuclear weapons capability. Many observers in Iran regarded the speech as 'inciting' the Arab states against Iran[89] and the British Ambassador was subsequently summoned by the Iranian Foreign Ministry.[90]

Notwithstanding government rhetoric, financial sanctions against Iran affected the economy and increased the pressure on the government from key trade stakeholders, most notably the *bazaaris*. Politically, the impact of sanctions witnessed the formation of a bi-partisan front against President Ahmadinejad.[91] Therefore, Iranian diplomacy catered as much to a foreign audience as it did towards a domestic constituency. As much as the Iranian government wanted to maintain negotiations with the P5+1, it wanted to do so on its own terms. Coupling counter-initiatives with missile tests and volatile rhetoric failed, however. It neither translated into diplomatic capital nor did it impress political stakeholders at home.

EU and US diplomacy

Prior to the UN Security Council resolution in September, US National Security Adviser Tony Lake told the FCO that the US would 'sharpen the choices for Iran'. It was decided that sanctions would continue to be a tool to compel the regime to engage directly with the US, with enrichment suspension being the crucial contingency.[92] In the light of the 2007 NIE, France, Britain and the US also wanted a confession from Iran.[93] However, as the Iranians rightly interpreted, there was no consensus among the P5+1 about the future direction of multilateral diplomacy towards Iran. Notwithstanding private US assurances to the Chinese that the Russian–Georgian crisis in August would not affect P5+1's posture,[94] the fallout of the conflict did effectively limit further measures against Iran in the short term. The Iranian Foreign Minister was quick to side with the Russian government, hoping that it would translate into a Russian veto against new sanctions at the UN Security Council.[95] More significantly, the German government's prerequisites for its support of the new measures were so extensive that, according to the FCO's Director for Political Affairs, they rendered any prospect for joint E-3 progress very difficult.[96] The German government remained opposed to EU measures and insisted on a broad-based multilateral coalition.[97] Chancellor Merkel's cabinet, much like other key powers, largely saw the period of transition between US administrations, in the words of the FCO, 'as a time to go slow and exercise caution until clear USG leadership on Iran emerges'.[98] Consultations on non-proliferation between French, British and US officials in November 2008 focused on the pace of Iran's nuclear programme and the issue of covert facilities and the need for the EU members to overcome legal hurdles in implementing financial measures against Iran.[99] To the FCO, 2009 was seen as a critical year for Iran, during which international pressure would gain more traction, causing Iran to eventually accept the June 2008 package.[100]

As the EU had largely abandoned diplomatic engagement and started to check Iranian nuclear capabilities on US terms, the EU had effectively ceased to serve the role of honest broker in the US–Iran–EU triangle. Conversations between David Miliband and his Turkish counterpart, Ali Babacan, in November 2008 had already indicated the Turkish government's self-perceived role as emerging mediator in the nuclear deal, which would ultimately lead to the joint Turkish–Brazilian deal in May 2010. To Babacan, diplomatic engagement with Iran had not brought any results, as previous offers had not been properly presented to Iran. Moreover, he was convinced that there were too many participants in the process, and therefore engagement had to be limited to a core group of interlocutors. Babacan made it clear to Miliband that Iran 'must see itself as a real partner in the talks' rather than being cornered by the international community.[101]

Conclusion

Essentially, the June proposal failed because of the irreconcilability of US and Iranian positions, with the former demanding enrichment cessation as a precondition for talks and the latter insisting on it as a fundamental and non-negotiable right under the NPT. Both sides were entering pre-negotiations with a perceived sense of strength. Initially confident about its position, the Iranian delegation's non-paper failed to address any areas of concern to the P5 + 1. In fact, Iranian authorities increased the number of centrifuges by November, thus defying one of the core demands of the P5 + 1 and previous UN Security Council resolutions. However, as the dynamics of domestic politics – partly impacted by sanctions – dictated a return to the negotiation table and the Iranian government communicated its interest in taking talks further, the EU and US government had already started implementing punitive measures and were drafting another UN Security Council resolution. Consultations between French, British and US officials indicate that the US-backed June proposal was never intended to test the Iranians or to be used as a means to resolve underlying issues; rather, it was a *casus* for more punitive sanctions. In this light, none of the parties engaged in any meaningful diplomacy.

5 Engagement with Iran
The Obama years (2009–2012)

Introduction

It was widely expected that the election of Barrack Obama in November 2008 would herald a sea-change in US foreign policy. While the Obama Presidency indeed shed the unilateral penchant of the Bush administration and again embraced international institutionalism, US diplomacy towards Iran continued to be informed by a realist mindset. Obama's 2009 *Naw Ruz* address to the Iranian government and people was followed by a much-celebrated speech in Cairo in June 2009 entitled 'New Beginning', which called for new improved mutual understanding and relations between the Muslim World and the West. Both speeches reflected a change in rhetoric as well as commitment to pragmatism in diplomacy, and largely set up a framework of engagement with Iran. Private messages from President Obama to the Supreme Leader eventually paved the way for the first high-level meeting between US and Iranian officials since the Islamic Revolution in the autumn of 2009.

However, entering engagement with the Iranians under the pressure of Israel and with domestic opposition, diplomacy was not given sufficient time and was soon abandoned in favour of a policy of containment.

In the consciousness of Iran's unprecedented crisis of legitimacy at home following the presidential elections in Iran in June 2009, and after the successful mobilization of all UN Security Council members, the threat of multilateral punitive measures in the event of continuous inflexibility on the part of the Iranians was credible and meant to instil leverage during negotiations. To the Iranians, the extension of sanctions and the passing of new ones prior to negotiations meant a continuation of US diplomacy towards Iran rather than a break with past tools of statecraft.

As the Iranian government started to abandon the agreement in Geneva and the human rights situation continued to deteriorate dramatically, the US government insisted on its set 'year-end deadline' for Iran to show concrete steps towards the course of engagement. Notwithstanding the Turkish–Brazilian channel, which effectively brought the Iranians back to the negotiation table, the Obama administration started to abandon its commitment to maintaining a dialogue with Iran in favour of punitive measures. Disclosed US diplomatic cables confirm that Obama's engagement strategy with Iran was implemented with the clear conviction that it would fail. The so-called 'dual-track' policy of simultaneously applying pressure while professing a commitment to negotiations was largely undermined by focusing almost entirely on the pressure track while never giving quiet diplomacy, as thirty years of animosity would warrant, any real chance to work. To Iran's Supreme Leader, the approach under the Obama administration was in no way different from previous ones: 'These [US overture] statements may seem soft, but in reality there is a cast iron fist underneath a velvet glove.'[1]

Setting the stage for engagement

On 20 March 2009, President Obama's *Naw Ruz* message marked a break with the rhetoric of the previous administration as, for the first time, a US President addressed both the Iranian people and the Iranian government and effectively called for engagement:

> So in this season of new beginnings I would like to speak clearly to Iran's leaders. We have serious differences that have grown over time. My administration is now committed to diplomacy that addresses the full range of issues before us, and to pursuing constructive ties among the United States, Iran and the international community. This process will not be advanced by threats. We seek instead engagement that is honest and grounded in mutual respect.[2]

However, prior to Obama's offer of engagement, he had extended sanctions against Iran for one year, on the grounds that it continued to pose a threat to US national security. The US sanctions would have lapsed without the President's formal notice of renewal.[3] What would become Obama's so-called 'dual-track approach', a policy of engagement coupled with sanctions, was immediately rejected by Khamenei, who responded in the following terms:

> For you to say that we will both talk to Iran and simultaneously exert pressure on her, both threats and appeasement, our nation hates this approach. One cannot treat our nation in this way. We have no experience of this new president and administration. We will wait and see. If you change your attitude we will change too. If you do not change then our nation will build on its experience of the past thirty years.

Without concrete signs of goodwill, US overtures were dismissed as 'deception or intimidation'.[4] The Iranian government expected that lifting sanctions would be a meaningful gesture towards engagement.[5] Tehran's official response to Obama's speech at Cairo University reflected hardline discourse and self-perception of Iranian power. A 2009 editorial in *Keyhan*, the Supreme Leader's mouthpiece, rejected Obama's exhortation to non-proliferation in the region and highlighted Iranian conditions for resuming official relations with the United States:

> Obama pretend[s] that his country is ready to take the first steps in the process of normalizing ties with Iran and is not setting any conditions for this but the truth is that Iran has pre-conditions that are completely logical. [Washington] has to release Iran's blocked assets, put the commander of the *Vincennes* naval warship on trial, extradite escaped criminals to Iran and [i]f America wants to get close to Iran in the issues connected with the Middle East region, it has to accept the legal Hamas government that has emerged as a result of the public's votes and officially recognize Lebanon's Hezbollah.... Otherwise Islamic Iran would not be able to put the fate of Muslims to a debate with America, which is responsible for many calamities and misfortunes in the Islamic world.[6]

The key architect of Obama's 'dual-track approach' was Dennis Ross, who had been appointed Special Advisor for the Gulf and Southwest Asia in January 2009. To the Iranians, Ross, a co-founder of the neo-conservative think-tank the Washington Institute for Near East Policy (to which he returned in 2011, after his appointment) and lacking any real expertise on Iran, displayed Zionist credentials rather than diplomatic pedigree.[7] From the onset, Obama's approach inspired little confidence as to many in Iran it was merely a continuation of a coercive approach which had prevented any sustainable engagement between both countries for over thirty years.

Several features of the 'dual-track approach' as well as outside factors made it difficult for engagement to gain any meaningful momentum.

First, time was treated as one of the most important variables in Iran's nuclear programme as well as engagement. Highly sceptical that 'engagement would lead to an acceptable resolution', the Israeli government effectively gave the Obama administration a tight window for diplomacy. In a June 2009 meeting, Israeli Defence Minister Barak estimated that:

> a window between six and eighteen months from now in which stopping Iran from acquiring nuclear weapons might still be viable. After that, he said, any military solution would result in unacceptable collateral damage. He also expressed concern that should Iran develop nuclear capabilities, other rogue states and/or terrorist groups would not be far behind.[8]

Given the confirmed progress of enrichment activities and the refusal of Iranian authorities for IAEA inspectors to inspect the heavy water reactor at Arak for a second time in February 2009, officials in the Obama administration feared that time was running out.[9] In fact, at a secret meeting of nuclear experts discussing Iran's progress at the British Mission to the IAEA in April 2009, the US representative claimed that 'although centrifuge operations in 2008 were mediocre, Iran had now demonstrated centrifuge operations such that it had the technical ability to produce highly enriched uranium if it so chose'. There was disagreement between the French and British representatives over Iran's stockpile of uranium. The French estimated that 'Iran's current uranium stockpile was dwindling, with less than 100 tons of uranium remaining, and that Iran had significantly slowed down operations at the UCF during 2008 and 2009, most likely to preserve its declining stockpile'. British experts argued, however, that the 'current uranium shortage will not have a near term impact on operations at Natanz, since Iran has plenty of UF6 to keep existing centrifuges running for several years.'[10] The British representative estimated that the IR-1 (P-1) cascades at the fuel enrichment plant (FEP) performed at an average level of 0.6 separative work units (SWU) per machine-year during 2008, and therefore concluded that after five years Iran could possess twenty tons of low-enriched uranium hexafluoride (UF6) with eight units of 3,000 centrifuge machines, at Iran's current pace of installation – approximately two cascades per month – and operation. The US representative claimed that this was about two-thirds of the amount needed for a single annual fuel reload for a Bushehr-type reactor.[11] The representatives agreed that Iran would need 1.5 tons of low-enriched UF6 to make an initial bomb and then another ton for each subsequent device. The British representative calculated that by 2014, Iran would have amassed twenty tons – effectively enough uranium for nineteen warheads.[12]

Mindful of the perceived pace of enrichment activities, the contingency of implementing engagement under an agreed-upon deadline was further reinforced in numerous high-level meetings between the Israeli and US governments, as well as by the lobbying efforts of the American Israel Public Affairs Committee (AIPAC) on Capitol Hill.[13] Notwithstanding the Obama administration's public rejection to establishing timetables, it eventually adopted a mindset which equated negotiations and diplomacy itself as a means by the Iranian government to buy time, rather than treating it as an effective conflict resolution effort. This particular attitude was reinforced in a May 2009 meeting between a US congressional delegation, US Embassy officials and the Israeli Defence Forces Intelligence Chief:

> Iran is in the position of wanting to pay only a minimum cost for its current program. It does not want to be North Korea or what Iraq was before 2003. Iran intends to keep resolutions and sanctions at a certain manageable level and continue to produce low enriched uranium until there is enough for several bombs. The Israel official stated that Iran could decide to produce a bomb by 2010, but Iran is waiting for the right time in the future and that there are some who will always doubt it despite the evidence.[14]

When the US administration abandoned dialogue in favour of a return to containment by the end of 2009, President Obama had effectively invested less than six months in engagement in order to settle over thirty years of mutual mistrust and animosity.

Second, the fallout of the presidential elections in Iran in June 2009 caught the US administration and the EU largely off guard and made it more difficult, in particular for the Obama administration, to anchor engagement within the domestic body politic. Prior to the elections, EU and US officials anticipated that Ahmadinejad would be denied a second term. Several moderate conservatives, all vetted by the Supreme Leader, were seen as likely contenders for the office of president. In March 2009, a Tehran-based contact, close to Khamenei, advised the US government via an FCO channel to wait to engage Iran until after the elections. Citing Ahmadinejad's lack of interest in improving relations with the US, he argued that direct outreach to Iran should happen after June 'so as to minimize the chances of boosting Ahmadinejad's prestige'. If the US did act before June, the interlocutor advised: 'use channels controlled by the Supreme Leader, not by Ahmadinejad'.[15]

Within days after the election and the protests which ensued, US and European diplomats were told by Iranian interlocutors from within the reformist camp that the elections were rigged on orders by the Supreme Leader's Office. On 19 June, a German diplomat hosted a senior cleric, brother of ex-IRGC commander and the Supreme Leader's military adviser Rehman Safavi, in his residence in London. At the meeting, which was also attended by Norwegian, British, Spanish and Japanese diplomats, the cleric advised that

> a majority of leaders within the government of Iran and the IRGC want the United States, while continuing to avoid interference in Iran, to continue and even strengthen its public messages on human rights, so as to support popular protests in Iran and prevent any consolidation of Ahmadinejad's electoral win.[16]

Conscious of the 'political coup' by conservatives but unsure – in the words of the US Embassy in London – whether these narratives reflect more the agenda of aggrieved candidates seeking a major redress rather than 'facts on the grounds', as well as still waiting for the senior clergy in Qom to side with Mousavi and Rafsanjani, the EU and the US government largely focused on the deteriorating human rights situation rather than questioning the outcome of the elections.[17]

Lastly, the regional balance of power and the so-called proxy wars between Iran and the US in Afghanistan and Iraq, and regional dynamics after the Arab Spring in 2011, remained a key variable informing US diplomacy towards Iran. While supporting the Kabul government and reconstruction efforts, the US administration was aware that the Iranian government maintained contact with some elements of the Taliban, members of the opposition and the country's *Shi'a* constituents.[18] As much as a Taliban resurgence was seen as contrary to Iranian strategic interests, Tehran was equally reluctant to see a democratic and secular Afghanistan allied with the West.[19] According to US intelligence reports, clandestine efforts by Iran included both material and financial support against NATO interests and the Afghan government.[20] As Iranian diplomats, alongside their US counterparts, were pledging their support for combating terrorism and assisting reconstruction in Afghanistan at the Shanghai Cooperation Organization in March

2009, US intelligence reported a concerted campaign by Iranian intelligence to undermine efforts for stability and democracy. Disclosed cables note that Iranian clandestine efforts included large-scale attempts to bribe members of the Afghan parliament to back 'anti-Coalition policies' and payments to kill Afghan officials. Just two weeks prior to President Obama's *Naw Ruz* address to Iran in 2009, the US State Department described Iranian policy in Afghanistan as a 'dedicated effort to influence Afghan attitudes towards Coalition forces and other issues'. Certain members of the Afghan parliament were said to be acting on Iranian orders, accepting bribes or political support to promote Iran's political agenda. Iranian intelligence infiltration in parliamentary affairs as well as among the opposition was considered to be extensive. As Hillary Clinton publicly denounced Iran as 'heading towards a military dictatorship' after the elections, the US Ambassador to Afghanistan rejected the Afghan government's offer to mediate on the grounds that

> Iran evidently is not ready to engage with us. Even though we believe that many Iranians desire more normal relations with the United States, the Iranian government appears out of touch with its people, in particular an increasingly angry middle class.'[21]

Iranian policy in Iraq also constituted a factor which determined US diplomacy. The US-led invasion created a power vacuum, with Syria, Saudi Arabia and Iran competing for their own spheres of influence. Iran in particular was singled out by Iraq's leading cleric, Ayatollah Hussein Al Sadr, in a private meeting with the Deputy Secretary of State, warning of 'undue Iranian influence' at all government levels.[22] According to the British Ambassador to Iran in 2007, Iran regarded Iraq as a tool in its broader strategy 'to counteract the US threat by seeking to exploit perceived US vulnerability there', and ultimately preventing any future threats from Iraq (i.e. from the Iraqi government, the US or terrorist groups).[23]

US military intelligence reports indicated that the IRGC was implementing a proxy war against US forces by establishing covert relations with militia, parities and charitable organizations gathering intelligence for Iran, smuggling lethal aid and conducting attacks against US interests under Iranian direction.[24] Iraqi government agencies, in particular in Basrah, were infiltrated by Iranian agents, and singled out as the biggest problem to security in 2008.[25]

To US diplomats, Iranian support of Iraq's *Shi'a* insurgency was not just a matter of tactical assaults against certain US interests but was seen as a larger strategy to secure the eventual defeat of the United States and increase Iranian influence in Iraq. As noted in a US intelligence assessment:

> Although it is often said that the US did Iran a favor by ridding it of the Taliban and Saddam Hussein, Iran actually views the US as a bigger threat than either of these. Iran is likely prioritizing its threats. It is therefore willing to deal with groups it considers enemies in order to counter its

perceived most significant threat, the US, with the expectation that it can handle the lesser threats down the road.[26]

After US and Iraqi forces neutralized *Shi'a* and *Sunni* militias in 2007–2008 as part of the surge, the US–Iranian stand-off in Iraq continued (notwithstanding President Obama's decision to seek engagement with Iran). IRGC networks maintained presence in Iraq, operating under the immediate strategic guidance of the Supreme Leader. An intelligence assessment in November 2009 reported that

> it is not uncommon for the IRIG to finance and support competing *Shi'a*, Kurdish, and to some extent, *Sunni* entities, with the aim of developing the Iraqi body politic's dependency on Tehran's largesse. While exact figures are unknown, Tehran's financial assistance to Iraqi surrogates is estimated at US$100–200 million annually, with US$70 million going to ISCI/Badr coffers.[27]

Iran had also shifted to shaping the Iraqi political landscape in general and dedicated its efforts in securing a *Shi'a*-dominated and preferably Islamist government in Iraq.[28]

As the Obama administration was struggling to anchor engagement with Israel and in Congress, Arab Gulf states increased their alarmist rhetoric on Iran and secretly called for military action rather than engagement.[29] Diplomatic correspondence between the US government and regional states reflected an Arab front demanding the US government to check Iranian influence in the region. Cautioning against 'appeasement', areas of concern centred on alleged Iranian subversive efforts in the region, its meddling in Yemen, Afghanistan and Iraq, Bahrain, Syria and support for Hamas and Hezbollah.[30]

Subject to Israel's contingencies for engagement as well as demands from regional allies and mindful of what many in the Pentagon and Department of State considered to be a regional balance of power shifting in favour of Iran, the Obama administration decided to engage Iran at a time of its greatest domestic crisis of legitimacy. As the US government opened diplomatic channels to Iran, it continued to check Iranian influence in the region by underwriting security and further upgrading the military capabilities of its regional allies. What US Secretary of State Hillary Clinton called a 'defence umbrella' in July 2009 reflected the US government's continuous commitment to extended deterrence in the Persian Gulf and would eventually lead to the largest arms deal in US history with Saudi Arabia in 2010.[31] Implementing engagement under a spectrum of sanctions, extended deterrence and multilateral negotiations evidently failed to break with a history of mutual mistrust. Failing to incorporate Iranian security perceptions, a Cold War mindset informed US policy, and Arab states were rallied against Iran while excluding any comprehensive negotiations with Iranian interlocutors over mutually acceptable collective security arrangements in the region. As American diplomats in Baghdad noted in September 2009:

In the longer term, we will need to flesh out ideas for a post-GCC security architecture that includes Iraq more fully, develops ways to contain Iranian regional influence, and shapes the special position Iraq will likely occupy in the Gulf in ways that further our interests and those of our Gulf partners. The challenge for us is to convince Iraq neighbors, particularly the Sunni Arab governments, that relations with a new Iraq are not a zero-sum game, where if Iraq wins, they lose. We still have work to convince them that a strong, stable, democratic (and inevitably *Shi'a*-led) Iraq is the best guarantee that Iraq will be able to shake Iranian manipulation and see its future bound up with that of the West and its moderate Arab neighbors.[32]

Subject to the same forces of this regional security dilemma, the Iranians too continued to put a premium on deterrence and coercion vis-à-vis their Arab neighbours.[33]

The 2009 Geneva deal

When the Obama administration agreed to engage Iran without preconditions, a US president had finally recognized the most important variable in the nuclear talks and seemed to have decoupled diplomatic pragmatism from the ideological gridlock, which had kept both states in a state of mutual hostility since 1979. For the first time, US and Iranian diplomats would be able to directly communicate their respective areas of concern as well as outline avenues for potential cooperation. However, the P5+1, and the US in particular, entered negotiations with the concrete priorities of suspension and managing, if not checking, Iran's regional ambitions. A main concern for the US government was what the US Ambassador to the IAEA referred to an Iranian interlocutor, in January 2009, as 'the inherent risk that [negotiations] would be a device by which Tehran would be able to buy time to further its nuclear development'. To the US, engagement would be implemented in order to enforce suspension as outlined in UNSC resolutions and would ultimately reach a suspension of enrichment.[34] As much as the Iranian government expected the West's recognition of its rights to nuclear power as a major regional if not global power, the EU and the US government perceived past nuclear proposals to have already recognized Iran's non-military rights contingent on verifiable contingency.[35]

Prior to the meeting in Geneva in October between the P5+1 and the Iranian delegation, the French, British and US governments disclosed intelligence, during a briefing at the IAEA, which indicated that the Atomic Energy Organization of Iran had secretly constructed another underground enrichment facility underneath an IRGC military base near the city of Qom. Intelligence estimates put the number of centrifuges at 3,000, but assessed that it would not be operational until 2010. In fact, Iran's Permanent Mission to the IAEA had sent a letter to the agency in September indicating that it was in the process of 'constructing a pilot fuel enrichment facility and that the required infrastructure has been established'. However, according to European and US intelligence, this facility was too small to be viable for the production of fuel for a nuclear power reactor, but rather 'may be well suited for a military purpose'.[36] In a letter to the IAEA in October 2009, the Iranian government would later explain the reasons for the construction of an underground enrichment facility:

> As a result of the augmentation of the threats of military attacks against Iran, the Islamic Republic of Iran decided to establish contingency centres for various organizations and activities ...
>
> The Natanz Enrichment Plant was among the targets threatened with military attacks. Therefore, the Atomic Energy Organization requested the Passive Defence Organization to allocate one of those aforementioned centres for the purpose of [a] contingency enrichment plant, so that the enrichment activities shall not be suspended in the case of any military attack. In this respect, the Fordow site, being one of those constructed and prepared centres, [was] allocated to the Atomic Energy Organization of Iran (AEOI) in the second half of 2007. The construction of the Fordow Fuel Enrichment Plant then started. The construction is still ongoing. Thus the plant is not yet ready for operation and it is planned to be operational in 2011.[37]

Notwithstanding Iran's claim, the disclosure was meant to increase pressure on Iran. The disclosure of the Fordow facility was largely used as leverage in the negotiations in Geneva. The covert facility confirmed to British Prime Minister Gordon Brown Iran's 'serial deception of many years' and prompted French President, Nicholas Sarkozy to give Iran a two-month deadline to meet international demands.[38] At a meeting of the P5 + 1 at the United Nations in New York in September, it was agreed that, given these new developments, the burden was now on Iran to prove the exclusively peaceful nature of its nuclear programme. The Foreign Ministers of the P5 + 1 agreed that the process in Geneva must be taken seriously by the Iranians to address their nuclear programme.[39] Overall the EU-3 and the US government felt confident that they had carefully calibrated the balance of power prior to talks. As US Secretary of Defence Robert M. Gates put it prior to the talks: 'The Iranians are in a very bad spot now.' President Obama's gambit in Poland on missile defence (changing it from a system based in Eastern Europe to a sea-based system) would eventually result in a Russian *quid pro quo* on Iran at the UN Security Council following the failure of the Geneva talks, supporting the passing of UNSC 1929 in June 2010. China had also been swayed as the Saudi government effectively gave assurances that they would supply China with oil should Iranian crude be cut off. US diplomatic channels directly guided the increase of Sino-Saudi trade and thus largely succeeded in building a consensus at the UN Security Council to increase punitive measures against Iran.[40] As part of Obama's carrot and stick approach, the US Treasury Department announced days prior to the Geneva talks that the United States had been working on a 'comprehensive' Iran sanctions plan, which would entail punitive financial measures against Iran with the 'largest possible international coalition'.[41] Rather than providing leverage, the Iranian government felt that the US, much like previous administrations, was negotiating in bad faith and entered negotiations with the demand for UN sanctions to be lifted as a sign of goodwill.[42]

During a private meeting between the US Under Secretary of State and EU Political and Security Committee (PSC) Ambassadors in November 2009, the UD official summarized the three concrete actions asked from Iran: (1) supporting the IAEA's proposal for refuelling the TRR; (2) facilitating the IAEA's full investigation of the then recently disclosed clandestine uranium enrichment plant near Qom; (3) and agreeing to a follow-on meeting between P5 + 1 Political Directors and Iranian representatives by the end of October, explicitly focused on nuclear issues but open to discussion of any issues raised by any party.[43]

Negotiations between the P5 + 1 and Iran in Geneva on 1 October 2009 resulted in a deal in which the Iranian delegation agreed to ship 1,200 kilos of 3.5 per cent low-enriched uranium (LEU), which represented approximately 75 per cent of Iran's LEU stockpile, to Russia before the end of 2009, where technicians would enrich it to 20 per cent, a process which would have produced about 120 kg of 20 per cent enriched uranium for the TRR fuel rods. The LEU would then go to France for fabrication into fuel rods. French authorities would subsequently ship the rods (120 kg of 20 per cent enriched uranium) to Iran for use in the Tehran Research Reactor, which produces medical isotopes, about one year after the conclusion of the agreement.[44] The deal was largely the product of discussions over arrangements to supply the Tehran Research Reactor, initiated by a formal request of Iran's Permanent Representative to the IAEA, Ali Asghar Soltani, when he requested assistance in refuelling the reactor on 2 June 2009.[45] Under the terms of the Geneva agreement, Iran would receive much-needed fuel for this reactor while outsourcing some of the enrichment process to Russia and France and would thus effectively reduce its stockpile. The US government treated the deal as a win–win scenario. It would have reduced the LEU stock below the level required to produce nuclear weapons by outsourcing the enrichment process to a third country, but would have provided Iran with enough enriched material, required for peaceful use in nuclear power reactors. The agreement also tacitly acknowledged Iran's right to produce enriched uranium as neither European nor US diplomats insisted that Iran should abandon its enrichment programme altogether.[46]

Much to the surprise to the Iranian delegation, US diplomats also brought up the issue of the detained American hikers in Iran. Iranian officials would later tell the Austrian Ambassador that it was the wrong time and perceived as not being connected in any way to the nuclear negotiations.[47]

Many political stakeholders in Iran, including the opposition, considered that the deal would have deprived the country of the very leverage it had gained over the years.[48] As Ahmadinejad was facing mounting domestic protests after the contested 2009 presidential elections, the fuel-swap deal quickly became subject to domestic politics. Former nuclear negotiator Hassan Rowhani called the West's conditions for supplying fuel to Iran illegal.[49]

Notwithstanding the President's attempts to sell the agreement in speech as 'an opportunity to Iran to gauge the honesty of the IAEA and Western powers',[50] he eventually also distanced himself from the deal. Upon returning to Tehran, Jalili even stated that 'the issue of enrichment suspension in the country was in no terms brought up during talks'.[51] Ali Larijani, the *Majlis* Speaker, questioned whether Iran should trust sending its LEU stockpile abroad:

> My guess is that the Americans have made a secret deal with certain countries to take enriched uranium away from us under the pretext of providing nuclear fuel,' he told the Iranian Students News Agency October 24, adding, 'I see no links between providing the fuel for the Tehran reactor and sending Iran's LEU abroad.'[52]

Former AEOI President Reza Amrollahi, an ally of Rafsanjani, questioned in an interview whether it made sense for Iran 'to give up all its enriched uranium in exchange for receiving [only] 30 kg of 20 per cent enriched uranium after a two-year wait'. Amrollahi claimed that

> only 300 kg of Iranian fuel would be needed to make this 30 kg of 20 per cent enriched fuel, so where is the rest [i.e. of the 1,000 kg of Iran's 3.5 per cent enriched fuel to be exported] going, and what guarantees do we have for getting this 20 percent enriched fuel?

He concluded his TV interview saying 'given that the TRR's remaining operational life was no more than fifteen years, getting fuel for this reactor wasn't worth all the risk'.[53]

The Iranian government eventually failed to formally respond to the offer but rather started to propose alternatives. Reflecting his government's unwillingness to surrender a major portion of the LEU stockpile, Foreign Minister Manouchehr Mottaki suggested a gradual fuel swap on Iranian territory, soon amended to an exchange of the AEOI's low-enriched uranium for 20 per cent enriched uranium on Turkish territory. Further effectively eliminating the confidence-building element of the fuel-swap offer, Foreign Ministry Spokesman Ramin Mehman-parast stated in an interview that 'Iran never said it would only exchange fuel' but that it would rather buy fuel alongside continued enrichment. Citing the lack of guarantees by Western powers and the twelve-month period to build fuel rods in Russia and France, Iran's national security planners apparently interpreted this as one year of increased vulnerability to attack.[54]

Given the extent of infighting in Iran and unpredictability about the course of politics in the country, it was difficult for Western diplomats to gauge diplomatic signalling coming from Iran. The departing Austrian Ambassador to Iran debriefed US officials in December 2009 and explained 'the lack of follow-through in the wake of the talks as a probable decision by Supreme Leader Khamenei that the West was not trustworthy or that Iran could get more from the P5 + 1 than the six offered in Geneva.' Moreover, Larijani's outspoken rejection of the Geneva deal was interpreted by him as 'an exercise of Larijani's first opportunity to undermine Ahmadinejad after he was pressured to disavow himself of knowledge that Iranian prisoners were being raped in jail, which lost him credibility with the Iranian public'.[55] During what the Ambassador believed to have been the first meeting between Rafsanjani and a Westerner since the election, Rafsanjani – speaking in the presence of over a dozen minders from the government – avoided talking about the nuclear negotiations but asked the West to condemn the election results and the human rights situation in the aftermath.[56]

The domestic environment caused Ahmadinejad to distance himself again from the deal as he went on to announce the purported production of the first batch of 20 per cent enriched LEU. He reminded President Obama that the conditions of the deal violated IAEA statutes: '[T]hey wanted to take our fuel so that they could delay Iran's capabilities in making a nuclear bomb. These were pitiless statements. These statements reminded us of the Bush Administration and [its] bullying era.[57]

Beneath the defiant rhetoric vis-à-vis the United States was an embattled president who was unable to work out a mutually acceptable fuel swap arrangement. In a November 2009 meeting between the Assistant Secretary of State and Turkish Foreign Minister Davutoglu, the US envoy was told that the Turkish regarded Ahmadinejad as 'more flexible' than others inside the Iranian government, but that he was facing 'huge pressures' after the US and EU member states sold the deal to domestic audiences as succeeding in 'weakening Iran's nuclear capability, which [was] interpreted by some circles in Iran as a virtual defeat'. According to Davutoglu, Ahmadinejad was ready to send a delegation to Vienna to work out the specifics of this proposal but was facing serious domestic problems.[58] To Ahmadinejad the core of the issue was psychological rather than a question of substance. While his government agreed to the proposal, he was cautious 'to manage the public perception'. To that end, Mottaki's 'Kish proposal' aimed at saving face, as explained by Davutoglu:

> Accordingly, the Iranians are proposing that the first 400 kilos be transferred to Kish Island – thereby keeping it on Iranian soil – and would receive right away an equivalent amount (30–50 kilos) of enriched fuel. The second stage would focus on the management of Iranian public opinion, after which Tehran would proceed with the Turkey option for the remaining 800 kilos, probably in two tranches. Davutoglu said Baradei agreed to consider this.[59]

The reports by the IAEA in November 2009 and February 2010 centred on the Fordow facility after Iran had given inspectors access to the facility between 24 and 29 October. EU-3 and US reading of the reports confirmed again that the facility made no sense in the context of Iran's civilian programme: 'it is too small to support a civilian power program but suitably sized for a weapons program'.[60] The IAEA Board's resolution against Iran on 27 November 2009 called on Iran to immediately suspend construction of the Fordow facility and provide clarification regarding the purpose of the plant.[61] During his debrief in

Vienna, the Austrian Ambassador to Iran described Iran's reaction to the resolution in the following terms:

> [...] Iran probably has whiplash from the international community's response to the Fordow Fuel Enrichment Plant (FFEP), which will complicate our efforts to press Iran into compliance with its obligations. Although IAEA Director General El Baradei said after the first inspection of the FFEP that it was nothing more than 'a hole in a mountain', the IAEA Board of Governors passed a resolution against Iran, citing the FFEP as one of its main points ... [he] argued that this probably leads Iran to believe that the international community is not serious about the issue, and that, rather, this is 'a game'.[62]

During a technical briefing prior to the resolution, on 18 November, the Director of Division of Operations B in the Department of Safeguards reiterated the Director General's report on Iran. While noting Iran's cooperation on access to all operating facilities and to IR-40, preliminary DIV on Darkhovin and notification of the Fordow facility, the briefing focused largely on Fordow, Iran's violation of Code 3.1 and outstanding questions on PMD.[63] In the meeting, Soltani questioned the expediency of his government's cooperation with the IAEA and threatened to reconsider Iran's cooperation given that the Secretariat, in his eyes, had mishandled sensitive information, which was voluntarily given from Iran and only led to more pressure from the P5+1 and the Agency and put facilities, including Qom and Darkhovin, under the threat of attack. He further argued that the Agency had

> no right to pass judgement on the rationale/purpose of Iran's nuclear programme, that Iran's intentions are not subject to review under its Comprehensive Safeguards Agreement, and thus, are not subject to investigation by the IAEA. The IAEA should not express that it is 'happy or sad' about information or what the inspectors have seen in Iran.[64]

Informed by this mindset, President Ahmadinejad called on the AEOI to build ten more enrichment sites in January 2010, and in February it started to increase the enrichment level of its LEU to 20 per cent (specifying a pilot plant of a single IR-1 centrifuge cascade) which purportedly was intended as fuel for the TRR.[65] The perceived failure of the Geneva talks, and particular the stated increase to 20 per cent enrichment levels, caused the US government and the EU to focus on the

> political message ... that this gambit is a pretext for 20 per cent enrichment in violation of UNSCRs as Iran has had plenty of opportunity to accept the TRR offer (despite Iran trying to pin the failure of the TRR deal on the other parties).[66]

During consultations between representatives from the US, EU-3, Spain, Japan, Australia, Canada and New Zealand at the US Mission to the IAEA in February

2010, it was agreed that this was a 'provocative move in defiance of UNSCRs and Board requirements'.[67] To the French Deputy Head of Mission at the IAEA, Iran lacked the technical capacity to provide fuel assemblies for the TRR from the 20 per cent enriched uranium and, therefore, had 'no peaceful use for the higher enrichment level'.[68] With French and German insistence, it was decided that 'Iran's announcement merits a political response that is UNSC action'. In the consciousness that they could 'easily get bogged down in safeguards legalities' at the IAEA Board, it was decided to work towards a resolution at the UN Security Council instead.[69] During German-hosted P5+1 informal pre-Board consultations on 26 February, the Russian Ambassador agreed with the EU-3–US assessment and viewed the Director General's February report on Iran as confirming that the Board resolution in November had not been groundless. A diplomatic cable on the meeting further noted that 'the Russian Ambassador also expressed concern that Iran has been successful in imposing "its interpretation" of events, including with respect to the Tehran Research Reactor (TRR) deal, on ill-informed G-77/NAM delegations'.[70] While the Chinese Ambassador attributed the more critical tone of the report to Amano's influence rather than Iran's actions, US diplomats appreciated Russia's shift towards adopting a tougher stance on Iran.[71] During the meeting the German Ambassador interpreted Iran's cooperation with the IAEA's request to upgrade the safeguards approach at Natanz before proceeding to 20 per cent enrichment 'as another example of Iran testing the red lines of its safeguard agreement'.[72]

Given Iran's decision to move towards 20 per cent and faced with Iran's failure to reciprocate positively to any of the provisions of the Geneva deal, coupled with the deteriorating human rights situation, the EU publicly urged the parties to remain in contact, but had already began redirecting diplomatic pressure on human rights at the UN Human Rights Council as well as initiating EU sanctions against Iran. The US government viewed the Universal Periodic Review at the UN Human Rights Council as an effective tool to increase pressure on Iran.[73]

The Turkish–Brazilian initiative

As the EU and the United States effectively started to abandon engagement and gradually shifted to a policy of outright containment, Turkish and Brazilian backchannels continued to work at bringing the Iranians back to the negotiating table. Eventually, in May 2010, a joint Brazilian–Turkish diplomatic initiative, which was patterned after the so-called 'Baradei proposal' for refuelling the Tehran Research Reactor, persuaded Iran to relinquish approximately half of its stockpile of LEU, send it to Turkey for storage and receive within a year the equivalent quantity of fuel for a small research reactor that produces medical isotopes. The so-called 'Tehran Declaration' agreed on the following key points:

- The three countries 'recall the right of all State Parties, including the Islamic Republic of Iran, to develop research, production and use of nuclear energy (as well as nuclear fuel cycle including enrichment activities).'

- Iran transfers 1,200 kg of LEU to be held in escrow in Turkey within one month.
- Pending their approval of the Tehran Declaration, the IAEA, France, Russia and the United States (the Vienna Group) would agree to provide 120 kg of 20 per cent enriched uranium fuel to Iran within one year.
- If the terms were not filled by the Vienna Group, Turkey would transfer the LEU back to Iran (which maintains legal possession of the material).[74]

While similar to the original Geneva deal, this fuel swap failed to stipulate whether or not Iran would get its low-enriched uranium back, nor did it offer to cease enrichment throughout the period. By this time, Iran had also significantly increased its overall stockpile; the LEU could be diverted into weapon-capable material.[75] Because of the timing of this deal, the Obama administration was quick to interpret Iranian motives as trying to find a way to impede what Secretary of State Clinton termed 'international unity' regarding the nuclear programme.[76] In fact, as early as November 2009, the US government secretly tried to dissuade the Turkish government from mediating as it was perceived that they were effectively enabling the Iranian government to play for time without delivering any tangible compromises.[77] What the US Ambassador to Turkey called the 'Turks' neo-posturing'[78] in the Middle East was seen as going contrary to US interests as it effectively represented an impediment to assembling and sustaining a multilateral consensus against Iran's nuclear programme and was, therefore, never seen as a viable mediating backchannel. Likewise the office of EU foreign policy chief Catherine Ashton also called the Tehran Declaration 'a move in the right direction' but dismissed it as it effectively failed 'to answer all of the concerns raised over Iran's nuclear programme'.[79] By and large, the EU-3 and the US regarded themselves to be in the driver's seat and were reluctant to allow Brazil and Turkey to take on a more assertive role towards Iran, even at the expense of a potential diplomatic breakthrough.[80]

Rather than seeking a return to the negotiation table, the EU and the Obama administration decided to dedicate diplomacy on increasing pressure at the IAEA Board and UN Security Council and impose unilateral sanctions in tandem with the European Union. Following the breakdown of talks and Iran's increase to 20 per cent, EU member states started to focus almost entirely on Iran's violation of its commitments to the UN and IAEA. Reaffirming a consensus by EU Foreign Ministers to continue with the dual-track approach and push for more EU sanctions, the Belgian MFA's Special Envoy for Disarmament and Non Proliferation, privately summarized his government's perceptions on Iran to US diplomats in Brussels:

> Iran's step is very provocative, and comes at a time when the world needs a signal of Iran's willingness to cooperate. The practical uselessness of the enrichment process, in view of Iran's lack of capacity to fabricate reactor elements, indicates Iran's real intent. The history of clandestine operations and intelligence reports about the real nature of Iran's nuclear program

make it impossible to trust Iran, he said. He said he never thought that the time President Obama gave Iran to negotiate in good faith would produce results.[81]

With the arrival of a new Director General, Yukiya Amano, in December 2009, and in the light of his first critical report on Iran in February 2010, the US Permanent Representative to the IAEA felt hopeful that Amano, unlike his predecessor, would be a valuable ally against Iran.[82] Concerns raised by the EU, the United States and the IAEA centred on Iran's decision to increase enrichment to 20 per cent; the failure to clarify possible military dimensions (which, contrary to the findings of the 2007 NIE, seemed to have continued beyond 2004); failure to substantiate the chronology and purpose of the Fordow plant; and failure to apply Code 3.1 Modified and the Additional Protocol.[83]

Istanbul talks 2011

Three talks organized by the EU in Istanbul concluded in January 2011 and failed to break the stalemate as the Iranians demanded an end of sanctions and enrichment continuation as preconditions for talks, while the P5 + 1 continued to employ punitive means as the only viable policy option to sway Iran to make meaningful concessions.[84] Iran was offered a revised version of the Geneva deal, which required Iran to send out 2.8 tonnes of low-enriched uranium – constituting of nearly 90 per cent of its LEU stockpile – and 40 kg of uranium which it had already enriched to 20 per cent. Considering the fact that President Ahmadinejad was unable to garner domestic support for the Geneva deal (which required Iran to ship out 75 per cent of LEU) and that Iran had not then enriched up to 20 per cent, this negotiation formula was impossible for the Iranian delegation to accept.[85] The Iranian delegation demanded that the international community first recognize its right to enrich nuclear fuel and that the UN lift all sanctions as a precondition for negotiations. Iran's maximalist position was made clear by President Ahmadinejad's statement on what his governments expected from the P5 + 1 in Istanbul:

> If they come and say: in the name of God, we stay out of the matter of the nuclear rights of the Iranian nation, we give up hostility and want to cooperate with Iran, we will say very well, that is it. However, it is very difficult for them along with their arrogant spirit, it is not that easy for them. They think they take privileges, they sit down and hold discussions. I think that this process will last for two or three months and that these talks can be repeated several times. However, as a result, they will have no other option, but to accept the law and recognize the nuclear rights of the Iranian nation and then they will go and deal with their immoral deeds, their resolutions and sanctions and expand their cooperation with Iran. I believe, God willing, this path will be continued. Iran's nuclear issue is finished. We do not have any problems. If they have problems, they should solve their problems and

cooperate [with Iran]. I predict that the negotiations will be a step forward. I hope these talks will be positive and constructive.[86]

French Foreign Minister Michèle Alliot-Marie called Iran's conditions 'completely unacceptable' because lifting sanctions and recognizing their right to enrichment was impossible given Iran's failure of cooperation with the IAEA.[87] In fact, the German government regarded Iranian demands for easing of sanctions as vindication that these measures were working. Reciprocating Iranian cooperation with sanctions relief was not seen as an acceptable formula.[88]

Following the failure in Geneva and the EU-3/US rejection of the Turkish–Brazilian initiative, all sides had again reverted to implemented positional bargaining, entering the talks in Istanbul with maximalist positions. During a conference in Sweden one month later, Iran's Deputy Foreign Minister extended an official invitation to Marc Grossman, the US Special Representative for Afghanistan and Pakistan, to visit Iran for talks on cooperation in Afghanistan. Washington purportedly dismissed the offer.[89] Overall, the failures of the Geneva deal, Tehran Declaration and Istanbul talks in 2011 created a deadlock which would continue throughout 2011 and 2012.

The Iranian government revived the 2009 fuel-swap deal just before the 2011 plenary session of the UN General Assembly. AEOI head Fereydoun Abbasi reiterated an offer to allow IAEA supervision for five years but made it contingent on the lifting of sanctions and without applying the provisions of Code 3.1.[90] Ahmadinejad's offer was also conditional on the US supply of fuel for the Tehran research reactor and reiterated that Iran would continue enriching LEU. But Ahmadinejad's fiercely anti-American UN address (which accused the US government of plotting the 9/11 attacks) catered more for domestic consumption than serving as an accommodating gesture with the United States.[91]

The IAEA report on Iran, released in November 2011, was interpreted by US Ambassador to the UN Susan Rice as further evidence 'that Iran has carried out activities ... relevant to the development of a nuclear explosive device'.[92] To Washington, the IAEA report confirmed its own intelligence (as most of it was a source for the report, Iranian policymakers dismissed the report as a fabrication).[93] Controversy over the IAEA report, the US government's accusation that the IRGC plotted to kill the Saudi Ambassador to the United States, reports about Iranian involvement in terrorist attacks against Israeli diplomats in Delhi, Bangkok and Tbilisi,[94] assassinations of Iranian scientists and other attempts of sabotage of Iran's nuclear infrastructure by foreign intelligence, and the British threat to impose sanctions on the Iranian Central Bank set the scene for the storming of the British embassy in Tehran at the end of November.[95] The breaking of official diplomatic relations with Britain, Iran's renewed threats to close the Strait of Hormuz and the European Council's unprecedented decision to impose an embargo on Iranian oil from June 2012 (until then, the EU had imported 20 per cent of Iran's oil) resembled Cold War strategies rather than constructive engagement.[96]

Plane spare parts for uranium: the Baghdad talks 2012

EU-3 governments seemed vindicated concerning the impact of their dual-track approach when Iran eventually responded to an October 2011 letter from Catherine Ashton and agreed to a further round of talks in Baghdad in 2012. Iran had agreed to the talks without previous preconditions and committed to actually talking about the nuclear programme.[97] The talks in Baghdad between the P5+1 and Iran in May and in Moscow in June 2012, however, failed to produce any agreement. The P5+1 delegation reiterated previous demands to cap uranium enrichment at the 5 per cent level and demanded that the HEU stockpile be shipped out to a third country. The Iranian government was again asked to halt all activities at the underground enrichment plant in Fordow. Previous offers were again presented to the Iranians, including the supply of fuel for the TRR, safety upgrades for the plant and much-needed spare parts for Iran's ageing and sanctioned civilian air fleet. As in Istanbul, sanctions relief was not part of the P5+1 offer but rather a vital measure to be implemented. US Secretary of State Hillary Clinton stated that 'as we lay the groundwork for these talks, we will keep up the pressure'. She said, 'All of our sanctions will remain in place and continue to move forward during this period.'[98]

The IAEA report on Iran in November 2012 found that Iran had stepped up its production of uranium enriched to 20 per cent purity, and had installed an additional 644 centrifuges at Fordow and 991 at Natanz. The report also noted that Iran had produced 232 kg of 20 per cent material, of which 96 kg were converted or slated for conversion to uranium oxide powder, purportedly for the production of fuel plates for its Tehran Research Reactor. Iran also continued to move forward with work on the Arak heavy water reactor. The report further noted that Iran was not fully cooperating with the Agency's investigation into the potential military dimension of its nuclear activities.[99] By the end of 2012, the sanctions regime against Iran had virtually cut it off from global markets and international capital flows.[100] Most importantly, July oil exports sank to 930,000 barrels per day, compared to 2011's average of 2.1 million barrels per day. Total oil production fell to 2.9 million barrels per day, which marked the lowest since 1989.[101] When the Rial lost over half of its value against the dollar in October, the US State Department spokesperson gave credit to the policy of isolation:

> Our understanding is that the Iranian currency has dropped to a historic low today against the dollar in informal currency trading, this despite some frantic efforts by the Iranian government last week to try to prop it up, rearrange the way it dealt with these issues.... From our perspective, this speaks to the unrelenting and increasingly successful international pressure that we are all bringing to bear on the Iranian economy. It is under incredible strain. Iran is increasingly cut off from the global financial system.[102]

Maintaining publicly that sanctions were not having an impact on the economy, the Supreme Leader and the government continued to reiterate that sanctions were not about brining Iran back to the negotiation table but for it to surrender to the dictates of US hegemony.[103] As long as both sides consider themselves to be in a position of strength and continue to follow positional negotiation strategies, the stalemate is unlikely to be broken. Only a graduated approach based on reciprocity and balanced concessions can create a joint value.

Conclusion

Why did negotiations fail and ultimately lead all parties to adopt confrontational foreign policies? Despite US overtures to engage with Iran through the P5+1 negotiation platform, the Obama administration's dual-track approach continued to rely on the same coercive tools of statecraft that have been employed against Iran for over three decades by the US government. Conscious of domestic opposition to 'appeasing Iran' and pressure by regional allies, diplomacy was a means to check Iranian nuclear capabilities rather than being used as a channel to work on mutual areas of concern and interest.[104] Giving engagement effectively only a window of less than six months (as demanded by the Israeli government), diplomacy evidently failed to break over thirty years of mutual hostility and mistrust.[105] Following the breakdown of the Geneva talks, the Turkish Foreign Minister urged the Americans to give 'more time for the engagement track to bear fruit'. While the Turks acknowledged 'the need to consider the coercive track in the absence of a reply from Iran', they 'warned against a public shift in emphasizing that track, saying carrots and sticks don't work with the Iranians. They'll just look for their own stick in response.'[106] Notwithstanding Turkish pleas to give engagement more time, the US government considered a return to more coercive diplomacy the only expedient alternative. During consultations with the Chinese Foreign Minister, Under Secretary of State Burns interpreted the events of 2009 as follows:

> [...] the US had sought creative solutions to build confidence with Iran, including on the Tehran Research Reactor proposal, but that Iran's failure to follow through on the understandings reached in Geneva, including on its commitment to meet with P5 + 1 countries for talks on its nuclear program, had been disappointing. At the end of 2009, [...] the US would have to ask what more we could do to push forward the diplomatic track, and how we should begin to make clear to Iran the consequences of Iran's failure to follow through on its commitments.[107]

The Iranian government, plagued by the country's greatest crisis of legitimacy, was caught between reciprocating the Geneva deal in 2009 and catering to domestic political pressure with equated compromise in the face of coercive Western diplomacy as defeat. Partisan politics aside, the two most important aspects of the initiative, which made it difficult for any Iranian administration to accept, were the risk of relinquishing its LEU stockpile and being dependent on unreliable foreign partners (particularly Russia) and the lack of linkage to a broader set of Iranian strategic interests. The offer of nuclear fuel assurance was essentially not attractive because, as one Japanese diplomat put it during a British-hosted nuclear fuel conference, '[it] only took the view of the supplier'. Given the lack of trust, it was argued by Japanese and South Korean representatives that 'no potential customer state should be asked to forgo rights under Article IV of the NPT'.[108] Shipping Iran's LEU abroad without any linkage to an incentive of strategic value to Iran was seen as virtual defeat by stakeholders across Iran's factions. The lack of linkage to a broader set of Iranian strategic interests but rather using diplomatic outreach with the primary objective of checking Iran's nuclear programme made it impossible for the Iranian government to agree to the initiative. After all, the entire nuclear programme was closely linked to Iran's prestige and role as regional power. For the Iranians, Western diplomacy was not 'business-like' and effectively failed to offer 'cash for cash'.[109] At a minimum, the lifting of sanctions (as demanded by Iranian delegations during talks) was seen as a meaningful incentive. What the Iranians really wanted, and what Iranian interlocutors had continuously reiterated in private meetings with EU and US officials, was the broadening of engagement to a broad range of strategic concerns. As a senior cleric told US officials in January 2009:

> XXXXXXXXXXXX said general regime distrust of the US, cumulative since the 1979 revolution, has created the general conviction in Tehran that the USG's nuclear end game is 'zero enrichment' of any type by Iran. XXXXXXXXXXXX argued USG needs to be clearer in its messaging; he said 'domestic opponents of reconciliation will exploit every opening in your offer ... (the USG in effect) must sell it to the Iranian people'. In this regard XXXXXXXXXXXX recommended USG use the concrete example of an existing US technology light water reactor, perhaps in Brazil, as a center-piece of its public approach. XXXXXXXXXXXX noted the regime's propaganda success in marrying the nuclear confrontation to themes of nationalism, and concluded that nuclear enrichment 'suspension' is a formula on which no one in Iran's political establishment, including Supreme Leader Khamenei, is able to back down, either now or in the future.[110]

Eventually, Iran's decision to repudiate the Geneva deal altogether and increase enrichment to 20 per cent constituted a game-changer for the EU and US government and subsequently redirected diplomacy towards containment, thus causing all parties involved to abandon constructive engagement altogether. Thus, all parties entered the talks in Istanbul and Baghdad and Moscow, in 2011 and 2012 respectively, with maximalist positions. The Obama administration found itself at the height of the presidential campaign and had moved the goal-posts that had been agreed to in Istanbul. Lacking vital political space before President Obama's re-election in November, the US saw little expediency in reciprocating Iranian concessions.[111] As key stakeholders of Iranian security and foreign policy indicated willingness for bilateral negotiations with the United States, President Obama may be able to manoeuvre and discreetly reach out to the Iranian government.

6 Not one iota of retreat

EU, US and Iranian nuclear diplomacy

Introduction

Engagement with Iran has to be seen within three distinct periods: the Critical Dialogue (1992–1997) and Comprehensive Dialogue (1998–2003) (under Presidents Rafsanjani and Khatami), the period from 2003 until 2005 in which engagement was championed by the EU-3 and represented an effort to avoid another US-led war in the Middle East,[1] and the period of coercive nuclear diplomacy (2005–2012), which has been the main focus of this book. It was only during the period of coercive diplomacy that the US government participated (both passively and actively) in the P5 + 1 framework.

The Critical Dialogue pursued by the European Union between 1992 and 1997 represented the CFSP in its infancy and failed to make any linkage between areas of concern and relations with the EU. Rather than demanding meaningful changes on the human rights situation, Iran's role in the Israel–Palestine conflict, support for terrorism or the *fatwa* against Salman Rushdie, good bilateral relations became an end in themselves rather than an incentive, as originally stated at the Edinburgh Summit in 1992. It was only Britain which, because of the death threat against a British citizen, actively pursued engagement and eventually managed to resolve the Rushdie affair in 1999.[2] Coming out of the Iran–Iraq war, President Rafsanjani was genuinely seeking détente with the West in an effort to develop Iran's political economy. The technocrat's tactic was to create an economic stake for the West in Iran, rather than to follow an agenda for political reform which could have positively impacted the situation of human rights in Iran.

With the election of President Mohammed Khatami, the EU dealt with a new Iranian government which genuinely sought détente abroad and political and economic reform at home. Appreciating these changes in Iranian politics, the EU launched the Comprehensive Dialogue (1998–2003). The framework of this dialogue contained political and economic incentives (TCA with the EU) for Iran in exchange for the realization of European demands for change. The human rights dialogue in particular was implemented through a multi-track approach involving international and Iranian NGOs and activists. This dialogue proved a valuable forum for activists and the reformist movement, which advocated democratization and protection of human rights from within an Islamic discourse.[3] Notwithstanding the reformist government's efforts at political change, the disclosure of undeclared nuclear sites and Natanz and Arak caused a priority shift towards security concerns.[4]

Confident about the efficacy of engagement and established channels of communication with Iran, from 2002 onwards Germany, France and Britain dedicated considerable diplomatic effort in finding a diplomatic solution, leading to the Tehran Declaration in 2003 and the Paris Agreement of 2004, in which Iran committed to signing of the Additional Protocol of the NPT.

The period of coercive diplomacy started in 2005, when the Iranian government resumed enrichment owing to the perceived failure on the part of the EU to deliver promised rewards. Numerous initiatives since then had failed to reach any mutually acceptable long-term agreement, causing the EU-3 and the US to bring Iran before the UN Security Council in 2006. With Iran defying six UN Security Council resolutions, engagement had become an exercise in coercive diplomacy by all sides involved. To the EU-3 and the United States, engagement had morphed into containment, backed by Cold War-like deterrence and economic warfare. As Iran has found itself under siege both economically and politically, nationalism and the experiences of past foreign domination coupled with its own perceived role in the region have informed its diplomatic manoeuvring.

EU diplomacy

As EU engagement with Iran started to focus solely on the nuclear programme in 2002, the neo-conservative machinery of the Bush administration advocated the use of military force as instrument of first choice for dealing with security-related foreign policy challenges. Whereas the European Council's final declaration in 2003 reaffirmed the EU's commitments 'to making effective multilateralism a central element of its external action, with at its heart a strong UN',[5] key stakeholders of the Bush doctrine politicized and misrepresented intelligence on WMDs in Iraq and lobbied support for the invasion among its European allies. Notwithstanding the deep divisions within the EU about the US-led invasion of Iraq in 2003, efforts by US officials to exchange intelligence with Europeans on Iran's alleged nuclear weapons programme in order to 'generate deeper understanding of the risks posed by WMD to ... European security'[6] failed to convince key decision-makers in EU member states about the urgency of the Iranian case. Having effectively employed established communication channels with Iran and extended incentives for compliance with European demands, by the end of 2003 European policymakers and officials felt confident that Europe's soft-power diplomacy would carry far-reaching political dividends. As a senior Italian FM official put it to US diplomats in December 2003: 'Iran has received a warning from the [international community] on its nuclear program and will therefore be more cautious in the future, he averred. Under the right conditions, Iran could be used as a tool to promote regional stability.'[7] Both the EU-brokered Tehran Declaration of 2003 and the Paris Agreement in 2004 were seen by Europeans as a first step towards concluding the nuclear file. However, to Europe engagement was a means to dismantle the enrichment programme altogether. Cessation of enrichment was indefinite rather than the confidence-building measure the Iranians perceived it to be. As the Non Proliferation Chief at the Dutch Foreign Ministry privately expressed it to US officials in November 2003:

> [He] raised the issue of the desired end-state, i.e., if the goal is elimination of the Iranian weapons program, now that the Iranians are providing some measure of cooperation it will be difficult to agree on which elements of the fuel cycle are peaceful and which support a weapons program. Concerning a technical finding of noncompliance ... [he] thought it might be possible but said it could be disadvantageous for follow-on actions because it would take the initiative away from the BoG. [He] said that given that an additional report was possible owing to the need to confirm details such as the source of HEU and LEU contamination the results of this might provide even more diplomatic leverage for a noncompliance finding.[8]

Iranian demands for talks about the Trade and Cooperation Agreement (TCA) with the EU to resume and other rewards in strategic areas to materialize following the Tehran Declaration of 2003 and Paris Agreement were dismissed. Solana's Iran/Iraq policy adviser, privately indicated that signing the Additional Protocol was not sufficient for the EU to deliver the rewards as 'signing the agreement is one thing; it's the implementation that counts and that will take a long time'. In December 2003, Foreign Ministers of the EU-3 decided not to resume talks for a TCA until, as the EU official put it, 'Iran delivers something major – such as agreeing to permanently end – vice suspend – its uranium enrichment program'. The official added that the 'EU has explicitly not set any specific benchmarks for resuming the TCA talks. To do so would only encourage Iranian bargaining to try to strike a better deal.'[9] EU Commission staffers and member states officials genuinely felt that the economic incentives offered would dissuade the Iranians from permanently giving up enrichment. With Iran's eventual resumption of enrichment activities in 2005, the IAEA passed a non-compliance resolution against Iran which brought the nuclear programme before the UN Security Council in 2006. Since then, EU-3 diplomacy has centred on applying economic and political pressure on Iran and denying any technical access. While still forwarding more incentives and prospects of strategic cooperation in a myriad of areas important to Iran, European diplomacy (in tandem with the US) offered fuel supply assurances to ensure reliable and constant access on the international market. The shift from the IAEA to the UN Security Council was seen as vital by the EU-3 as the case was no longer of a technical nature but rather needed the Council's enforcement capabilities. Iran's quest to master all stages of the nuclear cycle had to be checked and the authority of the IAEA reinforced. By doing so it was believed that it would ultimately discourage other countries from developing their own enrichment and reprocessing capabilities. More importantly, European credibility was at stake. Faced with Iranian defiance of EU-3 diplomatic initiatives, European leaders had few altern-ative but to bring Iran before the Security Council.[10] As conservative govern-ments in Britain, France and Germany were eager to recalibrate the transatlantic alliance and found themselves adopting a more hawkish stance towards Iran, the EU-3 channel was regarded by Paris, Berlin and London as the sole diplomatic authority in negotiations.[11] To that end, the British Permanent Representative to the IAEA saw the IAEA Secretary General as 'infuriatingly inconstant' and his mediating efforts as an attempt to assume 'the mantle of international saviour rather than international servant'.[12] As such, acting on behalf of the EU, Javier Solana presented offers for a negotiated solution in 2006 and 2008, both of which were backed by the US government and the UN Security Council. The Iranian government rejected both and presented counter-proposals which were unacceptable to the EU-3. As a result, the UN Security Council imposed sanc-tions against Iran.[13] The 2009 fuel-swap deal offered by the P5 + 1 failed owing to the political fallout which the Iranian presidential elections had caused. According to the Austrian Ambassador to Iran during a debrief of US diplomats in December 2009, President Ahmadinejad and Jalili came to Switzerland with the spirit of compromise and were willing to get to an agreement, particularly because the embattled president wanted to claim responsibility for a diplomatic breakthrough with the West. However, according to the Ambassador, Iran's sub-sequent failure to follow through the brokered deal was due to a decision by Khamenei that the West was not trustworthy and was also undermined by exten-sive post-election infighting.[14]

Subsequent major initiatives supported by the EU-3 in 2011 (Istanbul talks in January) and in 2012 (Baghdad talks in May and Moscow talks in June) were based on the fuel-swap deal and effectively compelled Iran to agree to P5 + 1 proposals. It was made clear by the EU High Representative for Foreign Affairs and Security Policy, Catherine Ashton, that no punitive measures would be lifted before meaningful confidence-building measures were implemented by Iran. Sanctions relief had become an incentive. Findings by the IAEA in October 2011 on activities concerning undisclosed activities related to the development of nuclear payload for a missile further confirmed to EU leaders that the sanctions constituted the only way forward.[15]

By the end of 2012, EU diplomacy towards Iran looked more like contain-ment than engagement. While in 1996, when President Bill Clinton passed the Iran Libya Sanctions Act, the EU Commission and member states dismissed isolation as a viable strategy and condemned the extraterritorial legislation,[16] the EU is now passing its own sanctions legislation in accordance with US law. This is the result of years of lobbying by the US State Department and US Treasury to align EU member states to US policy. After nearly a decade of, what the US Embassy to the EU referred to as 'strategic outreach' to member states and EU institutions about the efficacy of sanctions as part of a foreign policy toolkit, the Lisbon Treaty (entered into force 1 December 2009) consol-idated certain EU Commission and European Council Secretariat foreign policy responsibilities and strengthened the legality of EU-wide targeted sanctions.[17] Most EU member states were resisting the Bush administration's demand for sanctions until 2006, when Iran was referred to the UN Security Council. Reluctance was informed by economic interest as well as political concerns that punitive measures would upset the political balance and strengthen the hardliners rather than actually sway the Iranians in any meaningful way.[18] While the French and British governments were more inclined to use sanctions against Iran (described as 'hawkish' with regard to their policy on sanctions by the US Mission to the EU),[19] to other member states, most notably Italy and Germany, economic interests and investments in Iran had long prevailed over linking political demands to punitive measures. In particular, the German government's embrace of EU-wide sanctions against Iran represented a watershed moment in engagement. Germany has traditionally been Iran's most reliable partner, both politically and in economic terms, and has therefore been resisting imposing sanctions. By 2010, the German government privately admitted to US officials that 'Tehran would not respond to engagement' and agreed to pursue the 'pressure track'.[20] However, the Germans wanted sanctions to target the regime and to minimize the impact on the population at large. In a January 2010 meeting between German Foreign Ministry officials and House Foreign Affairs Committee Staff, German Foreign Ministry officials indicated that denying access to exploration and extraction technology could be an effective tactic, since it would more directly 'impact the government's pocketbook and ability to buy friends abroad', stressing that the EU and US 'need measures that do not generate a commiseration effect from other countries'.[21] Belgian officials too cautioned US diplomats against strong, adverse domestic reactions to sanctions, Belgian Special Envoy for Disarmament and Non Proliferation required sanctions to be as firmly based in international law as possible, 'because the Iranians, no less than the Russians, take a formalistic approach to such matters'. To the Belgian government appropriate linkages included 'banks, the Revolutionary Guards, insurance companies and the Iranian national bank'.[22] In October 2012, one senior European officials told the *Washington Post* that the goal of tightened sanctions was 'to bring the Iranian economy to its knees, and to make it in a way that really hurts the regime more than the population. That is very difficult.'[23] Making this distinction indeed proved difficult as sanctions started to have a significant impact on the Iranian economy. Far from targeting the ruling elite, sanctions have started to negatively impact the private sector and thus jeopardize the living standards of the country's middle class, with basic services deteriorating and inflation and unemployment rising.[24] The EU is using sanctions to compel Iran to halt all 20 per cent enrichment activities, to transfer all of its stock of 20 per cent enriched uranium to a third country under IAEA supervision and to shut down the Fordow facility.[25] As of 2012, EU sanctions against Iran included a wide array of financial and trade restrictions. The following list represents the most important restrictive measures adopted by the European Council:

- Export and import ban on arms.
- Export and import ban on goods and technology related to nuclear enrichment or nuclear weapon systems, including concerning nuclear materials and facilities, certain chemicals, electronics, sensors and lasers, navigation and avionics.
- Ban on investment by Iranian nationals and entities in uranium mining and production of nuclear material and technology within the EU.
- Ban on imports of crude oil and petroleum products from Iran. The prohibition concerns import, purchase and transport of such products as well as related finance and insurance.
- Ban on imports of petrochemical products from Iran.
- Export and import ban on dual-use goods and technology, for instance telecommunication systems and equipment; information security systems and equipment; nuclear technology and low-enriched uranium.
- Export ban on key equipment and technology for the oil and gas industries, that is for exploration and production of oil and natural gas, refining and liquefaction of natural gas, and for the petrochemical industry in Iran. Ban on financial and technical assistance for such transactions.
- Ban on investment in the Iranian oil and gas industries (exploration and production of oil and gas, refining and liquefaction of natural gas) and in the Iranian petrochemical industry. This means no credits, loans, new investment in and joint ventures with such companies in Iran.
- No new medium- or long-term commitments by EU member states for financial support for trade with Iran.
- Member states must not give new grants and concessional loans to the government of Iran. Prohibition to provide insurance and re-insurance to the Iranian government and Iranian entities (except health and travel insurance).
- Enhanced monitoring over the activities of EU financial institutions with Iranian banks and their branches, including the Iranian central bank.
- Restrictions on financial transfers to and from Iran. Banks must notify transfers above €10,000 to national authorities and request prior authorization for transactions above €40,000 (with humanitarian exemptions). Only permitted if it does not contribute to nuclear enrichment or weapons development.
- Prohibition for Iranian banks to open branches and create joint ventures in the EU. EU financial institutions may not open branches or bank accounts in Iran, either.
- Ban on the issuance of and trade in Iranian government or public bonds with the Iranian government, central bank and Iranian banks.
- Member states must require their nationals to exercise vigilance over business with entities incorporated in Iran, including those of the Iranian Revolutionary Guard Corps (IRGC) and of the Islamic Republic of Iran Shipping Lines (IRISL).
- National customs authorities must require prior information about all cargo to and from Iran. Such cargo can be inspected to ensure that trade restrictions are respected. Prohibited goods can be seized by member states.

- Cargo flights operated by Iranian carriers or coming from Iran may not have access to EU airports (except mixed passenger and cargo flights). No maintenance services to Iranian cargo aircraft or servicing to Iranian vessels may be provided if there are suspicions that it carries prohibited goods.
- Visa bans on persons designated by the UN or associated with or providing support for Iran's proliferation-sensitive nuclear activities or for the development of nuclear weapon delivery systems, for instance by acquiring prohibited goods and technology or by assisting listed persons or entities in violating UN and EU provisions; and other members of the IRGC.
- Asset freeze on entities associated with Iran's proliferation-sensitive nuclear activities or the development of nuclear weapon delivery systems, for instance by acquiring prohibited goods and technology or by assisting listed persons or entities in violating UN and EU provisions; and senior members and entities of IRGC and the IRISL.[26]

The EU established a multilateral negotiation framework, which allowed Iranian, EU and US diplomats to discuss areas of mutual concern. However, unable to break the stalemate through negotiations and risking the EU-3's credibility at the world stage, punitive measures adopted by the Council and implemented by all member states are not only aiming at checking Iranian weapon, nuclear and dual-use capabilities but are effectively attempting to coerce the Iranian government into making concessions by means of economic warfare. Engagement pursued by the EU has become containment – a policy which is less diplomatic strategy and more an end goal itself.[27]

US diplomacy

US–Iran relations between 2000 and 2008 were subject to the Bush administration's three main national security interests in the Middle East: defeating terrorism, promoting democracy and stopping the development of weapons of mass destruction.[28] As the US found itself in a post-9/11 unipolar moment of military strength and had troops deployed in Iraq, the Persian Gulf, Central Asia and Afghanistan, diplomacy towards Iran mainly consisted of threats.[29] Casting Iran as part of the 'axis of evil' set the foundation for US diplomacy towards Iran. Still informed by a 'regime change' mindset, President Bush kept the 'military option' on the table and resisted Khatami's 2003 diplomatic overtures.[30] To the Bush administration, the dismantling of Libya's WMD arsenal in 2004, following the US invasion of Iraq, proved that Iran would only respond to pressure.[31]

While Bush's policy towards Iran was publicly more conciliatory during his second term, it did not represent a change from previous administrations. Notwithstanding bilateral encounters between US and Iranian delegations on Iraqi and Afghan security, US participation in multilateral negotiations on the nuclear programme were seen as reward rather than means to achieve an agreement. Key neo-conservative stakeholders upheld the narrative that Iran had an active clandestine nuclear weapons programme and that Iran had taken advantage of engagement to advance the programme. To that end, the US State Department dedicated substantial efforts to move Iran before the UN Security Council.[32] Subsequent UNSC Resolutions 1737, 1747 and 1803 as well as US Government Executive Orders 13224 and 13382 effectively identified the international financial sector as a conduit for Iran's proliferation activities and provided the legal context in denying Iran's commercial and financial institutions from operating globally.[33] By the end of the Bush administration, US containment of Iran had finally been sanctioned by the UN Security Council and was implemented by its European allies.

The Obama administration's decision to directly engage Iran and participate in the P5+1 talks did not represent a sea-change in US policy towards Iran. While Obama's diplomacy emerged within a new liberal framework of commitment to multilateralism and the abolition of nuclear weapons, engagement was implemented through a 'dual-track approach' employing both pressure and diplomacy. Following the short window of engagement in 2009, it was decided that Iran was refusing to engage seriously on the TRR proposal and that the pressure track was necessary, in the words of the Under Secretary of State to his Russian counterpart to 'reinforce the credibility of the P5+1 process and sending a broader message to nuclear aspirant states'.[34] Subsequently, prioritizing his domestic agenda, the Obama administration focused more on the pressure track, which was underwritten by 'smart power'. Overall, coercive diplomacy towards Iran seemed expedient given the domestic arena and, once again, made good politics but constituted poorly designed foreign policy. Essentially, US diplomacy towards Iran remained informed by the realist objective to maintain US hegemony in the region. A nuclear-armed Iran was seen as jeopardizing the regional balance of power, which has been created and maintained by US power since the end of the Second World War.

Coercive diplomacy to maintain US dominance in the Middle East

During a 2012 speech on foreign policy, President Obama declared:

> my policy is not containment; my policy is to prevent them from getting a nuclear weapon – because if they get a nuclear weapon that could trigger an arms race in the region, it would undermine our non-proliferation goals, it could potentially fall into the hands of terrorists.[35]

In September 2012, the US Senate joined the President and passed a resolution 'reject[ing] any United States policy that would rely on efforts to contain a nuclear weapons-capable Iran', thereby lowering the threshold of a military pre-emptive attack – albeit in ambiguous terms.[36] Notwithstanding lessons from the Cold War about the dynamics of mutually assured destruction, the US government embraced the premise (largely championed by Israel) that the logic of nuclear deterrence only applied to rational actors and Iran's radicals would act in unpredictable ways even at the risk of national annihilation. As Israel and other pro-Israel stakeholders in Washington upheld this narrative, both the Bush and Obama administrations employed Cold War concepts of conventional extended deterrence, sabotage and economic warfare.

In strategic terms, US diplomacy towards Iran was based on power balancing and has been aiming at preventing Iran from acquiring nuclear weapons capability by means of checking its conventional procurement efforts and forestalling an Axis-like alliance between Iran and Persian Gulf states or outside nuclear states. Resisting Iranian calls for an indigenous collective security system in the region, Persian Gulf security remained underwritten by US power balancing.[37] Having effectively declared US leadership in efforts to abolish nuclear weapons, President Obama adopted an abolitionist policy in which the bomb no longer featured as the core foundation of US national security and world order. However, beneath this declaration US security policy remained anchored in deterrence, underwritten by its superiority in conventional military power. As President Obama himself declared: 'Make no mistake: As long as these weapons exist, the United States will maintain a safe, secure and effective arsenal to deter any adversary, and guarantee that defense to our allies.'[38] Declaring abolition of nuclear weapons its policy in the distant future while not explicitly committing US disarmament to any verifiable timeframe is security policy anchored in realism:

> an American call for eventual abolition in the distant future is strategically cost-free and serves American national interests. There are so many excess nuclear warheads that Washington can make cuts ostensibly for the purpose of incremental disarmament while maintaining the world's most effective nuclear arsenal for many years.[39]

The three main principles behind the US government's nuclear and disarmament policy centred on (1) strengthening the non-proliferation regime, including ratification of the CTBT treaty; (2) reducing the US nuclear arsenal (by pledging new START negotiations with Russia); and (3) maintaining a nuclear deterrence. To that end, plans for missile defence systems in Europe to protect the southern flank of Europe, given the fast pace of Iran's missile development, were part of US security architecture.[40]

In the region, US extended deterrence of the Gulf Cooperation States (GCC) is solely aimed at checking Iranian ambitions. The GCC states, most notably the UEA and Saudi Arabia, consider Iran its primary external threat, one that is existential in nature, and have viewed diplomatic efforts to end the nuclear programme with scepticism. To many military leaders in the Gulf, the logic of war with Iran has dominated strategic thinking and planning, causing a large-scale effort to build up respective forces of GCC members.[41] Close defence relationships among the GCC, backed by US military power and political support, has allowed Gulf states to suppress the political revolt in Bahrain in 2011 in the wake of the Arab Spring. When the GCC sent Saudi forces to Bahrain in 2011 in order to protect the government from a *Shi'a* revolt, which was partly backed by

Iran, the GCC effectively deterred Iran from further intervening in Bahrain.[42] In a private meeting between US officials and the UAE Chief of Staff during a plenary session of the Gulf Security Dialogue in 2009, the Assistant Secretary of Defence for International Security Affairs reiterated the close defence coordination between both states:

> Diplomacy is only one tool. The USG wants to help provide the UAE with defensive capabilities and our troop presence here should help act as a deterrent to Iran. We don't want to signal that we will give up on diplomacy, yet in parallel to that effort we intend to keep the pressure on Iran. We appreciate the candor of our defense engagement with the UAE. We are dealing with an unpredictable foe and need to take all precautions ... that our message to Iran is that threats against our allies will not go unanswered. We need to be prepared in case deterrence does not work, with the realization that with or without nuclear weapons Iran seeks to be a dominant power in the region.[43]

International relations of the Middle East since the Arab Spring have been dominated by indigenous movements for democratization and political reform, on one side, and the rivalry of two blocs of players. On the one side, outsiders – the US, Russia and China – seek to enhance their influence and restrain threats while major regional players – Saudi Arabia, Iran, Egypt, Turkey – seek regional leadership.[44] Within this environment of power-balancing, US diplomacy towards Iran has been largely guided by *realpolitik* rather than approached with a depoliticized conflict resolution mindset. To that end, the conflicts in Yemen, Syria and the Palestinian Territories have been defined by the US and Israel as the latest manifestation of Iranian expansionism.[45]

Even though a power-balancing situation makes for a difficult if not impossible win–win negotiation framework, three elements of US foreign policy towards Iran stand out as major diplomatic pitfalls: (1) a foreign policy in which sanctions have ceased to be part of a diplomatic toolkit but rather become an end in themselves; (2) double standards, using the military threat emanating from America's closest ally, Israel, as deterrent and providing a nuclear armed state, India, with nuclear fuel while denying the technology to Iran; (3) supporting and actively participating in a policy of sabotage and cyber warfare against Iran's nuclear and security infrastructure.

The US sanctions regime against Iran has been in place since President Carter issued Executive Order 12170 following the storm on the US Embassy in Tehran. Successive administrations have added a myriad of punitive measures targeting Iran's commercial, financial and energy sector and inevitably negatively affecting the lives of ordinary Iranians. Key legislation has remained the Iran Libya Sanctions Act (1996) which became the Iran Sanctions Act (ISA) in 2010, and Clinton's Executive Order 12957, prohibiting any trade with Iran. President Bush's Executive Order 13382 froze the assets of individuals linked to the nuclear programme.[46] Under the Obama administration, the Comprehensive Iran Sanctions, Accountability, and Divestment Act (CISADA) strengthened existing sanctions against Iran's energy sector and penalized foreign financial institutions who engage in specified transactions with Iran by limiting their access to the US financial system, effectively seeking to reduce foreign investment in Iran. ISA and CISADA were further expanded with the passage of the Iran Threat Reduction and Syria Human Rights Act which was signed into law by President Obama on 10 August 2012.[47] Sanctions had a significant impact on Iran's economy, most notably causing Iran's oil exports to drop, severing its most important commercial ties with Western states and blocking access to foreign investment and hard currency. During and since the breakdown of talks in May 2012, the US government and EU-3 have been demanding that Iran should commit to three irreversible steps: (1) stop enriching uranium to the twenty per cent level; (2) ship out Iran's existing stockpile of enriched uranium; (3) shut down the underground nuclear enrichment facility in Fordow.[48] Iran's nine-step proposal in October 2012, which called for the US and EU to reciprocate Iran's graduated cessation of enrichment by dismantling sanctions alongside each step, was dismissed by the Obama administration on the grounds that Iran could not be trusted. As one senior Obama administration official put it: 'the way they have structured it, you can move the fuel around, and it stays inside the country. ... They could restart the program in a nanosecond. They don't have to answer any questions from the inspectors.'[49] Since 2010, the Obama administration has effectively been compelling Iran to agree to a formula rather than offering incentives or agreeing to an easing of sanctions in exchange for concessions. By refusing to ease sanctions on Iran in any meaningful way, the P5+1 offered no reciprocity in return for Iranian compliance. Literature on diplomacy and sanctions confirms that for coercive diplomacy to succeed there must be 'tit for tat' – clear benefits for cooperation – and that those benefits are realized when the coerced state cooperates.[50] On the breakdown of the Baghdad talks in May 2012, one Iranian diplomat said that the steps 'were meant to be reciprocal, simultaneous, and ... balanced in their value to each side ... instead, Iran was told there would be "consideration" of easing sanctions "later", after Iran made concessions'. Echoing this sentiment, the former adviser to Iranian nuclear negotiations teams from 2004 to 2006, Kaveh Afrasiabi, emphasized that 'Iran cannot be expected to make big concessions for the sake of a pittance', and that one could 'achieve concrete progress only if there is symmetry of compromise on both sides'.[51]

Second, the US maintains amicable relations with Israel and India, two nuclear weapons states which are still in a state of war with their respective neighbours, and, in the case of Israel, in violation of several UN Security Council resolutions. During an IAEA Board session in November 2009, Iran's Permanent Representative criticized perceived US double standards, noting that: 'if Iran were not in the NPT, it would benefit from complete freedom from inspection and control, punitive measures [*sic*] and, in fact, would be rewarded if it acquired and developed nuclear weapons'.[52] Making concerted diplomatic advances to help India improve its nuclear non-proliferation credentials a top priority, the Bush administration signed the US–Indian Peaceful Atomic Energy Cooperation Act on 18 December 2006. Under this agreement, India pledged to separate its civil and military nuclear facilities and to place its civil nuclear facilities under IAEA safeguards. In exchange, the US agreed to work towards full civil nuclear cooperation with India.[53] With the official conclusion of the nuclear deal in 2008, India had effectively won international acceptance of its nuclear weapons programme, making it the only state with nuclear weapons which is not a member of the NPT to engage in nuclear commerce on the global market.[54] Showing its commitment to a transformed US–Indian relationship, the Indian government voted for the 'non-compliance' resolution against Iran at the IAEA Board in September 2005 and then voted to refer Iran to the UN Security Council in February 2006.[55] During a meeting between a US Ambassador and a German State Secretary at the United Nations in March 2006, the diplomatic backlash of the agreement was discussed:

> The German official asked if the recently announced US–India civilian nuclear energy deal would have an impact on our collective ability to deal with the Iranian threat. The Ambassador [...] said that there would not be any 'real world spillover'. The two governments bore no comparison to one another – India was seeking to move towards the IAEA, while Iran is making a deliberate, strategic choice to move away from the non-proliferation regime, having signed and then broken its NPT commitments. Iran's actions posed a real threat of proliferation, in the region and beyond.[56]

Washington's relationship with Israel is far more complex and has constituted a major strategic variable within the context of multilateral diplomacy towards Iran. In 1996, Prime Minister Benjamin Netanyahu addressed the US Congress, warning that a nuclear armed Iran would have 'catastrophic consequences, not only for my country, and not only for the Middle East, but for all mankind'. In 2012, he challenged President Obama and said 'Those in the international community who refuse to put red lines before Iran don't have a moral right to place a red light before Israel.' During his speech before the UN General Assembly he presented a cartoon depicting a bomb and declared that Iran must not be allowed to enrich to 20 per cent.[57] For over a decade, Israel has not only upheld the narrative of Iran's clandestine nuclear weapons programme but has also maintained an aggressive military posture and has escalated talk of a preventive military strike of Iran's nuclear and key military sites, similar to the Israeli Air Force's operations in Iraq in 1981 and Syria in 2007.[58] Far from censuring its strongest ally in the region and exerting pressure on Israel to refrain from engaging in military threats, successive US governments have effectively been coerced into adopting an unprecedented sanctions regime against the very country which has continuously been threatened with a military attack.[59] What was much more detrimental to multilateral nuclear diplomacy was the fact that the military threat from Israel was used as part of a US foreign policy toolkit in its posture towards

Iran and was also used to convince Russia and China to stand behind the EU-3 – the US dual-track approach.[60]

As Iran continues to increase its HEU stockpile, the Israeli government maintains that important elements of the nuclear programme will soon be beyond conventional military capabilities, and therefore there must be action before, in the words of Israel Minister of Defence Ehud Barak, Iran reaches the 'zone of immunity'.[61] Questioning the expediency of diplomacy towards Iran, in particular Obama's decision to engage, Israeli Prime Ministers have continuously pushed the US government to implement 'crippling sanctions' and warned that 'time was running out'.[62] During a private meeting between Senator John McCain and Benjamin Netanyahu in 2010, the Prime Minister argued that 'only sanctions felt by the general public would make a difference since the public will blame the regime. The Iranian regime is a detested tyranny and sanctions can help make it even more detested.'[63] Commending Congress on the passing of the Iran Threat Reduction and Syria Human Rights Act of 2012 (H.R. 1905) in August 2012, the American Israel Public Affairs Committee, which wrote most of the sanctions against Iran and lobbied for them, credited itself that 'the totality of US sanctions on Iran will now represent the strongest set of sanctions to isolate any country in the world during peacetime'.[64] Within the context of problem-solving negotiations, Israel has acted as spoiler and has continuously worked towards drawing the US, Israel and Iran towards military confrontation. As a result, it has succeeded in stalling its own peace process with the Palestinians.[65]

Lastly, the US is supporting and actively engaging in covert activities, involving sabotage, cyber warfare and targeted assassinations of Iranian nuclear scientists and officials. The *New Yorker* reports that, beneath the veneer of seeking a diplomatic solution, the Joint Special Operations Command by orders of President Bush conducted training for members of the Mujahideen-e-Khalq (MEK), an armed dissident Iranian opposition then designated a foreign terrorist organization by the US State Department. According to a retired US general, MEK members received 'standard training ... in commo, crypto [cryptography], small-unit tactics, and weaponry [for] six months'.[66] The killing of Mostafa Ahmadi-Roshan, a Tehran-based chemist, by a motor-cycle-borne assassin in January 2012 marked the fifth Iranian scientist to be assassinated.[67] In May 2012, Iranian authorities hanged Majid Jamali Fashi, who had been sentenced for the 2010 killing of Tehran University physics professor Masoud Ali Mohammadi. Fashi confessed that he had been recruited and trained by Mossad to carry out the murder. In August, Iranian state TV broadcast the confessions of more than a dozen suspects in connection with the assassination campaign, stating that they had been trained in Israel to 'place magnetic bombs on cars – the method used in the killing of the scientists'.[68] The Iranian intelligence ministry's charge that the CIA, Mossad and Britain's MI6 are behind the assassination campaign seemed vindicated to many in Iran when US Secretary of State Hillary Clinton announced two months later that the US government had removed the MEK from its terrorist list. Interpreting the move as a hostile act, the Iranian Foreign

Ministry said that 'Washington [had] entered a new phase of hostility towards Iran by removing the terrorist Mojahedin-e Khalq Organization (MKO) from the list of terrorist groups'.[69]

The most large-scale act of sabotage against Iran's nuclear programme came in the form of a cyber attack orchestrated by US and Israeli intelligence. Operation 'Olympic Games' had started under Bush in 2006 and was accelerated under President Obama upon his taking office, with the aim of destroying critical infrastructure of Iran's nuclear programme. The strategic objective was twofold: to retard Iran's progress in enriching and to moot the need for a kinetic attack on Iran's nuclear installations by Israeli forces.[70] Former CIA Director Michael Hayden called the Stuxnet worm

> the first attack of a major nature in which a cyber attack was used to effect physical destruction. And no matter what you think of the effects – and I think destroying a cascade of Iranian centrifuges is an unalloyed good – you can't help but describe it as an attack on critical infrastructure.[71]

While publicly downplaying the extent of damage caused by Stuxnet, President Ahmadinejad admitted that the attack had set back the programme. A 23 per cent decline in the number of operating centrifuges during the period from mid-2009 to mid-2010 may have been a result of Stuxnet.[72] Experts believe that the attack set back Iran's nuclear programme by at least two years, and in January 2011 Meir Dagan (then serving Israeli intelligence chief) declared that Iran would not reach nuclear capability until 2015 owing to the measures deployed against them.[73]

Overall, after trying engagement with Iran for a short period in 2009, which did not allow either party to address mutual areas of concern created by over three decades of hostility, the Obama administration continued with a policy of coercive diplomacy towards Iran. By essentially implementing a foreign policy based on political isolation and deterrence, sanctions and sabotage, the US government has been compelling rather than engaging Iran.

In this environment, US coercive diplomacy is meant to raise Iran's cost of prolonging the nuclear programme. Rather than providing meaningful incentives, backed by a political willingness to address underlying roots of mutual hostility and commit itself to a cycle of reciprocity, US diplomacy has become a 'policy of compellence'.[74]

Iranian diplomacy

Ever since the death of Iran's revolutionary leader Ruhollah Khomeini in 1989, the country's foreign policy has been torn between the myriad of political actors and rival factions in the country. These underlying ideological and partisan divides have resulted in competing visions and policies of maintaining internal and external security on one side and diplomatic initiatives aimed at restoring Iran's legitimate place within the international community on the other. The nuclear negotiations have to be viewed within this contested domestic environment, particular following the 2009 presidential elections. For over two decades, Iranian foreign policy has failed to craft and implement sustainable strategies which are strategically expedient for all domestic actors while at the same time acceptable to outside powers. Conscious of the way history has, time and again, treated Iran not as an equal but as a rather strategic asset to outside powers, Iran's main foreign policy determinant has been a 'quest for independence and freedom'.[75] In terms of security, this has largely translated into Iran relying on conventional military deterrence and an asymmetrical threat posture across the region as a means of securing territorial integrity and security. The leadership has, however, always maintained throughout negotiations that Iran would never seek to weaponize its nuclear programme. This claim has been anchored by three core arguments, which were stipulated by the Iranian Foreign Ministry during a conference on security in May 2008.

First, Ayatollah Khomeini issued a *fatwa* against the production, stockpiling and use of nuclear weapons. Iranian negotiators have continuously referred to this verdict and the Supreme Leader Ali Khamenei himself has repeatedly endorsed the ruling.[76] Addressing a crowd of Iranian nuclear scientists, in February 2012, he stated:

> Nuclear weapons are not at all beneficial to us. Moreover, from an ideological *fiqhi* [Islamic jurisprudential] perspective, we consider developing nuclear weapons as unlawful. We consider using such weapons as big sin. We also believe that keeping such weapons is futile and dangerous, and we will never go after them.[77]

Second, Iranian government officials claim that a nuclear bomb cannot guarantee Iran's security. On the contrary, it would constitute a new source of national, regional and international insecurity.

Third, with reference to the IAEA's inspection regime, which Iran claims has investigated its nuclear programme more rigorously than it has investigated any other member state's nuclear programme, Iranian officials maintain that 'the IAEA confirmed that Iran is not diverting nuclear material', and found only that it cannot verify the absence of undeclared nuclear material in Iran, which, according to the Iranian Foreign Ministry 'puts Iran in the same category in the IAEA's eyes as forty-five other member states, including Germany'.[78]

With reference to the NPT and the fact that Argentina, Brazil, Germany, Japan and the Netherlands, as well as the five nuclear weapons parties (China, France, Russia, Britain and the US), have their own enrichment programmes, Iran has maintained that it is not breaching NPT rules by engaging in enrichment, because this is sanctioned under the regime as well as carried out under IAEA supervision.[79] It is important to emphasize that when Iran was brought before the UN Security Council in 2006, it was because the Board had determined that Iran had violated its safeguards agreement. The question whether Iran had in fact violated the NPT remains unclear as neither does the treaty itself provide for a mechanism for determining whether a state party has violated its obligations, nor can the UN Security Council adjudicate a state's treaty violation.[80] Notwithstanding lack of IAEA mechanisms to determine such violations, the US State Department argued in a 2005 report that Iran had violated Article II of the NPT:

> The breadth of Iran's nuclear development efforts, the secrecy and deceptions with which they have been conducted for nearly twenty years, its redundant and surreptitious procurement channels, Iran's persistent failure to comply with its obligations to report to the IAEA and to apply safeguards to such activities, and the lack of a reasonable economic justification for this program leads us to conclude that Iran is pursuing an effort to manufacture nuclear weapons, and has sought and received assistance in this effort in violation of Article II of the NPT.[81]

By November 2012, Iran has been in violation of six UN Security Council resolutions (Resolutions 1696 (2006); 1737 (2006); 1747 (2007), 1803 (2008) 1835 (2008) and 1929 (2010)), which had been imposed in response to the alleged proliferation risks the programme represented and Iran's failure to meet the requirements of the IAEA following its 2005 resolution of non-compliance. The IAEA's key concerns are:

- Failure to suspend its enrichment- and heavy water-related programmes, as required by the UNSC and IAEA Board. Instead, Iran has increased its stockpile of low-enriched uranium hexafluoride (UF6) product at Natanz (FEP). In November 2012, Iran's total 3.5 per cent low-enriched uranium (LEU) production at the FEP was 7,611 kg. According to the ISIS, this total amount of 3.5 per cent UF6, if further enriched to weapon grade, is enough to make, in theory, six or seven nuclear weapons. Iran has also designated two, tandem cascades at the smaller, above-ground Pilot Fuel Enrichment Plant for the production of LEU enriched to nearly 20 per cent uranium-235, which it claims is for the Tehran Research Reactor (TRR).[82]
- Iran has not suspended work on all heavy water-related projects, including the construction of the heavy water moderated research reactor at Arak. Although it is obliged to suspend all enrichment-related activities and heavy water-related projects, Iran is conducting a number of activities at UCF, the Fuel Manufacturing Plant (FMP) and the Fuel Plate Fabrication Plant (FPFP) at Isfahan.[83]
- The underground facility in Fordow is complete. According to the ISIS report, all 2,784 IR-1 centrifuges (sixteen cascades of 174 each) have been installed (which is the maximum number it was designed to hold), though only four cascades are operating and another four are fully equipped, vacuum-tested and ready to begin operating.[84]
- Iran is not implementing the provisions of the modified Code 3.1 of the Subsidiary Arrangements General Part to Iran's Safeguards Agreement, which

provides for the submission to the IAEA of design information for new facilities as soon as the decision to construct, or to authorize construction of a new facility has been taken. To that end, Iran has also refused to answer the IAEA's questions or provide the requested level of access, which includes providing access to documents and individuals associated with the decision of new facilities (e.g. Fordow FFEP).[85]

• Iran's has failed to address the IAEA's questions concerning possible military dimensions to the nuclear programme. IAEA reports since 2010 have noted that there are indications that Iranian nuclear weaponization work may have continued beyond 2004 and suggest that weapon-related programmes projects are being implemented in Iran. To that end, Iran has continued to refuse IAEA inspectors permission to enter the Parchin military site, where the IAEA has evidence from member states 'indicat[ing] that Iran constructed a large explosives containment vessel in which to conduct hydrodynamic experiments' relevant to nuclear weapons development.[86]

In July 2012, President Ahmadinejad told an audience in Iran that the government would not 'retreat even one iota from their rights, principles and values against the declining materialistic powers. The enemy deals a blow to the Iranian nations step by step; but, in return, it receives a stronger, heavier blow.'[87] Since Iran resumed enriching in 2005, and the subsequent referral to the UN Security Council, Tehran's security policy has been informed by a mindset that conciliation and concession are a sign of weakness, essentially resembling German diplomacy in the late nineteenth and early twentieth centuries, which historian Harold Nicholson likened to an ideology of *Einkreisung* – 'encirclement'.[88] Acting within the framework of the Supreme Leader's mandate, Iran's nuclear negotiators Hassan Rowhani (2003–2005), Ali Larijani (2005–2007) and Saeed Jalili (2007–to date)[89] used negotiations to present maximalist positions and project power. In his memoirs, Rowhani himself acknowledges that Iran's technological progress was meant to create realities on the ground in order to improve Iran's bargaining positions: 'We can say that 20 per cent enrichment has in some ways created increased deterrence', adding that, 'given the heavy cost paid', the nuclear programme 'should have progressed more'.[90] To that end, Iran has been using negotiations to buy time. Rather than committing to implementing initial steps put forward in EU-3 and later P5 + 1 proposals, the Iranian government offered new initiatives for talks, pushing deadlines and effectively increasing its stockpile.

To many in Iran, Western diplomacy has began to mirror British diplomacy during the Mossadeq era (1951–1953) when the British government, following nationalization of Iran's oil industry by Prime Minister Mossadeq, sought to destabilize the government through an oil embargo.[91] In the end, 'Operation Ajax', a covert operation coordinated by CIA and MI6, succeeded, as it facilitated royalist forces to overthrow Mossadeq's government in favour of the Shah.[92] The coup and extensive US support would help the Shah to transform the country into an authoritarian monarchy, which in the long run led to the rise of

Khomeini and resulted in the Islamic Revolution of 1979. By the end of 2012, the unprecedented sanctions regime coupled with other tools of coercive state-craft has virtually cut Iran off from the global economy and increased pressure on the government from a variety of factions. But so far it has not translated into the change of policy demanded by the P5 + 1. Rather than changing course and testing initiatives on the table, Iran has made structural and tactical moves designed to manage a 'siege economy' at home and demonstrate its assertive military defence posture externally.[93] Far from addressing the core issues, the leadership remains distrustful of Western commitments and continues to promote Iranian interests around the Middle East through the 'axis of resistance'.[94] As Iran is seeking a regional leadership position following the Arab Spring in 2011 and continues to underwrite its allies in the Levant, including the embattled Syrian regime, unchecked mastery of the nuclear fuel cycle is seen by many states in and outside the Middle East as further emboldening a revisionist and unpredictable regime.

Conclusion

The narrative of nuclear negotiations between Iran and the West seems to confirm the basic premise of realism. Parties involved continue to perceive each other as adversaries rather than partners seeking a mutually acceptable agreement. Diplomatic tools employed by the EU-3, the US government and Iran have been those of coercive persuasion rather than communication and concession. Multilateral negotiations have never left the realm of Westphalian-style diplomacy aiming at checking each other's capabilities and limiting respective choices. The EU-3 and US have continued to insist on suspending enrichment indefinitely and have not trusted the IAEA to be the sole authority on Iranian compliance; in fact, during the time of El Baradei, they did not trust the Director General to represent a neutral intermediary. Overall, following Iran's resumption of enrichment in 2005, the EU-3 followed the US example and started to implement a threatening non-constructive negotiation style. From then, the process was not so much about joint problem-sharing and problem-solving by seeking a solution which would have accommodated everyone adequately, but rather about maintaining positions and compelling Iran to accept their demands. Likewise, from 2005 onwards, Iran has never tested EU-3 sponsored offers and commitments in any meaningful way and started to use progress in its nuclear programme as diplomatic capital. Driven by the ambition to be recognized as an equal power and informed by a strong sense of nationalism and independence, it has continued to procure its conventional military capabilities and to underwrite its proxies in the region.

At the core of the stalemate lies a fundamental lack of trust and reciprocity

Trust could never be established because all parties involved (in particular Iran and the US) never accepted that their own security does not require the insecurity of the other state. Caught in this Cold War-like mindset, both adopted policies that reinforced this security dilemma.[1] Failing to reflect on the actual causes of conflict, none of the parties sought to eliminate undermining factors causing this lack of trust (e.g. selective and distorted perceptions, negative attitudes and images, poor communication and a competitive win–lose orientation, which attempted to force or extract capitulation from the adversary).[2] This failure is best summed up by a British FCO Minister's statement during his testimony before the House of Lords, when he described Iran's lack of trust vis-à-vis Europe and the US without realizing or perhaps admitting that the West too has been subject to the very same mindset in its dealings with Iran:

> They are a signatory to the NPT as part of the bargain between nuclear and non-nuclear powers. We have no issue with Iran developing civil nuclear power. It is something that we would encourage. We think it has much to do with their internal issues. There are books and many serious articles written by lots of people about how people get into a position of having an institutionalised enemy and having a position from which they cannot budge because the regime actually depends on having this track. Perhaps they find it difficult to contemplate another course of action and remain stable – I do not know. I think we are all in the business of trying to discern why, with the degree of risk and concern there is, Iran is not as open as it could be to satisfying international concerns. If it has a peaceful nuclear programme, show everybody. That is what we all want to see. Do not hide anything. Why they should be engaged on the track, despite all the powers ranged against them, is a question for someone else to answer more definitively.[3]

Reciprocity is the second most important variable for conflict resolution and has been missing in this relationship. The success behind constructive engagement lies in the ability of the West to show Iran that, by entering into dialogue about changes of political behaviour or allegiance to international regimes (NPT or human rights), a new good might be jointly created. Iran has never felt that it would gain much from ceasing enrichment as proposals have never reflected proportional reciprocity.[4] Proposals by the EU-3 fell short of Iranian expectations and were perceived as imbalanced given what it was asked to concede. In turn, Iranian demands were made as it continued to disregard confidence-building conditions and continued with enrichment activities. Once incentives put forward by the EU (and backed by the US) ended as a result of these actions and punitive measures were imposed, Iran demanded that sanctions should stop before concessions were made, while the P5+1 insisted that sanctions relief could only come upon full Iranian compliance (which had to be determined by the P5+1).

Breaking the stalemate

By the end of 2012, the conflict over Iran's nuclear programme has reached a mutually hurting stalemate. In past conflicts, this stalemate brought along a mutual acknowledgement that a negotiated settlement might be better for all parties involved, rather than continuing with existing policies.[5] This means that while coercive means and compellence are unlikely to stop Iran from enriching or pursuing other activities related to the nuclear programme, sanctions will continue to isolate Iran further from global markets and create an embargo-torn siege economy and political crisis. Western diplomacy, with the most powerful political, economic and military assets at its disposal, continues to face down Iran, while Iran remains defiant and champions resistance and independence. In order to make a shift from this *zero-sum* to a *positive-sum* environment, all stakeholders must engage in a joint problem-solving approach. Conflict literature refers to this moment as 'ripeness', a concept which essentially refers to a political settlement contingent on several key variables:[6]

1 All sides must have something to gain

Given the volatility of current relations between Iran and the West, in particular the US, respective stakeholders should not regard or demand the issue with a winning mentality, effectively seeking only ways to overcome and to get what their governments want by the end of negotiations.[7] Rather, diplomacy should represent a clear conciliatory mentality, advocating a solution which is to be found with and not against the other state. With the stakes raised high on all sides, saving face is fundamental in finding an agreement. An international agreement must, therefore, clearly reflect the interests of all vested parties. In this context, Iran is unlikely to commit to any accord that fails to address fundamental economic, political and security interests. Likewise, the EU and the US would only agree to a deal that provides the necessary objective and verifiable safeguards on Iran's nuclear intention and capabilities. The EU-3 and the US should grant Iran its right to continue enrichment (to a certain percentage) and processing activities. Thus, Western powers would settle for a second-best and workable alternative rather than continued to strive for an unattainable 'victory over Iran'. Yet such major concession must be met by Iran's commitment to full cooperation with all of the outstanding requests by the IAEA for access to information, personnel and nuclear sites. An international inspections regime must be established in order to maintain transparency and cooperation with the IAEA and ultimately build international confidence in the peaceful nature of the programme. The narrative has shown that all sides have entered negotiations with maximalist positions, demanding concessions from the other side without committing to concessions themselves. Therefore, an international accord, which could unite all parties must reflect the security, economic and political priorities of both Iran and the EU-3 and US government. As even Otto von Bismarck – the very statesman behind *realpolitik* – pointed out, 'In politics no one does anything for another, unless he also finds it in his own interest to do so.'[8]

2 All sides must have leaders capable of making an agreement

Only Nixon could go to China: perhaps only Obama can go to Iran. A crucial variable in the nuclear negotiations has always been US–Iranian relations (or rather the lack thereof). Opening diplomatic channels of communications (even only military-to-military communications as recommended by US military officials in order to prevent a 'war by accident') and especially putting forward the prospect of re-establishing relations has been a taboo in both Iranian and US politics. The narrative showed that past initiatives at détente largely failed owing to mutual mistrust that the other side would not be able to anchor any rapprochement within the respective domestic body politic. In conflict resolution literature, this problem is commonly referred to as the 'two-level game'. Here, interactions between governments happen at two levels:

> At the national level, domestic groups pursue their interests by pressuring the government to adopt favourable policies, and politicians seek power by constructing coalitions among those groups. At the international level, national governments seek to maximize their own ability to satisfy domestic pressures, while minimizing the adverse consequences of foreign developments.[9]

So, the important question is: which US and Iranian statesmen can negotiate outcomes that are acceptable to both domestic and foreign audiences? There is certainly no love lost between the Islamic Republic and the Democratic Party, and the narrative has demonstrated that President Obama as well as Congress continued with many of the previous policies towards Iran. Moreover, as the US government is preparing to support Syria's rebels and overthrow Iran's strongest Arab ally, engaging the US will prove difficult to legitimize before a hardline audience in Iran without appearing to be effectively capitulating before US power. Nonetheless, Barack Obama won a second term and pushed through most of his domestic policy priorities. Even though Congress is likely to act as spoiler in some respect,[10] President Obama enjoys enough momentum to initiate an opening and commit the US to an international agreement with Iran. It will, however, be difficult to 'separate the people from the problem' as long as Ahmadinejad is in the President's Office. Even though security and foreign policy is the Supreme Leader's prerogative, a settlement between Iran and the US seems unlikely under Ahmadinejad's tenure. Not only would shaking hands with Ahmadinejad, Israel's alleged greatest foe, prove a difficult photo op for any American president, Ali Khamenei is unlikely to grant his fallen-out-of-grace president the triumph of commanding an accord with the West, and with the US in particular. Carefully vetted candidates will run in the next presidential elections in June 2013. As the Green Movement and prominent members of the reformists have been removed from Iran's veneer of competitive politics, a pragmatist conservative president is likely to have the mandate as well as the support of the Supreme Leader to ease tensions and negotiate a mutually acceptable agreement.

3 The settlement must include enough compromise on the part of both sides so that leaders can persuade their domestic audiences that the national interest was protected

It is important to emphasize the meaning of diplomacy in the context of international cooperation. Seen as the profession of persuasion, the history of diplomacy has shown us – as has this narrative – that the exercise of power features prominently during negotiations. As the Israel–Palestine conflict continues to demonstrate, unequal distribution of power among states, which allows one side to dominate negotiations and influence the outcome reflecting mainly the interests of the more powerful party, rarely produces sustainable peace agreements in international relations. In the words of Harold Nicholson, 'Diplomacy ... in its essence is ... the art of negotiation is essentially a mercantile art. The foundation of good diplomacy is the same as the foundation of good business – namely credit, confidence, consideration and compromise.'[11]

The narrative on nuclear negotiations with Iran shows a lack of commitment to both compromise and proportional reciprocity by all parties. European and American policymakers know full well that suspension of uranium enrichment unilaterally, or complete suspension, would be an unacceptable demand for the Iranians. By the same token, if the Iranians insist on enrichment on Iranian territory, Iran must provide objective assurances within the framework of an international inspections regime. What is needed is another 'grand bargain'. The Chinese advocated such a thaw of relations during Obama's first term. Following the Obama administration's decision to engage Iran and having learned that Iran's leadership had discreetly expressed willingness to resume bilateral contacts after the 2008 elections, the Chinese government encouraged both countries to enter into direct negotiations. Such major détente between the US and Iran, however, required that sanctions give way to depoliticized and discreet talks between Iran and the US.[12] The Director of the Centre for Middle East Studies at the PRC's Ministry of Foreign Affairs-affiliated China Institute for International Studies envisioned such a grand bargain in the following terms:

> Li cited unnamed contacts in the United States 'with close access to policymakers on Iran' to support his belief that the United States would be willing to accept some internationally supervised uranium enrichment by Iran. This would be a concession, Li said, that 'the Europeans would have great difficulty accepting'. To make such a concession diplomatically palatable, Li continued, the United States in return would expect Iran's cessation of support for Hamas and Hizbollah, among other terrorist groups in the region, and its cooperation in Iraq and Afghanistan. In addition, Li suggested, the United States would expect Iran to agree to a stricter IAEA safeguard agreement that would control Iran's nuclear activities and include terms that would be integrated into the NPT as a basis for further safeguards governing all NPT signatory countries. He stated that before agreeing to a low level of Iranian enrichment activity, the United States would insist Iran implement a six-to-twelve-month freeze on nuclear enrichment activities.[13]

4 Both sides must have access to a mutuality acceptable process

However, for such a grand bargain or any other international accord to materialize, the US and Iran have to engage in bilateral talks. The nuclear impasse will not be resolved as long as Tehran and Washington refuse to talk to one another. In the US in particular, the reluctance to open dialogue with Iran but rather to continue with isolation cuts across the entire political spectrum. In 2011, the Iran Threat Reduction Act of 2011 (H.R. 1905), passed by the House of Representatives, included a clause which would have effectively outlawed diplomacy with Iran. The section read: 'No person employed with the United States Government may contact in an official or unofficial capacity any person that ... is an agent, instrumentality, or official of, is affiliated with, or is serving as a representative of the Government of Iran.'[14] The perception that 'silence' coupled with sanctions sometimes 'speaks louder than words' has informed US diplomacy towards Iran ever since 1979. A US State Department cable describing a meeting between US and Swiss officials in 2007 epitomizes this mindset. Following Swiss efforts to persuade Iran to return to negotiations in February 2007, the US Ambassador to Switzerland told the Swiss State Secretary of Foreign Affairs to step back because, given Switzerland's status as a US protecting power, his government's actions risked sending mixed messages to Iran:

> the Ambassador observed that, since Switzerland's position was now well known, now would be an opportune time to rest. Tehran knew what it needed to do to begin negotiations. Swiss silence would speak louder than words. Certainly, Iranian officials might reach out to the Swiss, but it would be helpful if Switzerland itself did not pursue more dialogue. Sanctions were starting to bite and international pressure was getting to Iran. The international community needed to allow the P5+1 track to have an effect.[15]

Thus, a fundamental prerequisite for any agreement would be principled negotiations between the US and Iran in order to resolve a wide range of issues that have not been addressed in over three decades of broken relations, most of which are, in fact, the result of a lack of diplomatic relations. Like the discreet channels between Palestinians and Israelis, which were hosted in Norway and led to the Oslo Accords in 1993, talks between the US and Iran have first to be conducted in secret. What conflict resolution literature calls a 'core group of agreers' that come together and gradually expand membership describes a tactic of building a coalition across both warring parties large enough to make a stable agreement no broader than necessary to cover the issue – a tactic of participant instrumentalism.[16] The Chinese, who time and again have indicated a willingness to act as mediator between Iran and the US, fittingly suggested to the US a 'Nixon in China moment'. An unofficial visit to Iran, along the lines of Henry Kissinger's June 2009 trip to China to discuss North Korea sanctions or former President Clinton's August 2009 visit to Pyongyang to effect the release of the two American journalists, would allow for discreet and informal discussions on a range of areas of mutual concern and interest.[17]

Power politics and conflict resolution

Unfortunately, EU/US relations with Iran have become a textbook case of game theory's 'Prisoner's Dilemma'. The paradox of game theory is, as Jervis suggests, that

> even if each side prefers mutual cooperation to mutual defection (and each knows that this is the other state's preference) the result can still be non cooperation because each part is driven by the hope of gaining its first choice – which would be to exploit the other – and its fear that if it cooperates, the other will exploit it.[18]

The narrative of the nuclear negotiations, confirms that in the absence of communicating respective interests, state preferences prohibit cooperation, despite a certain degree of convergence of interests between them. Notwithstanding the merits of trust and reciprocity in conflict resolution approaches with the fundamental premise that rewards tend to spawn more rewards and punishment to spawn more punishment,[19] neither side has so far been willing to test the other's commitment to honour agreements. As long as all states involved are driven by this mindset, sanctions will remain in place, Iran will continue to defy Western demands and the stalemate is unlikely to be broken.

Notes

Introduction

1 See Oliver Richmond, *Maintaining Order, Making Peace* (New York: Palgrave, 2002), pp. 41–75.
2 Alexandra Homolar, 'Rebels without a conscience: the evolution of the Rogue States Narrative in US Security Policy', *European Journal of International Relations* 17, 4 (December 2011), pp. 705–727.
3 For Larijani's statement on Iranian security perceptions at the Munich Security Conference, see Disclosed US Diplomatic Cable, *Ref ID: 09 MUNICH22, Munich Security Conference – Focus On Iran*, Origin: Consulate Munich (10 February 2009), Classification: Unclassified.

1 Setting the scene: constructive engagement with Iran

1 Mary Casey, 'The EU is set to impose new sanctions on Iran' (15 October 2012) Foreign Policy, http://mideast.foreignpolicy.com/posts/2012/10/15/the_eu_is_set_to_impose_new_sanctions_on_iran (website accessed 5 February 2013).
2 Cited in Trita Parsi, 'Israel's diplomatic scare game', *The Nation* (10 August 2012), www.nation.com.pk/pakistan-news-newspaper-daily-english-online/international/10-Aug-2012/israel-s-diplomatic-scare-game (website accessed 5 February 2013).
3 The concept of constructive engagement is regarded as widely ambiguous among policymakers and scholars. Often condemned as doing nothing more than pursuing a solicitous policy towards authoritarian regimes, constructive engagement is, therefore, regarded as a controversial foreign policy option: one that is determined by economic interests rather than genuine interest to change certain state behaviour. For a discourse on opposing US and European policies towards so-called rogue states, see Richard N. Haas, *Transatlantic Tensions: The US, Europe and Problem Countries* (Washington, DC: Brookings, 1999).
4 It is interesting to note that it was actually the European Union's policy of Critical Dialogue towards Iran, which translated into German as *Kritischer Dialog*, that turned out to be the first usable term describing a policy referred to in the English language as constructive engagement. See Richard N. Haas and Meghan L. O'Sullivan, *Honey and Vinegar – Incentives, Sanctions and Foreign Policy* (Washington, DC: Brookings, 2000), p. 1.
5 See Jeffrey Herbst, 'Incentives and domestic reform in South Africa', in David Cortright (ed.), *The Price of Peace – Incentives and International Conflict Prevention* (New York: Rowman and Littlefield, 1997), pp. 205–222; Audie Klotz, 'Norms reconstituting interests: global racial equality and US sanctions against South Africa', *International Organization* 49, 3 (Summer 1995), pp. 451–478.
6 Christopher Coker, *The United States and South Africa 1968–1985: Constructive*

Engagement and its Critics (Durham, NC: Duke University Press, 1986), pp. 154–158.

7   Ibid., p. 155.

8   Ibid., pp. 111–114; see also Michael Clough, 'Beyond constructive engagement', *Foreign Policy* 61 (Winter 1985–1986), pp. 3–24.

9   Alexander George, *Bridging the Gap: Theory and Practice in Foreign Policy* (Washington, DC: US Institute for Peace, 1993), pp. 50–51.

10 See ibid, p. 50.

11 J. L. Richardson, 'New perspectives in appeasement: some implications for international relations', *World Politics* 40, 3 (April 1988), p. 290; see also John W. Wheeler-Bennett, *Munich: Prologue to Tragedy* (London: Macmillan, 1948); Lewis B. Namier, *Diplomatic Prelude* (London: Macmillan, 1948); Winston Churchill, *The Second World War, I: The Gathering Storm* (London: Cassell, 1948).

12 J. L. Richardson, 'New perspectives in appeasement', p. 291.

13 Hans Morgenthau, *Politics among Nations*, 3rd edn (New York: Macmillan, 1967), p. 96.

14 Evan Luard, 'Conciliation and deterrence: a comparison of political strategies in the interwar and postwar period', *World Politics* 19, 2 (January 1967), p. 186.

15 William R. Rock, *British Appeasement in the 1930s* (London: Edward Arnold, 1984), p. 99.

16 William R. Rock, *British Appeasement in the 1930s*, pp. 99–100.

17 Alexander George and Gordon A. Craig, *Force and Statecraft: Diplomatic Problems of our Time*, 3rd edn (Oxford: Oxford University Press, 1995), p. 157.

18 Ibid., p. 254.

19 Ibid., p. 254.

20 Willy Brandt, *A Peace Policy for Europe* (London: Weidenfeld and Nicolson, 1969), p. 104.

21 Alexander George and Gordon A. Craig, *Force and Statecraft: Diplomatic Problems of our Time*, p. 256.

22 Oliver Richmond, *Maintaining Order, Making Peace* (New York: Palgrave, 2002), pp. 41–74.

23 Alexander George, *Bridging the Gap: Theory and Practice in Foreign Policy*, p. 48.

24 Henry A. Kissinger, *A World Restored* (London: Gollancz, 1973), p. 1. See also Alexander George, *Bridging the Gap: Theory and Practice in Foreign Policy*, p. 48; George distinguishes between 'revolutionary' or 'outlaw' states and 'revisionist' states, which seek merely to rectify the status quo and do not reject the norms and practices of the international system.

25 Oliver Richmond, *Maintaining Order, Making Peace* (London: Palgrave, 2002), pp. 41–75.

26 Friends Committee on National Legislation, 'Constructive engagement with Libya' (February 2004), http://fcnl.org/resources/newsletter/feb04/constructive_engagement_with_libya/ (website accessed 1 November 2012).

27 David E. Sanger, 'In US–Libya nuclear deal, a Qaddafi threat faded away', *New York Times* (1 March 2011), www.nytimes.com/2011/03/02/world/middleeast/02arms.html (website accessed 5 February 2013).

28 Disclosed US Diplomatic Cable, *Senator Reviews Bilateral Relationship With Senior Libyan Officials* (31 August 2006) published on website www.cablegatesearch.net/cable.php?id=06TRIPOLI454 (website accessed 8 August 2012).

29 Oliver Richmond, *Maintaining Order, Making Peace*, pp. 41–74.

30 Daniel Druckman, 'Negotiating in the international context', in I. William Zartman (ed.), *Peacemaking in International Conflict: Methods and Techniques* (Washington, DC: United States Institute of Peace, 2007), pp. 147–148.

31 G. R. Berridge, 'Human nature, good faith, and diplomacy', *Review of International Studies* 27, 4 (October 2001), p. 556.

32 Harold Nicholson, *Diplomacy* (Georgetown: Institute for the Study of Diplomacy, 1988), p. 25.
33 For example, see Kissinger's statement after the SALT negotiations ('The way to use this freeze is for us to catch up. ... If we don't do this, we don't deserve to be in office'), cited in John Lewis Gaddis, *Strategies of Containment: A Critical Appraisal of Postwar American National Security* (Oxford: Oxford University Press, 1982), p. 325.
34 Jonathan Monten, 'Thucydides and modern realism', *International Studies Quarterly* 50, 1 (March 2006), pp. 6–12.
35 In 1997, the US President's Export Council reported a total of seventy-three countries that were under some form of unilateral economic sanctions. For an analysis on the use and efficacy of US laws and executive orders imposing various sanctions against states (in particular Iran and Libya). see Troy Lavers, 'Law as a smart bomb or just a limited tool of coercion: considering extra-territorial economic sanctions', *RUSI Journal* 146, 5 (October 2001), p. 17.
36 See Gary C. Hufbauer, Jeffrey J. Schott and Kimberly A. Elliott, *Economic Sanctions Reconsidered: History and Current Policy* (Washington, DC: Peterson Institute for International Economics, 1990), pp. 92–93; see also Robert Pape, 'Why sanctions still do not work', *International Security* 23 (Summer 1998), pp. 66–77; David A. Baldwin, *Economic Statecraft* (Princeton: Princeton University Press, 1985), pp. 130–144. Concerning British–Iranian relations and the sanctions debate, it should be noted that the imposition of sanctions against Iran by Britain in 1951 (together with covert operations) proved effective for Britain to achieve stated policy goals. The success of sanctions in this historical case mainly derived from the fact that while oil rents were fundamental for the survival of the Iranian economy, Britain and other major Western powers were able to substitute oil imports from Iraq, Kuwait and Qatar. See Makio Miyagwa, *Do Economic Sanctions Work?* (London: Macmillan, 1992), pp. 30–33.
37 Natasha Bahrami and Trita Parsi, 'Blunt instrument sanctions don't promote democratic change', *Boston Review* (6 February 2012), www.bostonreview.net/BR37.1/trita_parsi_natasha_bahrami_iran_sanctions.php (website accessed 12 October 2012).
38 Meghan L. O´Sullivan, *Shrewd Sanctions: Statecraft and State Sponsors of Terrorism* (Washington, DC: Brookings, 2003), p. 27.
39 For the human impact of UN sanctions on the Iraqi population see Denis Halliday, 'Sanctions have an impact on all of us', *Middle East Report* 209 (Winter 1998), p. 3; Roger Normand, 'Iraqi sanctions, human rights and humanitarian law', *Middle East Report* 200 (July–September 1996), pp. 40–46.
40 Geoffrey Kemp, 'Europe's Middle East challenges', *The Washington Quarterly* 27, 1 (2003–2004), p. 163.
41 See Mark Leonard, 'Why the US needs the EU', *Time* (28 February 2005).
42 Joseph S. Nye 'The changing nature of world power', *Political Science Quarterly* 105, 2 (Summer 1990), p. 181.
43 Joseph S. Nye, *Soft Power: The Means to Success in World Politics* (New York: Public Affairs, 2004), pp. 80–81.
44 Disclosed US Diplomatic Cable, *The EU and Sanctions (Introducing the EU, Part VII)* (23 February 2010) published on website www.cablegatesearch.net/cable.php?id=10BRUSSELS211 (website accessed 8 August 2012).
45 William Long, *Economic Incentives and Bilateral Cooperation* (Ann Arbor: University of Michigan Press, 1996), p. 9; Robert Axelrod, *The Evolution of Cooperation* (New York: Basic Books, 1984), pp. 7–26.
46 John Ruggie, 'International responses to technology: concepts and trends', *International Organization* 29 (Summer 1979), p. 559, quoted in Stephen Haggard and Beth A. Simmons, 'Theories of international regimes', *International Organization* 41, 3 (Summer 1987), p. 492.

47 John Ruggie quoted in Stephen Krasner, *International Regimes* (Ithaca: Ithaca University Press, 1983), p. 2.

48 See Philip Everts and Guido Walraven (eds), *The Politics of Persuasion: Implementation of Foreign Policy by the Netherlands* (Aldershot, Hants: Avebury, 1989), pp. 77–78; Robert A. Dahl and Bruce Stinebrickner, *Modern Political Analysis* (New York: Prentice Hall), p. 45. See Joanne Gowa, 'Anarchy, egoism, and third images: the evolution of cooperation and international relations', *International Organization* 40, 1 (Winter 1986), pp. 169–170.

49 See Hugh Miall, Oliver Ramsbotham and Tom Woodhouse, *Contemporary Conflict Resolution* (Cambridge: Polity Press, 1999), pp. 5–6.

50 Oliver P. Richmond, *Mediating in Cyprus: The Cypriot Communities and the United Nations* (London: Frank Cass, 1988), p. 7.

51 Ronald J. Fischer, 'Prenegotiation problem-solving discussions: enhancing the potential for successful negotiation', in Robert Matthews and Charles Pentland (eds), 'Getting to the table: processes of international prenegotiation', *International Journal* XLIV, 2 (Spring 1989), p. 442.

52 Eben A. Weitzman and Patricia Flynn Weitzman, 'Problem solving and decision making in conflict resolution', in Morton Deutsch, Peter T. Coleman and Eric C. Marcus (eds), *The Handbook of Conflict Resolution: Theory and Practice* (San Francisco: Jossey-Bass, 2000), p. 188.

53 J. Z. Rubin and D. G. Pruitt, *Social Conflict: Escalation, Stalemate and Settlement* (New York: McGraw-Hill, 1994), p. 169.

54 Roger Fischer and William Ury, 'Getting to yes', in David P. Barash (ed.), *Approaches to Peace: A Reader in Peace Studies* (Oxford: Oxford University Press, 2000), p. 71.

55 Ibid., p. 74.

56 Ronald J. Fischer, 'Prenegotiation problem-solving discussions: enhancing the potential for successful negotiation', p. 443.

57 G. R. Berridge, *Diplomacy: Theory and Practice* (London: Palgrave Macmillan, 2002), p. 46.

58 See I. William Zartman and Maureen R. Berman, *The Practical Negotiator* (New Haven, CT: Yale University Press, 1982), pp. 225–228.

59 Raymond Cohen, *Negotiating Across Cultures: International Communication in an Interdependent World* (Washington, DC: US Institute of Peace Press, 2000), p. 100.

60 I. William Zartman and Maureen R. Berman, *The Practical Negotiator*, p. 93.

61 A high-context culture communicates allusively rather than directly. As important as the explicit content of a message is the context in which it occurs, surrounding non-verbal cues and hinted-at nuances of meaning. Loss of face (humiliation before the group) is an excruciating penalty to be avoided at all costs. This negotiation style is therefore shame-orientated rather than guilt-orientated. Directness and especially contradiction are much disliked. It is also hard for speakers of this kind of culture to deliver a blunt no. See Raymond Cohen, *Negotiating Across Cultures: International Communication in an Interdependent World*, p. 32.

62 Low-context culture exemplified by the United States and Europe reserves a different role for language. What has to be said is stated explicitly. While politeness is obviously not precluded, negotiators of low-context cultures hardly see the need for contrived formulas and verbal embellishments. Hence, guilt not shame is the psychological price paid for misdemeanour. Ibid., p. 32.

63 Raymond Cohen, *Negotiating Across Cultures: International Communication in an Interdependent World*, p. 106.

64 Chris Patten, 'The Iranian choice – an opportunity to embrace the family of nations', *The Iranian Journal of International Affairs* XV, 1 and 2 (Spring–Summer 2003), p. 129.

65 Ibid., p. 131.

66 European Council in Edinburgh (11–12 December 1992), 'European Council, Conclusions of the Presidency', *RAPID, DOC/92/8*.

67 Ibid., paragraph 15–17.

68 Matthias Struwe, 'The policy of Critical Dialogue: an analysis of European human rights policy towards Iran from 1992–1999', *Durham Middle East Paper Series No. 60* (Durham, NC: Centre for Middle Eastern and Islamic Studies, 1998), pp. 1–2.

69 Ibid., pp. 1–2.

70 See Peter Rudolf, 'Critical engagement: the European Union and Iran', in Richard N. Haas (ed.), *Transatlantic Tensions: The US, Europe and Problem Countries* (Washington, DC: Brookings, 1999), p. 87.

71 'Iran Politik der Bundesregierung; Antwort der Bundesregierung auf die Grosse Anfrage', *Deutscher Bundestag, Drucksache 13/3483* (16 January 1996).

72 See 'Declaration by the Presidency on behalf of the European Union on Iran', *RAPID PESC/97/32, 7009/97 (Presse 97)* (Brussels, 10 April 1997).

73 'Declaration by the European Union on Iran', *RAPID PESC/97/41, 7569/97 (Presse 125) E/41/97* (Luxembourg, 29 April 1997).

74 Commission of the European Communities, 'Communication from the Commission to the European Parliament and the Council–EU relations with the Islamic Republic of Iran', *COM (2001) 71 final* (Brussels, 7 February 2001); see also 'Declaration by the European Union on Iran', *RAPID PESC/97/41, 7569/97*.

75 Since human rights was one of the main areas where the European Parliament could exert pressure on the Commission, it played a crucial part in shaping EU public opinion on relations with Iran by consistently scrutinizing policies and developments and passing critical resolutions. See European Parliament, 'Resolution on human rights in the world in 1993–1994 and the Union's human rights policy', *Official Journal C126* (22 May 1995); European Parliament, 'Resolution on continued human rights violations in Iran', *Official Journal C166* (3 July 1995); European Parliament, 'Resolution on the violation of political and human rights in the Islamic Republic of Iran', *Official Journal C096* (1 April 1996); European Parliament, Resolution on Iran, *Official Journal C 176* (2 June 1997).

76 Foreign Minister Klaus Kinkel, 'Plenarprotokoll', *Deutscher Bundestag 13. Wahlperiode-104. Sitzung, Plenarprotokoll 13/104*, p. 9217.

77 Ibid., p. 9217.

78 Peter Rudolf, 'Critical engagement: the European Union and Iran', in Richard N. Haas, *Transatlantic Tensions: The US, Europe and Problem Countries* (Washington, DC: Brookings, 1999), p. 76.

79 Ibid., p. 76.

80 Interview with senior EU Commission Official, Commission of the European Union, St Andrews, 5 March 2005.

81 Bernd Kaussler, 'European Union constructive engagement with Iran: an exercise in conditional human rights diplomacy (2000–2004)' *Iranian Studies* 41, 3 (June 2008), pp. 269–270.

82 Ibid.

83 Ibid.

84 Ibid., pp. 269–295.

85 Martin Fletcher, 'Britain is appeasing Iran, Nobel Laureate Shirin Ebadi says', *The Times* (24 September 2009), available at: www.timesonline.co.uk/tol/news/world/middle_east/article6846763.ece (website accessed 12 March 2011).

86 Disclosed US Diplomatic Cable, *EU, Others, Frustrated With Iran Human Rights Dialogue* (7 December 2005) published on website www.cablegatesearch.net/cable.php?id=05BRUSSELS4323&version=1314919461 (website accessed 9 August 2012).

87 Bernd Kaussler, 'From engagement to containment: EU–Iran relations and the nuclear programme, 1992–2011', *Journal of Balkan and Near East Studies* 14, 1 (Spring 2012), pp. 53–57.

124 *Notes*

88 See Bernd Kaussler and Anthony Newkirk, 'Diplomacy in bad faith: American–Iranian relations today', *Diplomacy and Statecraft* 23, 2 (2012), pp. 347–380.

2 Old Europe's diplomacy: the 2004 Paris Agreement

1 Ali Ansari, *Confronting Iran: The Failure of American Foreign Policy and the Roots of Mistrust* (London: Hurst, 2006), p. 205.
2 See the statement by a senior Italian Ministry official: 'While those in power were not trustworthy, it would be important to find ways to engage the younger generation. Iranians he knew were eager for good relations with the United States.' Disclosed US Diplomatic Cable, *GOI Briefs USEU Amb on EU Presidency Briefs USEU Priorities* (28 August 2002) published on website www.cablegatesearch.net/cable.php?id=02ROME5255 (website accessed 15 August 2012).
3 Disclosed US Diplomatic Cable, *Italy Won't Force Iran WTO Accession Issue* (19 April 2002) published on website http://cables.mrkva.eu/cable.php?id=2801
4 Disclosed US Diplomatic Cable, *XX Discusses Non-Proliferation Issues* (6 August 2002) published on website www.cablegatesearch.net/cable.php?id=02ROME3855 (website accessed 1 September 2012).
5 See the statement by the spokesman for Iran's Atomic Energy Organization on the construction of the Bushehr nuclear reactor and the extraction of uranium in Saghand and Yazd; Fars News Agency (17 May 2003). The head of the Iranian Atomic Energy Organization, Gholamreza Aqazadeh, told UN diplomats that 'Iran, because of the unnecessary restrictions imposed, has not managed yet to take delivery of 100 tons of enriched uranium and 390 tons of depleted uranium from Germany for use at Bushehr'; IRNA (7 May 2003). The Iranian Foreign Minister, Kamal Kharrazi, supported a Syrian-sponsored UN Security Council resolution which called for a WMD-free Middle East; ISNA (17 May 2003).
6 See speech at Shahid Beheshti University, Voice of the Islamic Republic of Iran (12 May 2003).
7 'Bush administration contacts with Iran direct and indirect', *Middle East Forum* (10 November 2008), www.meforum.org/2011/bush-administration-contacts-with-iran (website accessed 14 May 2012).
8 Rajaee Bahram, 'Deciphering Iran: the political evolution of the Islamic Republic and US foreign policy after September 11', *Comparative Studies of South Asia, Africa and the Middle East* 24, 1 (2004), p. 166.
9 In a meeting with the Jordanian Foreign Minister, Sadr said that 'Iran supports the same outcome in Iraq as Jordan – the emergence of a strong, stable Iraqi state'. Disclosed US Diplomatic Cable, *Iranian Ambassador Tells GOI Iran Wouldn't Mind Seeing Saddam Go* (17 March 2003) published on website www.cablegatesearch.net/cable.php?id=02ROME3855 (website accessed 1 September 2012).
10 In a meeting with the Jordanian Foreign Minister, Sadr said that 'Iran supports the same outcome in Iraq as Jordan – the emergence of a strong, stable Iraqi state'. Disclosed US Diplomatic Cable, *Iranian Deputy FOMIN in Amman Talks Peace Process, Kharazi Expresses Concern about MEK on Jordanian-Iraq Border* (18 April 2003) published on website www.cablegatesearch.net/cable.php?id=03AMMAN2505 (website accessed 1 September 2012).
11 Disclosed US Diplomatic Cable, *Iraq: Iran Would Accept UN Sanctioned War in Iraq, Khatemi Tells Berlusconi* (28 April 2003) published on website www.cablegatesearch.net/cable.php?id=03ROME854 (website accessed 2 September 2012).
12 Gareth Porter, 'Understanding Iran's diplomatic strategy', *Al Jazeera* (27 April 2012), www.aljazeera.com/indepth/opinion/2012/04/2012422833676280.html (website accessed 12 May 2012).
13 Ibid.
14 See letter posted on Nicholas D. Kristof, 'On the ground', *New York Times* (27 April

2007), http://kristof.blogs.nytimes.com/2007/04/28/irans-proposal-for-a-grand-bargain/ (website accessed 15 May 2012).
15 Ibid.
16 Gareth Porter, 'Understanding Iran's diplomatic strategy'.
17 IAEA, Board of Governors, 'Implementation of the NPT Safeguards Agreement in the Islamic Republic of Iran: Report by the Director General', *GOV/2003/40* (6 June 2003), pp. 7–8.
18 Implementation of the NPT safeguards agreement in the Islamic Republic of Iran Report by the Director General, IAEA GOV/2003/40 (19 June 2003) www.iaea.org/Publications/Documents/Board/2003/gov2003-40.pdf (website accessed 1 October 2012).
19 Disclosed US Diplomatic Cable, *Iranian Nuclear Program: Canada Pushing Hard* (30 May 2003) published on website www.cablegatesearch.net/cable.php?id= 03OTTAWA1556 (website accessed 1 October 2012).
20 The US Ambassador to Kuwait told the Kuwaiti Foreign Minister that signing the AP was 'important but not sufficient'. He further 'emphasized that the burden of proof is on Iran to, inter alia, prove that it has not diverted nuclear material to non-peaceful purposes'. Disclosed US Diplomatic Cable, *Kuwaiti FM Discusses Iran/IAEA* (1 October 2003) published on website www.cablegatesearch.net/cable.php?id=03KUW AIT4534&version=1314919461 (website accessed 3 September 2012).
21 IAEA Board of Governors, 'Implementation of the NPT Safeguards Agreement in the Islamic Republic of Iran Resolution adopted by the Board on 12 September 2003', *GOV/2003/69* (12 September 2003), p. 2.
22 Ibid.
23 Council of the European Union, Brussels, 'European Council 16 and 17 October 2003, Presidency conclusions', *15188/03 POLGEN 77* (Brussels, 25 November 2003), p. 17.
24 Disclosed US Diplomatic Cable, *IAEA/Iran Dutch MFA on IAEA BoG Noncompliance Resolution* (4 September 2003) published on website www.cablegatesearch.net/cable.php?id=03THEHAGUE2173 (website accessed 7 September 2012).
25 The official said the Iranian Ministry of Foreign Affairs, Deputy Director General for International and Political Affairs Ali Asghar Soltanieh, told the Dutch Deputy Political Director that Iran enjoyed no benefits under the NPT. Ibid.
26 Bahman Nirumand, *Iran Report Nr. 09–2003* (Heinrich Böll Stiftung, September 2003), p. 15.
27 Farideh Farhi, 'Ahmadinejad's nuclear folly', MERIP (Fall 2009), www.merip.org/mer/mer252/farhi.html (website accessed 5 February 2013).
28 See BBC, 'Full text Iran Declaration' (21 October 2003), http://news.bbc.co.uk/2/hi/technology/3211036.stm (website accessed 15 June 2012).
29 Ibid.
30 Farideh Farhi, 'Ahmadinejad's nuclear folly'.
31 Ibid.
32 The NIE read in part:

> Our assessment that Iran halted the program in 2003 primarily in response to international pressure indicates Tehran's decisions are guided by a cost-benefit approach rather than a rush to a weapon irrespective of the political, economic, and military costs. This, in turn, suggests that some combination of threats of intensified international scrutiny and pressures, along with opportunities for Iran to achieve its security, prestige, and goals for regional influence in other ways, might – if perceived by Iran's leaders as credible – prompt Tehran to extend the current halt to its nuclear weapons program. It is difficult to specify what such a combination might be.
>
> (Office of the Director of National Intelligence (November 2007) www.dni.gov/press_releases/20071203_release.pdf)

33 See, for example, the statement by Basij which in an open letter accuses 'officials of dereliction of duty'; ISNA (24 October 2003), BBC Monitoring.
34 The Iranian Foreign Ministry also handed the names of detained persons suspected of being al-Qaeda members to the UN; Vision of the Islamic Republic of Iran Network 1 (26 October 2003), BBC Monitoring.
35 Council of the European Union, 'Statement by Javier Solana, EU High Representative for the CFSP, on the agreement on Iran's nuclear programme', *S0304/04* (Brussels, 15 November 2004).
36 Of particular importance was Iran's disclosure of plutonium production. The report read:

> Iran acknowledged the irradiation of depleted UO2 targets at TRR and subsequent plutonium separation experiments in a hot cell in the Nuclear Safety Building of TNRC between 1988 and 1992. Neither the activities nor the separated plutonium had been reported to the Agency previously.
> (IAEA Board of Governors, 'Implementation of the NPT Safeguards Agreement in the Islamic Republic of Iran, Report by the Director General', *GOV/2003/75* (10 November 2003), p. 10)

37 Ibid., p. 8.
38 For a timeline of US non-proliferation efforts towards Libya, see Kelsey Davenport, *Chronology of Libya's Disarmament and Relations with the United States*, www.armscontrol.org/factsheets/LibyaChronology (website accessed 17 September 2012).
39 Disclosed US Diplomatic Cable, *Spain, El Baradedi Tells Palacio IAEA Should Move Cautiously on Iran* (24 February 2004) published on website www.cablegatesearch.net/cable.php?id=04MADRID635 (website accessed 18 September 2012).
40 Disclosed US Diplomatic Cable, *Ref ID: 04ROME792 Iran/IAEA: Italy (Still) Sees the Glass as Half Full*, Origin: Embassy Rome (2 March 2004), Classification: Confidential.
41 Ibid.
42 Disclosed US Diplomatic Cable, *Ambassador's March 24 Meeting With Dutch Political Director: Iraq, GME, EU, China* (8 March 2004) published on website www.cablegatesearch.net/cable.php?id=04THEHAGUE787 (website accessed 18 September 2012).
43 The report further stated 'that Iran has been developing more sophisticated centrifuges than it had previously admitted, and that it has produced or acquired nuclear materials with very limited plausible civilian application'. House of Commons Foreign Affairs Committee, *Iran – Third Report of Session 2003–04 (19 March 2004) by authority of the House of Commons, London*, The Stationery Office HC 80, p. 22.
44 Barbara Slavin, 'Former Iranian negotiator faults his nation's nuclear diplomacy', *Al Monitor* (6 June 2012), www.al-monitor.com/pulse/originals/2012/al-monitor/moussavian-faults-ahmadinejad-se.html (website accessed 23 September 2012).
45 The Italian Foreign Ministry's Director for the Persian Gulf, told US officials that the 'international community must remain tough and vigilant regarding Iran's nuclear program, it must also continue to engage the Tehran regime'. In line with Italy's even-handed approach towards Iran, the Italian official told the US Embassy in Rome that the IC's message of nuclear restraint must be unconditional, but should be accompanied by offers to Iran to participate in regional initiatives, such as the GME. Dialogue, high-level political visits and trade arrangements were also helping to keep communications channels open. Disclosed US Diplomatic Cable, *EU, GAERC and Council – Italy on Board With US Positions on MEPP/IAEA, Balkans* (19 March 2004) published on website http://wikileaks.org/cable/2004/04/04ROME1692.html (website accesed 18 September 2012).
46 Disclosed US Diplomatic Cable, *Italy on Board With Iran/IAEA BoG Views* (30 April 2004) published on website www.cablegatesearch.net/cable.php?id=04ROME1692 (website accessed 18 September 2012).

47 Disclosed US Diplomatic Cable, *Iranian Diplomat Sounds Out the Brits* (18 June 2004) published on website www.cablegatesearch.net/cable.php?id=04ROME2363 (wesbite accessed 19 September 2012).

48 European Parliament, 'Briefing paper – External policies of the Union – The EU–Iran human rights dialogue' (June 2007) authored by Morten Kjærum, Executive Director Danish Centre for International Studies and Human Rights, DCISM Copenhagen, Denmark; www.europarl.europa.eu/committees/en/droi/studiesdownload.html?langua geDocument=EN&file=17651 (website accessed 12 July 2012).

49 Interview with EU official.

50 A Council resolution stated:

> the Council expressed its deep regret and disappointment that large numbers of candidates were prevented from standing in this year's parliamentary elections, including many sitting members of the Majlis, thus making a genuine democratic choice by the Iranian people impossible. This interference was a setback for the democratic process in Iran. The Council expressed the hope that Iran will return to the path of reform and democratisation.
>
> (EU External Action Service, 'Council conclusions – Iran – 2004–2008', www. eeas.europa.eu/iran/docs/iran_council_2004–08_en.pdf (website accessed 12 July 2012))

51 Interview with EU official.

52 Ali Ansari, *Confronting Iran: The Failure of American Foreign Policy and the Roots of Mistrust*, p. 134.

53 Walter Posch, 'Why Europe mustn't cede its leadership on Iran to the US', *Europe's World* (Spring 2009) www.europesworld.org/NewEnglish/Home/Article/tabid/191/ ArticleType/ArticleView/ArticleID/21351/language/en-US/WhyEuropemustntcedeit-sleadershiponIrantotheUS.aspx (website accessed 10 July 2012).

54 Disclosed US Diplomatic Cable, *Wishful Thinking? EU Hopes G8 Can Keep Iran Out of UNSC* (8 October 2004) published on website http://wikileaks.org/ cable/2004/10/04BRUSSELS4335.html (website accessed 18 September 2012); for a statement by the Iranian government see Jomhuri-ye Eslami website (27 October 2004) BBC Monitoring.

55 Ibid.

56 Europeans also favoured a G8 approach, in order to broaden the appeal for Iran but also to secure the support of Russia should a G8 initiative fail and Iran be referred to the UN Security Council; ibid.

57 Ibid.

58 Ibid.

59 Disclosed US Diplomatic Cable, *April 15 US EU Troika Consultations* (23 April 2004) published on website www.cablegatesearch.net/cable.php?id=04BRUSSELS 1766 (website accessed 18 September 2012).

60 Marina Ottaway and Thomas Carothers, 'The greater Middle East initiative: off to a false start', *Policy Brief No 29 March 2004*, Carnegie Endowment for International Peace, p. 2.

61 Disclosed US Diplomatic Cable, *Wishful Thinking? EU Hopes G8 Can Keep Iran Out of UNSC*.

62 Ibid.

63 Joseph Ferguson, 'Iran–US–Russia relations: a spring thaw after a freezing winter?' (July 2004), csis.org/files/media/csis/pubs/0402qus_russia.pdf (website accessed 1 August 2012); for US Representative Ron Paul's statement on this resolution see: www.ronpaularchive.com/2004/05/dont-start-a-war-with-iran/_(website accessed 13 February 2013).

64 IAEA, 'Communication dated 26 November 2004 received from the Permanent

Representatives of France, Germany, the Islamic Republic of Iran and the United Kingdom concerning the agreement signed in Paris on 15 November 2004', *INFCIRC/637* (26 November 2004), p. 3.

65 Ibid.

66 The resolution further concluded:

> all the declared nuclear material in Iran has been accounted for, and therefore such material is not diverted to prohibited activities. The Agency is, however, not yet in a position to conclude that there are no undeclared nuclear materials or activities in Iran.
>
> (IAEA Board of Governors, 'Implementation of the NPT Safeguards Agreement in the Islamic Republic of Iran', *GOV/2004/83* (15 November 2004), p. 23)

67 Disclosed US Diplomatic Cable, *Netherlands/EU Expectations for Dec 13 GAERC* (9 December 2004) published on website www.cablegatesearch.net/cable. php?id=04THEHAGUE3219 (website accessed 20 September 2012).

68 Disclosed US Diplomatic Cable, *EU//Iran WMD Rep Readout on Talks, Path Ahead For EU-3-Iran Dialogue* (23 December 2004) published on website www.cablegate-search.net/cable.php?id=04BRUSSELS5396 (website accessed 24 October 2012).

69 Ibid.

70 Ibid.

71 Ibid.

72 Ibid.

73 Disclosed US Diplomatic Cable, *EU-Iran French Readout of Paris Agreement Working Group Meetings January 17–18* (26 January 2006) published on website www.cablegatesearch.net/cable.php?id=05PARIS472&version=1314919461 (website accessed 24 October 2012); This position was reinforced by Rowhani's statement back in Iran: 'No documents, guarantees and resolutions could ever persuade Iran to ignore its legitimate and lawful right to gain access to nuclear technology for peaceful purposes'; *IRNA* (30 November 2004) BBC Monitoring.

74 Ibid.

75 See statement by Deputy Speaker Mohammad Reza Bahonar, Fars News Agency (7 December 2004), BBC Monitoring; also see editorial in *Jomhuri-ye Eslami* (20 November 2004), which accused the IRIB TV station of giving too much prominence to supporters of the Paris Agreement.

76 IRNA (24 November 2004), BBC Monitoring.

77 IRNA (29 November 2004), BBC Monitoring.

78 Ibid.

79 Scott Peterson, 'Imminent Iran nuclear threat? A timeline of warnings since 1979', *The Christian Science Monitor* (8 November 2011), www.csmonitor.com/World/Middle-East/2011/1108/Imminent-Iran-nuclear-threat-A-timeline-of-warnings-since-1979/Earliest-warnings-1979–84 (website accessed 2 August 2012); Bahaman Niruman, *Iran Report, 12/2004* (Heinrich Böll Stiftung), pp. 12–14; Semira N. Niko, 'Timeline of Iran's nuclear activities', *Iran Primer* (USIP, Washington, DC), http://iranprimer.usip.org/resource/timeline-irans-nuclear-activities (website accessed 1 August 2012).

80 Bahaman Niruman, *Iran Report, 12/2005* (Heinrich Böll Stiftung), p. 14.

81 The French government told the Bush administration that a US statement which would call for 'full cessation and dismantling of Iran's fissile material production efforts' would undermine EU-3 efforts 'because they are the exact terms that the EU-3 is pushing for in negotiations'; Disclosed US Diplomatic Cable, *Ref ID: 05PARIS1233 Iran/IAEA: France Will Raise Iran at the Feb 28 IAEA BoG Meeting, But Requests Amendment to US Statement*, Origin: Embassy Paris (25 February 2005), Classification: Confidential.

82 *IRNA* (7 June 2005) BBC Monitoring.

83 See *Tehran Times* (29 June 2005) BBC Monitoring.

84 Disclosed US Diplomatic Cable, *European Security Strategy in Context* (5 January 2004) published on website http://wikileaks.org/cable/2004/01/04BRUSSELS14.html (website accessed 25 October 2012).

85 See Tytti Erästö 'Transatlantic diplomacy in the Iranian nuclear issue – helping to build trust?' *European Security* 20, 3 (2001), pp. 405–430.

86 Disclosed US Diplomatic Cable, *Engaging the EU on the Middle East in 2005* (10 December 2004) published on website www.cablegatesearch.net/cable. php?id=04BRUSSELS5221 (website accessed 28 October 2012).

87 Disclosed US Diplomatic Cable, *European Security Strategy in Context.*

88 Disclosed US Diplomatic Cable, *Engaging the EU on the Middle East in 2005.*

89 FCO officials told US officials that, as a result, the British government was 'reasonably comfortable that member states would support referral to the UNSC if the EU-3 talks break down', Disclosed US Diplomatic Cable, *UK Plans for its EU Presidency: Middle East Issues* (16 June 2005) published on website www.cablegatesearch.net/ cable.php?id=05BRUSSELS2339 (website accessed 29 October 2012).

3 The Arc of Extremism: Amhmadinejad, the EU-3 and the Bush administration (2005–2007)

1 Disclosed US Diplomatic Cable, *EU Resumes Trade, Political Negotiations With Iran* (19 January 2005) published on website http://wikileaks.org/cable/2005/01/ 05BRUSSELS212.html (website accessed 10 June 2012).

2 Mohamed El Baradei, *The Age of Deception: Nuclear Diplomacy in Treacherous Times* (New York: Metropolitan Books, 2011), p. 142.

3 Ibid.

4 Disclosed US Diplomatic Cable, *Iran-EU-3: February 24 Meeting Between French President Chirac and Iranian Nuclear Negotiator Hassan Ruhani* (25 Feburary 2005) published on website www.cablegatesearch.net/cable.php?id=05PARIS1225 (website accessed 10 June 2012).

5 Ibid.

6 Seyed Hossein Mousavian, *The Iranian Nuclear Crisis: A Memoir* (Washington, DC: Carnegie Endowment for International Peace, 2012), p. 162.

7 Ibid.

8 Ibid.

9 Arms Control Association, 'History of official proposals on the Iranian nuclear issue', www.armscontrol.org/pdf/20050323_Iran_Proposal_Steering_Cmte.pdf; (website accessed 15 August 2012).

10 A cable states that the Italian FM official also refused to attend a visit to the Isfahan uranium conversion facility (UCF) and a zirconium production plant on the grounds that it would be misused for propaganda purposes as he was the only official from an EU country. Disclosed US Diplomatic Cable, *Iran Hosts Conference March 5–6 to Show its Nuclear Program is Irreversible* (18 March 2005) published on website www.cablegatesearch.net/cable.php?id=05PARIS1834 (website accessed 11 June 2012).

11 El Baradei, *The Age of Deception: Nuclear Diplomacy in Treacherous Times*, p. 142.

12 Disclosed US Diplomatic Cable, *REF05DUBLIN321, Irish Response to Demarches on March 16 GAERC*, Origin: Embassy Dublin (15 March 2005), Classification: Confidential.

13 Seyed Hossein Mousavian, *The Iranian Nuclear Crisis: A Memoir*, p. 168.

14 Bill Samii, 'Iran: Tehran opposes US pro-democracy initiatives', Radio Free Europe (22 April 2005); Heinrich Böll Stiftung, *Iran-Report Nr.04/2005*, p. 9.

15 Seyed Hossein Mousavian, *The Iranian Nuclear Crisis: A Memoir*, p. 168.

16 Arms Control Association, 'History of official proposals on the Iranian nuclear

issue', www.armscontrol.org/factsheets/Iran_Nuclear_Proposals (website accessed 30 August 2012).

17 Seyed Hossein Mousavian, *The Iranian Nuclear Crisis: A Memoir*, p. 169.

18 Disclosed US Diplomatic Cable, *Iran EU-3 Letter Warns Tehran Against Changes to Voluntary Suspension* (12 May 2005) published on website http://wikileaks.org/cable/2005/05/05PARIS3234.html (website accessed 12 June 2012).

19 Ibid.

20 Disclosed US Diplomatic Cable, *Undersecretary May 13 Discussions in Rome* (1 June 2005) published on website http://wikileaks.org/cable/2005/06/05ROME1859.html (website accessed 12 June 2012).

21 See political analysis by US Consulate in Dubai, citing excerpts of a pro-Rafsanjani election booklet; Disclosed US Diplomatic Cable, *Rafsanjani Vs. Qualibaf?* (19 April 2005) published on website www.cablegatesearch.net/cable.php?id=05 DUBAI1753 (website accessed 18 June 2012).

22 Disclosed US Diplomatic Cable, *Cheney's Visit, Comments on Iran and Democracy Earn Blanket Coverage in Local Press* (18 June 2005) published on website www.cablegatesearch.net/cable.php?id=05KUWAIT2900 (website accessed 19 June 2012).

23 Disclosed US Diplomatic Cable, *FM Fischer on Iran* (1 July 2005) published on website www.cablegatesearch.net/cable.php?id=05BERLIN2235&version=1314919 461 (website accessed 19 June 2012).

24 While many EU governments shared US concerns about legitimacy, it was noted that Ahmadinejad's margin of victory in the second round of voting was substantial. Disclosed US Diplomatic Cable, *Irish Reponse to Pre-GAERC Demarche* (15 July 2005) published on website www.cablegatesearch.net/cable.php?id=05DUBLIN884 (website accessed 27 June 2012).

25 Arms Control Association, 'History of official proposals on the Iranian nuclear issue', www.armscontrol.org/factsheets/Iran_Nuclear_Proposals; 'Message from Dr Rohani to E3/EU ministers July 18, 2005', www.armscontrol.org/pdf/20050718_ Iran_Rowhani_EU3.pdf (website accessed 1 September 2012).

26 Cited from Seyed Hossein Mousavian, *The Iranian Nuclear Crisis: A Memoir*, p. 172.

27 Ibid, p. 173.

28 Disclosed US Diplomatic Cable, *EU Political Directors Troika* (13 July 2005) published on website www.cablegatesearch.net/cable.php?id=05BRUSSELS2748 (website accessed 28 June 2012).

29 Ibid.; Disclosed US Diplomatic Cable, *Responses to EU-3 Requests – France* (28 July 2005) published on website www.cablegatesearch.net/cable.php?id=05PARIS 5214 (website accessed 5 July 2012).

30 See communication between the US government and the EU-3 on the removal of the seals by Iranian authorities, Disclosed US Diplomatic Cable, *Iran/EU-3 Letter from US to PolDirs* (20 July 2005) published on website www.cablegatesearch.net/cable. php?id=05PARIS5032 (website accessed 6 July 2012).

31 House of Commons, Foreign Affairs Select Committee, *Global Security: Iran – Fifth Report of Session 2007–2008 (HC 142)* (2 March 2008), p. 16.

32 IAEA Board of Governors, 'Implementation of the NPT Safeguards Agreement in the Islamic Republic of Iran and related Board resolutions. Resolution adopted on 11 August 2005', *GOV/2005/64* (11 August 2005), www.iaea.org/Publications/Documents/Board/2005/gov2005-64.pdf (website accessed 5 February 2013).

33 www.armscontrol.org/factsheets/Iran_Nuclear_Proposals; see also www.armscontrol.org/pdf/20050805_Iran_EU3_Proposal.pdf.

34 El Baradei, *The Age of Deception: Nuclear Diplomacy in Treacherous Times*, p. 144.

35 House of Commons, Foreign Affairs Select Committee, *Global Security: Iran – Fifth Report of Session 2007–2008 (HC 142)*, p. 17.

36 IRNA (10 August 2005), BBC Monitoring.
37 House of Commons, Foreign Affairs Select Committee, *Global Security: Iran – Fifth Report of Session 2007–2008 (HC 142)*, p. 17.
38 Seyed Hossein Mousavian, 'Iran and the West: the path to nuclear deadlock', *Global Dialogue* 8, 1–2 (Winter/Spring 2006), Nuclear Perils issue.
39 House of Commons Select Committee on Foreign Affairs *Written Evidence Session 2007–08 Foreign Affairs Committee Publication* (20 February 2008), www.publications.parliament.uk/pa/cm200708/cmselect/cmfaff/142/142we07.htm   (website accessed 1 November 2012).
40 Communication dated 2 February 2006 received from the Permanent Mission of the Islamic Republic of Iran to the Agency, IAEA INFCIRC/666 www.iaea.org/Publications/Documents/Infcircs/2006/infcirc666.pdf (website accessed 8 July 2012).
41 E'temad website (6 February, 2006), BBC Monitoring.
42 Robert O. Freedom, 'Russia, Iran, and the nuclear question: the Putin record', *Jerusalem Viewpoints No, 544* (6 Tamuz 5766/2 July 2006), Jerusalem Centre for Public Affairs, http://jcpa.org/jl/vp544.htm (website accessed 1 September 2012).
43 Disclosed US Diplomatic Cable, *Russian Ambassador Argues Russia Can't Support Iran Sanctions Because of Possible Iranian Retaliatory Moves* (14 November 2005) published on website www.cablegatesearch.net/cable.php?id=05ALGIERS2292 (website accessed 9 July 2012).
44 Disclosed US Diplomatic Cable, *Security Council Secretary on Larijani Talks* (25 January 2006) published on website www.cablegatesearch.net/cable.php?id= 06MOSCOW754 (website accessed 8 July 2012).
45 Ibid.
46 Ibid.
47 Ibid.
48 John Parker, 'Russia and the Iranian nuclear program: reply or breakthrough?' *Institute for National Strategic Studies, Strategic Perspectives No. 9* (March 2012), p. 4.
49 See TAR-TASS News Agency (9 January 2006); Ekho Moskvy Radio (9 January 2006), BBC Monitoring.
50 Farideh Farhi, 'Iran's national security and nuclear diplomacy: an insider's take' (7 August 2012), *LobeLog Foreign Policy*, www.lobelog.com/irans-national-security-and-nuclear-diplomacy-an-insiders-take/ (website accessed 28 September 2012).
51 House of Commons, Foreign Affairs Select Committee, *Minutes of Evidence* (8 February 2006) Session 2005–2006, www.publications.parliament.uk/pa/cm200506/cmselect/cmfaff/904/6020803.htm (website accessed 5 October 2012).
52 Disclosed US Diplomatic Cable, *US-EU-Canada Discussions of Iran* (3 November 2005) published on website www.cablegatesearch.net/cable.php?id=05OTTAWA32 83&version=1314919461 (website accessed 8 July 2012).
53 Disclosed US Diplomatic Cable, *French on January 30 GAERC: Hamas, Iran, Iraq, Belarus, Balkans* (17 January 2006) published on website www.cablegatesearch.net/cable.php?id=06PARIS535 (website accessed 12 July 2012).
54 Disclosed US Diplomatic Cable, *Iranian Government Reacts to IAEA Vote* (5 February 2006) published on website http://wikileaks.org/cable/2006/02/06DUBAI523.html (website accessed 12 July 2012).
55 IAEA Board of Governors, 'Implementation of the NPT Safeguards Agreement in the Islamic Republic of Iran', *GOV/2006/53* (31 August 2006).
56 Barbara Slavin, 'Watching Iran – how the Wikileaks disclosures could put a sweeping US effort to monitor the Islamic Republic in jeopardy', *Foreign Policy* (6 December 2010), www.foreignpolicy.com/articles/2010/12/06/watching_iran (website accessed 12 October 2012).
57 As noted in French editorials, see Disclosed US Diplomatic Cable, *Media Reaction Report – US Diplomacy – Iran Paris – Monday* (19 June 2006) published on website http://wikileaks.org/cable/2006/06/06PARIS4183.html (website accessed 13 July

2012). In a private meeting between Foreign Minister Mottaki and the Sultan of Oman on 5 June, Mottaki indicated that his government 'had paid careful attention to Condoleezza Rice's May 31 interview on CNN and found the language she used to be favorable'. Disclosed US Diplomatic Cable, *Readout on Sultan's June 5 Meeting with Iran FM* (6 June 2006) published on website http://wikileaks.org/cable/2006/06/06MUSCAT904.html (website accessed 12 July 2012).

58 See Glenn Kessler, 'Six powers reach accord on Iran plan', *Washington Post*, www.washingtonpost.com/wp-dyn/content/article/2006/06/01/AR2006060100363.html (website accessed 1 April 2012).

59 Council of the European Union, Elements of a Proposal to Iran, S202/06 as approved on 1 June 2006 at the meeting in Vienna of China, France, Germany, the Russian Federation, the United Kingdom, the United States of America and the European Union, www.consilium.europa.eu/ueDocs/cms_Data/docs/pressdata/en/reports/90569.pdf (website accessed 12 October 2012).

60 House of Commons, Select Committee on Foreign Affairs, *Inquiry: Global Security – Iran Memorandum by the Foreign and Commonwealth Office Session 2006–2007* (17 October 2007), www.publications.parliament.uk/pa/cm200607/cmselect/cmfaff/memo/496/ucm202.htm (website accessed 12 October 2012).

61 ISIS, 'Nuclear Iran – documents: Islamic Republic of Iran's response to the package presented on June 6, 2006', http://isis-online.org/publications/iran/responsetext.pdf (website accessed 12 October 2012).

62 Disclosed US Diplomatic Cable, *IAEA/Iran 'Like Minded' Discuss DG Report* (6 September 2006) published on website http://wikileaks.org/cable/2006/09/06UNVIEVIENNA659.html (website accessed 17 July 2012).

63 Disclosed US Diplomatic Cable, *Possible Iran Scenarios Leading Up to September 11 BOG* (21 August 2006) published on website http://wikileaks.org/cable/2006/08/06UNVIEVIENNA626.html (website accessed 18 July 2012).

64 The report noted Iran's ongoing P1 and P2 centrifuges programs, outstanding questions on plutonium experiments and a myriad of transparency questions on ongoing research and construction IAEA, *Implementation of the NPT Safeguards Agreement in the Islamic Republic of Iran Report by the Director General*, GOV/2006/38 (8 June 2006) www.iaea.org/Publications/Documents/Board/2006/gov2006-38.pdf (website accessed 26 July 2012).

65 As urged by El Baradei during a meeting with the Slovenian Prime Minister in August. Disclosed US Diplomatic Cable, *Demarche Delivered, EU Foreign Ministers and Iran* (31 August 2006) published on website www.cablegatesearch.net/cable.php?id=06LJUBLJANA563 (website accessed 24 July 2012).

66 Disclosed US Diplomatic Cable, *IAEA/Iran 'Like Minded' Discuss DG Report.*

67 Ibid.

68 Mohamed El Baradei, *The Age of Deception: Nuclear Diplomacy in Treacherous Times*, p. 204.

69 Disclosed US Diplomatic Cable, *September GAERC – Finnish Presidency Views* (14 September 2006) published on website http://wikileaks.org/cable/2006/09/ 06HELSINKI936.html (website accessed 20 July 2012). To Iran-watchers in the US State Department, public statements by President Ahmadinejad and Foreign Minister Mottaki in New York in September initially appeared to be laying the groundwork for the acceptance of the suspension contingency by stressing the temporary nature of any such action. 'President Ahmadinejad said that Iran is willing to negotiate under undefined fair and just conditions and Foreign Minister Mottaki said that Iran is currently seeking a way to make a balance between its rights and its commitments.' Disclosed US Diplomatic Cable, *Iran Hinting At Temporary Suspension* (16 September 2006) published on website www.cablegatesearch.net/cable.php?id=06DUBAI6065 (website accessed 21 July 2012).

70 The Russian representative saw 'virtue' in the drawing out of the dialogue with the

Iranians as, according to his view, this 'led to nuances within the ruling circles in Iran and a better understanding of the international community's position'. Calling Larijani a 'good interlocutor' who was not resisting a solution, the Russian official thought that prolonged dialogue would help Larijani 'bring others around within the government, while simultaneously revealing publicly the differences between competing actors'. Disclosed US Diplomatic Cable, *Russian Security Council Secretary on Iran, Frozen Conflicts, NATO, Ukraine, Boeing* (19 September 2006) published on website www.cablegatesearch.net/cable.php?id=06MOSCOW10439 (website accessed 24 July 2012).

71 Disclosed US Diplomatic Cable, *U/S with DFM on Iran, Afghanistan, India, Burma and UN Issues* (20 November 2006) published on website http://wikileaks.org/cable/2006/11/06TOKYO6635.html (website accessed 28 July 2012).

72 See discussions between Italian and Russian officials, Disclosed US Diplomatic Cable, *X Discusses Iran, Lebanon and Syria with Italians* (19 September 2006) published on website www.cablegatesearch.net/cable.php?id=06ROME2637 (website accessed 28. The Chinese government agreed with the United States that Iran needed to be penalized for its behaviour but stressed that the 'penalty should fit the crime'. Disclosed US Diplomatic Cable, *PRC Supports UNSC Action on Iran Differs on Scope* (20 November 2006) published on website www.cablegatesearch.net/cable.php?id=06BEIJING23933 (website accessed 28 July 2012).

73 UN Security Council, *Resolution 1737 (2006) S/RES/1737/2006* (27 December 2006), adopted by the Security Council at its 5612th meeting, on 23 December 2006, www.iaea.org/newscenter/focus/iaeairan/unsc_res1737-2006.pdf (link accessed 1 November 2012).

74 IRNA (27 December 2006), BBC Monitoring; Out of 203 present *Majlis* Deputies, 161 voted in favour of the bill, with fifteen undecided and fifteen against; Iranian Farhang Radio website (27 December 2006), BBC Monitoring.

75 The Egyptian President rebutted Ahmadinejad following his statement about being 'a nuclear country' saying that,

> nuclear states are only those that have military nuclear capabilities [...] the possession by some countries of peaceful nuclear technology or some of stages of the nuclear cycle or carrying out some peaceful nuclear activities does not mean by any means that it can call itself a nuclear state.
> Egypt Slams Iranian President, *Fox News* (25 December 2006) www.foxnews.com/printer_friendly_wires/2006Dec25/0,4675,EgyptIranNuclear,00.html (website accessed 1 August 2012).

76 By February 2007, Iran had informed the IAEA that two 164-machine cascades were installed at the facility in Natanz and were operating under vacuum; see House of Commons Select Committee on Foreign Affairs, *Written Evidence Session 2007–08, Foreign Affairs Committee Publication* (20 February 2008) www.publications.parliament.uk/pa/cm200708/cmselect/cmfaff/142/142we07.htm (website accessed 1 November 2012). During a February 2007 meeting between Italian Prime Minister Prodi and senior Italian FM officials, it appeared to the Italians that the Iranians were looking for a way out of the nuclear impasse, but were seeking a resolution, which would allow them to save face. As Larijani offered to stop enrichment that was in place (at 300 gas centrifuges as opposed to the stated 3,000) if the nuclear file was taken out of the UN Security Council and returned to the IAEA, the Italians reiterated that the resolution 'allows no enrichment, no nuclear industry'. Larijani presented a *fait accompli* and said that if the West's concern was about Iran mastering the technology it was too late, as it already had. Larijani reportedly asked Prodi: 'what they were supposed to do? Get amnesia?' Disclosed US Diplomatic Cable, *Larijani Visit to Italy: Looking for a Deal?* (26 February 2007) published on website http://wikileaks.org/cable/2007/02/07ROME386.html (website accessed 16 August 2012).

134 *Notes*

77 See Council of the European Union – *Iran Council Conclusions* (Brussels, 18 October 2006) www.consilium.europa.eu/uedocs/cmsUpload/st14149.en06.pdf (website accessed 1 November 2012).

78 Transcripts of the speech can be found at http://news.bbc.co.uk/2/hi/uk_news/politics/5236896.stm (website accessed 10 November 2012).

79 Ibid.

80 See assessment by German Embassy in Tehran and the Chinese Foreign Ministry, Disclosed US Diplomatic Cable, *Strong Domestic Pressure Driving Iran's Nuclear Program, China Looking After Economic Interests* (20 January 2006) published on website www.cablegatesearch.net/cable.php?id=06BEIJING1306 (website accessed 17 August 2012). Following a meeting between Iranian Foreign Minister Mottaki and the Dutch Foreign Minister on 7 December 2006, the desk officer for Iran at the Dutch Foreign Ministry told US officials that Mottaki's inflexibility on any of the issues raised by the Dutch 'confirmed Dutch suspicions that Mottaki and the Iranian Foreign Ministry in general exercised little real influence in Tehran'. Disclosed US Diplomatic Cable, *Ref ID: 06THE HAGUE2661, Netherlands/Iran: on Nukes, Middle East, and Human Rights* (27 December 2006) published on website www.cablegatesearch.net/cable.php?id=06THEHAGUE2661 (website accessed 18 August 2012).

81 Jeremy Pressman, 'The United States and the Israel Hezbollah War', *Middle East Brief No. 13* (Brandeis University, Brown Centre for Middle East Studies, November 2006), www.brandeis.edu/crown/publications/meb/MEB13.pdf (website accessed 1 October 2012).

82 See statement by President Ahmadinejad *IRNA* (16 July) BBC Monitoring

83 See Simon Tisdali, 'Iran's secret plan for Summer Offensive to force US out of Iraq', *The Guardian* (22 May 2007) www.guardian.co.uk/world/2007/may/22/iraq.topstories3 (website accessed 19 April 2012).

84 Mohamed El Baradei, *The Age of Deception: Nuclear Diplomacy in Treacherous Times*, p. 201.

85 See David E. Sanger and Michael R. Gordon, 'Rice says Bush authorized Iranians' arrest in Iraq', *New York Times* (13 January 2007) www.nytimes.com/2007/01/13/world/middleeast/13strategy.html (website accessed 1 November 2012).

86 for Iranian activities in Iraq since 2003, see Sam Dagher, 'Leaks depict Iranian opposition in post-Saddam Iraq', *Wall Street Journal* (30 November 2010) http://online.wsj.com/article/SB10001424052748703994904575646911886138950.html?mod=WSJEUROPE_hpp_MIDDLESecondNews (website accessed 20 April 2013).

87 House of Commons, Foreign Affairs Committee Foreign Policy *Aspects of the Detention of Naval Personnel by the Islamic Republic of Iran, Sixth Report of Session, 2006–07 Report, together with Formal Minutes, Oral and Written Evidence Ordered by the House of Commons to be printed 17 July 2007 HC 880 Incorporating HC 496–i/ii (2006–07)*, www.publications.parliament.uk/pa/cm200607/cmselect/cmfaff/880/880.pdf (website accessed 5 February 2013).

88 Barbara Slavin, 'US held Iranians as hostages officials say', *Washington Times* (15 July 2009), www.washingtontimes.com/news/2009/jul/15/iranians-held-by-us-were-envoys/#ixzz2AIf5m35W (website accessed 20 October 2012).

89 House of Commons, Foreign Affairs Committee Foreign Policy, *Aspects of the Detention of Naval Personnel by the Islamic Republic of Iran, Sixth Report of Session.*

90 Ibid.

91 In its report, the Foreign Affairs Committee stated that no evidence was made available to them that any deal was reached between the British government and Iran over the release of the detainees; ibid.

92 According to the account of the Omani Foreign Minister, who had been in correspondence with Larijani, moderates in Iran took charge of the crisis (heralded by Larijani himself) as they feared that

any attempt to capitalize on the British hostages would redound negatively, likely earn widespread condemnation in the international community, cast Iran in worse political light vis-à-vis the UK, and ultimately fail to produce positive results. In the end, the moderates prevailed when even the Supreme Leader saw the futility of prolonging the crisis.

(Disclosed US Diplomatic Cable, *Omani Foreign Minister Claims Iranian President Overruled in Release of British Captives; Renewed Efforts to Resolve Standoff with UNSC* (16 April 2007) published on website www.cablegatesearch. net/cable.php?id=07MUSCAT359&version=1292153820) (website accessed 2 October 2012).

93 *The Guardian*, 'US embassy cables: Iranian reformist dismisses sailor crisis as "political stunt"' (10 December 2010) www.guardian.co.uk/world/us-embassy-cables-documents/104753 (website accessed 3 October 2012).

94 Bernd Kaussler, 'From engagement to containment: EU–Iran relations and the nuclear programme, 1992–2011', *Journal of Balkan and Near Eastern Studies* 14, 1 (March 2012), p. 62.

95 Statement made by H.E. Mr. Manouchehr Mottaki, Foreign Minister of the Islamic Republic of Iran before the United Nations Security Council (March 24 2007) www. un.int/iran/statements/securitycouncil/articles/Statement_by_H.E._Mr._Mottaki.pdf (website accessed 1 November 2012).

96 UN Security Council Resolution 1737 (2006) www.un.org/News/Press/docs/2006/ sc8928.doc.htm (website accessed 1 November 2012).

97 James Dobbins, 'Engaging Iran', *USIP – The Iran Primer*, http://iranprimer.usip. org/resource/engaging-iran (website accessed 25 October 2012). Following the August meeting, the US Ambassador to Iraq noted in a cable that the talks with the Iranians were not fruitful, saying that 'Iranian Ambassador Qomi accused the US of working with Al Qaeda and the Ba'athists. They want to create the appearance of cooperating without cooperating.' Disclosed US Diplomatic Cable, *Talabani Discusses Leadership Meeting, Iran Talks, Iraqiyya, Withdrawal, Barzani intractability* (9 August 2007) published on website http://wikileaks.org/cable/2007/08/ 07BAGHDAD2657.htm (website accessed 25 October 2012).

98 The Ambassador advised the US government that the international community's best tool to change Iranian behaviour was 'unanimity and uncertainty'. As for the trilateral talks, he saw Iranian officials to be on a very short leash and would be required to stick to talking points, but 'the questions and points the US raises will likely spark useful internal debate over their interests. The Iranian side will return to the next meeting with at least some responses'. Disclosed US Diplomatic Cable, *British Ambassador to Iran: Iran Sees Us as its Biggest Strategic Issue* (30 November 2007) published on website http://wikileaks.org/cable/2007/11/07 BAGHDAD3903.html (website accessed 25 October 2012).

99 Larijani called for a US withdrawal from Iraq and emphasized that Iran posed no threat to the region. He called upon Arab Gulf states to join with Iran to seek regional solutions for regional security problems. Concerning the nuclear programme, Larijani warned that if the US succeeded in limiting Iran's nuclear programme, Arab countries would face the same fate, saying that: 'They will allow you to have a power plant, but they will keep the fuel.' Disclosed US Diplomatic Cable, *Reaction to Larijani's Proposal for Gulf-Iran Alliance* (12 July 2007) published on website www.cablegatesearch.net/cable.php?id=06IRANRPODUBAI16 (website accessed 28 October 2012).

100 see Ariel Zircuinick, 'WikiLeaks reveals 5 Arab countries concerned about Iran', *The Christian Science Monitor*, www.csmonitor.com/World/Middle-East/2010/1129/ WikiLeaks-reveals-5-Arab-countries-concerned-about-Iran/Saudi-Arabia (website accessed 20 April 2013).

101 Disclosed US Diplomatic Cable, *GCC Advisor: Visit to Isfahan Nuclear Facility Confirms Suspicion; GCC More Aware of Iranian Threat* (11 October 2006) published on website www.cablegatesearch.net/cable.php?id=06KUWAIT4071 (website accessed 10 November 2012).

4 Bigger Sticks and Bigger Carrots: the 2008 Proposal

1 See the statement by the Swedish representative during a meeting with US and EU members of the Conference on Disarmament/UN and Non-Proliferation Working Groups, Disclosed US Diplomatic Cable, *US and EU-27 Hold Third Dialogue on Verification and Compliance* (4 June 2007) published on website http://wikileaks.org/cable/2007/07/07BRUSSELS2170.html (website accessed 28 October 2011).

2 The 2007 US National Intelligence Estimate (NIE) judged 'with high confidence' that Iran halted its nuclear weapon programme in the autumn of 2003, but assessed 'with moderate-to-high confidence' that Iran 'at a minimum is keeping open the option to develop nuclear weapons'. The joint assessment of US intelligence agencies also assessed 'with moderate confidence that Iran probably would use covert facilities – rather than its declared nuclear sites – for the production of highly enriched uranium [HEU] for a weapon'. The NIE further concluded that Iran was unlikely to be 'capable of producing enough HEU for a weapon in late 2009, but [even that] was considered "highly unlikely"'. It judged with 'moderate confidence' that Iran would have enough HEU during the 2010–2015 timeframe; National Intelligence Council, *National Intelligence Estimate – Iran: Nuclear Intentions and Capabilities* (November 2007), pp. 6–9.

3 Disclosed US Diplomatic Cable, *French Presidency Strategic Adviser Discusses Iran's Nuclear Program* (13 December 2007) published on website www.cablegatesearch.net/cable.php?id=07PARIS4750 (website accessed 29 October 2011).

4 Disclosed US Diplomatic Cable, *US National Intelligence Estimate on Iran's Nuclear Program: UK Response* (12 April 2007) posted on *The Telegraph* (4 February 2011) www.telegraph.co.uk/news/wikileaks-files/london-wikileaks/8304937/U.S.-NATIONAL-INTELLIGENCE-ESTIMATE-ON-IRANS-NUCLEAR-PROGRAM-UK-RESPONSE.html (website accessed 29 October 2011).

5 Disclosed US Diplomatic Cable, *IAEA/Iran: UK and France Look Forward, DG to Meet Miliband* (21 December 2007) published on website www.cablegatesearch.net/cable.php?id=07UNVIEVIENNA778 (website accessed 15 December 2011).

6 Ibid.

7 Ibid.

8 IRNA (7 December 2007), BBC Monitoring.

9 Borujerdi further stated that

> this report will strengthen the positions of countries such as China and Russia, just as Al-Baradi's report did; and it will lead to the undermining of the stance of those countries pursuing policies contrary to the recommendations of this report in order to pass a third resolution [against Iran at the United Nations Security Council].
>
> (Quoted by the Islamic Republic of Iran News Network, 4 December; IRNA (4 December 2007), BBC Monitoring)

10 Disclosed US Diplomatic Cable, *Iran: the UK says EU Desire for Third UNSCR Means No Autonomous Measures Before March* (29 January 2008) posted on *The Telegraph*, www.telegraph.co.uk/news/wikileaks-files/london-wikileaks/8304960/IRAN-UK-SAYS-EU-DESIRE-FOR-THIRD-UNSCR-MEANS-NO-AUTONOMOUS-MEASURES-BEFORE-MARCH.html (website accessed 28 October 2011).

11 Disclosed US Diplomatic Cable, *El Bsradei on his Tehran Visit: sees Iranians as 'Relaxed' with 'Plausible' Answers* (18 January 2008) posted on *The Telegraph* (4

February 2011) www.telegraph.co.uk/news/wikileaks-files/london-wikileaks/8304957/EL-BARADEI-ON-HIS-TEHRAN-VISIT-SEES-IRANIANS-AS-RELAXED-WITH-PLAUSIBLE-ANSWERS.html (website accessed 28 October 2011).

12 Institute for Science and International Security, 'Briefing notes from February 2008 IAEA meeting regarding Iran's nuclear program' (11 April, 2008), www.isisnuclear-iran.org/assets/.../IAEA_Briefing_Weaponization.pdf (website accessed 9 December 2011).

13 Voice of the Islamic Republic of Iran (27 February 2008), BBC Monitoring.

14 Islamic Republic News Agency (28 February 2008).

15 During the Tehran Friday Prayer, Ayatollah Jannati declared:

> They [Americans] should be sorry for taking Iran's case to the UN Security Council under such circumstances, and issuing so many resolutions and sanctioning Iran. They are still thinking of adopting another resolution. Our people have an allegiance with their God, prophet and leader not to back down from their lawful positions.
> (Voice of the Islamic Republic of Iran (29 Feb 2008), BBC Monitoring)

16 Disclosed US Diplomatic Cable, *El Bsradei on his Tehran Visit: sees Iranians as 'Relaxed' with 'Plausible' Answers.*

17 Disclosed US Diplomatic Cable, *PDAS McNerney's October 24 Meeting at the Israel MFA on Iran: Situation in the IAEA and UNSC* (12 December 2007) posted on *The Telegraph* (2 February 2011) www.telegraph.co.uk/news/wikileaks-files/8314536/PDAS-MCNERNEYS-OCTOBER-24-MEETING-AT-THE-ISRAELI-MFA-ON-IRAN-SITATUATION-IN-THE-IAEA-AND-UNSC-CABLE-3-OF-5.html (website accessed 28 October 2011).

18 Ibid.

19 See Juan Cole, 'Lebanese press on Bush's Middle East Tour' (17 January 2008) posted on www.juancole.com/2008/01/lebanese-press-on-bushs-middle-east.html (website accessed 19 December 2011).

20 Joe Kay, 'Bush uses Abu Dhabi speech to escalate threats against Iran', *Tehran Times* (15 January 2008).

21 The Iranian Foreign and Defence Ministries dismissed the footage released by the US Department of Defence as propaganda. IRGC Commander Ali Fadavi referred to a routine incident in which Iranian patrol boats took control of the entry and exit of vessels in the Persian Gulf when they witnessed three US warships entering the waters of the region. The Iranian government insisted that their patrol's behaviour was in accordance with the 1982 Law of the Sea Convention concerning straits. The IRGC commander stressed that the release of the footage by the Pentagon had to be seen within the context of Bush's visit to the region and was

> in line with America's discriminative objectives against Iran. We assure you that nothing unusual has happened on that day and like any other occasion it was a control and identification for the entering and exiting vessels in the Strait of Hormuz.
> (Fars News Agency (7 January 2008; 9 January 2008; 10 January 2008))

See also IRNA and ISNA (8 January 2008), BBC Monitoring. According to an Iranian contact in the UK, Ali Fadavi independently planned and led the IRGC feint against US Navy warships. According to the contact, Ali Fadavi himself was 'the voice on the bridge' which made English-language contact with the bridge of US warships. The diplomatic cable from the US Embassy reads:

> Fadavi is said to have a reputation for brilliance and ideological extremism, and to be professionally jealous of his immediate superior, IRGC (Naval) commander Abbas Safari. After the incident, Fadavi was reportedly taken by former overall IRGC commander Rahim Safavi to Tehran to brief Supreme Leader Khamenei.

This account of what prompted the IRGC to confront US Navy ships in the Straits, if true, may suggest that senior IRGC officers enjoy significant de facto autonomy and may in future be willing to stage further dangerous provocations of US forces, perhaps without prior national-level guidance from Tehran.

(Disclosed US Diplomatic Cable, *Hormuz Straits Incident. Allegedly and IRGC Initiative* (15 January 2008) posted on *The Telegraph* (4 February 2012) www. telegraph.co.uk/news/wikileaks-files/london-wikileaks/8304955/HORMUZ-STRAITS-INCIDENT-ALLEGEDLY-AN-IRGC-INITIATIVE.html) (website accessed 28 October 2011).

22 MENAS, *Iran Strategic Focus* 4, 1 (January, 2008), p. 3.
23 The Russian Ambassador to the UN publicly stated that Russia would only back economic sanctions against Iran which would affect proliferation efforts, and reiterated that this would not affect Iran's normal economic relations; ITAR-TASS News Agency (27 February 2008), BBC Monitoring.
24 UN Security Council, *Resolution 1803 (2008) Adopted by the Security Council at its 5848th meeting, on 3 March 2008 S/RES/1803 (2008),* pp. 2–5.
25 Italy was considered by the US Treasury to be playing an 'unconstructive role within the EU and [was] slowing down EU efforts to establish autonomous sanctions'. Cameron expressed concern that other EU member states were not stopping their export credits to Iran. Disclosed US Diplomatic Cable, *Depsec Discusses Iran Sanctions, US Economy with Conservative Leader Cameron* (18 March 2008) posted on *The Telegraph* (4 February 2011) www.telegraph.co.uk/news/wikileaks-files/london-wikileaks/8304997/DEPSEC-TREASURY-DISCUSES-IRAN-SANCTIONS-U.S.-ECONOMY-WITH-CONSERVATIVE-PARTY-LEADER-CAMERON.html (website accessed 28 October 2011).
26 On 21 April 2007, OMV of Austria and NIOC, Petropas and NIGEC signed several contracts to participate in the development of gas liquefaction projects in Iran and to purchase LNG from the same scheme in Iran's South Pars gas field. MENAS, *Iran Strategic Focus* 3, 5 (May 2008), p. 7.
27 Iran reformist news outlets were quick to criticize the government's 'failed oil and gas policy', citing Iran's dependence on foreign technology in extracting gas in the South Pars field. See E'temad-e Melli (13 July 2008), BBC Monitoring.
28 On 21 May 2008, Foreign Minister Manuchehr Mottaki said Iran–China trade ties had increased noticeably in the previous three years from US$10 billion dollars annually to US$20 billion; IRNA (21 May 2008), BBC Monitoring.
29 Under the agreement, CNOOC is to purchase North Pars output for twenty-five years in the form of liquefied natural gas; Fars News Agency website (2 April 2008), BBC Monitoring.
30 This is reflected in the Iranian Oil Ministry's decision to award phases 19 and 20–21 to local companies rather than Russians; MENAS, *Iran Strategic Focus* 7, 7 (July 2008), p. 10.
31 Ibid.
32 Disclosed US Diplomatic Cable, *Iranian Importers/Exporters: Having More Problems With Financing Blame USG-Led Financial Measure* (3 November 2008) posted on *The Telegraph* (4 February 2011) www.telegraph.co.uk/news/wikileaks-files/london-wikileaks/8304784/IRANIAN-IMPORTERSEXPORTERS-HAVING-MORE-PROBLEMS-WITH-FINANCING-BLAME-USG-LED-FINANCIAL-MEASURES.html (website accessed 28 October 2011).
33 Speaking at the second Iran International Oil Refining Forum, Iranian Foreign Minister Manouchehr Mottaki said since Pakistan faced significant energy needs, his government was ready to provide security for the IPI gas pipeline project and called for its immediate implementation; Islamic Republic News Agency website (11 Oct 2008), BBC Monitoring.

34 MENAS, *Iran Strategic Focus* 4, 10 (October 2008), pp. 7–8; MENAS, *Iran Strategic Focus* 3, 7 (July 2007), pp. 7–8.

35 In a closed meeting in December 2007 between the US Embassy in Israel and Israeli officials, a Mossad representative expressed concern that the Nabucco Project was being used by Iran as a means to drive a wedge between Europe and the United States. In the meeting the US representatives were urged to convince the Europeans not to allow Iran to participate in the project. Disclosed US Diplomatic Cable, *PDAS McNerney's October 24 Discussion on Counter Proliferation, Finance and Iran with the Israeli MFA* (13 December 2007) posted on *The Telegraph* (2 February 2011) www. telegraph.co.uk/news/wikileaks-files/iran-wikileaks/8299141/PDAS-MCNERNEYS-OCTOBER-24-DISCUSSIONS-ON-COUNTERPROLIFERATION-FINANCE-AND-IRAN-WITH-THE-ISRAELI-MFA-CABLE-4-OF-5.html (website accessed 25 October 2011).

36 Despite sanctions and US efforts to discourage economic investments in the oil and gas sector, Russia's Gazprom announced on 20 February 2008 that it was seeking several joint developments in the South Pars and Kish gas fields and other oil production projects. On 12 March, Vietnam's Petro Vietnam and the National Iranian Oil Company (NIOC) signed a $115 million contract (over a period of four years) for developing the onshore Danan block. The next day, Indonesia's Pertamina signed a €300 million contract to establish a urea-ammonia petrochemical complex in southern Iran. NIOC continued to woo Chinese investors over various investments and ventures, including the North Pars gas field and a $2 billion deal signed in December 2007 with CNOOC. MENAS, *Iran Strategic Focus* 4, 3 (March, 2008), pp. 8–10; MENAS, *Iran Strategic Focus*, 4, 4 (April, 2008), pp. 6–9.

37 Farhang-e Ashti website (9 November 2008), BBC Monitoring.

38 Mehr News Agency (13 August, 2008), BBC Monitoring.

39 In a report by Iran's Central Bank, the number of people living below the poverty line had significantly increased since 2007. Farhang-e Ashti website (3 August 2008).

40 Mardom-Salari website (28 April 2008), BBC Monitoring; MENAS, *Iran Strategic Focus* 4, 5 (May, 2008), p. 1.

41 See Rowhani's speech at the Centre for Strategic Studies in Tehran (linked to the Expediency Council); Heinrich Böll Stiftung, *Iran Report Nr.03–2008*, pp. 5–6.

42 MENAS, *Iran Strategic Focus* 4, 3 (March, 2008), pp. 1–3; A visit by Mayor Ghalibaf to Japan was closely watched by the US State Department, which interpreted his rhetoric and potential policy as president as possibly being 'marginally less confrontational'. The Japanese government considered him an 'impressive and viable candidate'. Disclosed US Diplomatic Cable, *Ref ID: 08LONDON2789 Iran: Further Readout on Ghalibaf Visit to Japan* (4 November 2008), Destination: 08TOKYO2954.

43 Disclosed US Diplomatic Cable, *Demarche to UK on Iran's Parliamentary Elections* (13 March 2008) posted on *The Telegraph* (4 February 2011) www.telegraph. co.uk/news/wikileaks-files/london-wikileaks/8304991/DEMARCHE-TO-UK-ON-IRANS-PARLIAMENTARY-ELECTIONS.html (website accessed 25 October 2011).

44 Disclosed US Diplomatic Cable, *Iran: Foreign Secretary Says UK to Lead Financial Pressure on Iran* (13 May 2008) posted on *The Guardian* (13 December 2010) www.guardian.co.uk/world/us-embassy-cables-documents/155309

45 Disclosed US Diplomatic Cable, *Iranian Banks in London: UK Plans and Concerns* (14 May 2008) posted on *The Telegraph* (4 February 2011) www.telegraph.co.uk/ news/wikileaks-files/london-wikileaks/8299147/IRANIAN-BANKING-IN-LONDON-UK-PLANS-AND-CONCERNS.html (website accessed 25 October 2011).

46 Ibid. The FSA also expressed concerns over using classified evidence, as it would eventually become part of the public record if challenged by Iranian authorities in a British court.

47 Disclosed US Diplomatic Cable, *International Security Discussion with HMG* (3 June 2008) posted on *The Telegraph* (4 February 2011) www.telegraph.co.uk/news/wikileaks-files/london-wikileaks/8305077/INTERNATIONAL-SECURITY-DISCUSSIONS-WITH-HMG.html (website accessed 25 October 2011).
48 A FCO official also noted that the British strategy was to get agreement to the first two steps before attempting the much more controversial wider measures, which he expected to be a 'hell of a slog unless the Iranians do something really stupid'; ibid.
49 Ibid.
50 Disclosed US Diplomatic Cable, *U/S Jeffrey and A/S O'Brien Press UK on Iranian Banks* (9 June 2008) posted on *The Telegraph* (4 February 2011) www.telegraph.co.uk/news/wikileaks-files/london-wikileaks/8299149/US-JEFFERY-AND-AS-OBRIEN-PRESS-UK-ON-IRANIAN-BANKS.html (website accessed 21 October 2011).
51 MENAS, *Iran Strategic Focus* 4, 4 (April 2008), p. 1. In a December 2007 meeting, US Embassy officials in London met with an alleged ex-IRGC member who claimed to have been a long-term operative for the IRGC and provided in-depth details about Iran destabilizing activities in Iraq. He offered to serve as interlocutor of 'those inside Iran'. US officials could not verify the authenticity of his account and had no interest in further contact or engagement with him. Disclosed US Diplomatic Cable, *Ex-IRGC Member Lists Quds Force Fronts in Iraq, Claims to Represent Those Inside*, posted on *The Telegraph* (4 February 2011) www.telegraph.co.uk/news/wikileaks-files/london-wikileaks/8304942/IRAN-ALLEGED-EX-IRGC-MEMBER-LISTS-QUDS-FORCE-FRONTS-IN-IRAQ-CLAIMS-TO-REPRESENT-THOSE-INSIDE.html (website accessed 21 October 2011).
52 Joint letter by the EU-3+3 to Iranian Foreign Minister Mottaki (14 June 2008), www.fco.gov.uk/en/news/latest-news/?view=News&id=3772654 (website accessed 1 September 2011).
53 MENAS, *Iran Strategic Focus* 4, 1 (June 2008), p. 1.
54 Ibid.
55 According to Solana, his request to meet with Larijani and the Supreme Leader's Foreign Policy Adviser were rejected on instructions from President Ahmadinejad. In an apparent snub based on the fact that the EU lacked a Foreign Minister, the Iranian government refused to send a Foreign Minister-level representative to greet Solana at the airport. Instead, the German Ambassador welcomed him. US Disclosed Diplomatic Cable, *EU Readout of Solana Visit to Tehran* (28 December 2007) published on website www.telegraph.co.uk/news/wikileaks-files/london-wikileaks/8304942/IRAN-ALLEGED-EX-IRGC-MEMBER-LISTS-QUDS-FORCE-FRONTS-IN-IRAQ-CLAIMS-TO-REPRESENT-THOSE-INSIDE.html (website accessed 21 October 2011).
56 MENAS, *Iran Strategic Focus* 4, 2 (February, 2008), p. 2.
57 Disclosed US Diplomatic Cable, *Iran Nuclear: UK Commons Report Will Call For Dropping Suspension, FCO Discounts Report's Impact*, posted on *The Telegraph* (4 February 2011) www.telegraph.co.uk/news/wikileaks-files/london-wikileaks/8299142/IRAN-NUCLEAR-UK-COMMONS-REPORT-WILL-CALL-FOR-DROPPING-SUSPENSION-FCO-DISCOUNTS-REPORTS-IMPACT.html (website accessed 21 October 2011). The published version of the 'Global Security–Iran' report by the House Foreign Select Committee stated on the suspension clause:

We conclude that it seems very unlikely that Iran will accept the demand that it suspend enrichment before substantive talks can begin. It feels it got little reward for its previous suspension, and its present Government has ramped up nationalist feeling on this issue. This stalemate is in no-one's interest but simply pressing for a resumption of Iran–US dialogue without an end to President Ahmadinejad's defiance of UN resolutions will strengthen him and dismay and weaken reformers. We recommend therefore that the Government urges the current US Administration to change its policy and begin to engage directly with Iran on its nuclear programme, as the absence of such engagement has deprived the international community of a significant diplomatic tool. The international community has made clear that if Iran suspends dual use enrichment it can expect cooperation on civilian nuclear power and Condoleezza Rice has said she will meet the Iranians 'any time, any place'. If this positive offer is accepted then it would become possible to make progress towards a solution.

(House of Commons Foreign Affairs Committee, *Global Security: Iran Fifth Report of Session 2007–08 HC 142*, Incorporating HC 496-i, ii, iii Session 2006–07, published on 2 March 2008, p. 5)

58 The proposal in May 2008 envisioned a comprehensive negotiation framework in the fields of political, economic, security and nuclear cooperation with the P5+1. It did not, however, address issues on enrichment or details on how it would resolve concern relating to the nuclear programme at large. For the letter see www.armscontrol.org/system/files/IranProposal20May2008.pdf (website accessed 1 January 2012).

59 Disclosed US Diplomatic Cable, *Iran: FCO Readout on Solana in Tehran and PM Brown's Statement on Iranian Banks* (17 June 2008) posted on *The Telegraph* (4 February 2011) www.telegraph.co.uk/news/wikileaks-files/london-wikileaks/8305098/IRAN-FCO-READOUT-ON-SOLANA-IN-TEHRAN-AND-PM-BROWNS-STATEMENT-ON-IRANIAN-BANKS.html (website accessed 21 October 2011).

60 Ibid.

61 Disclosed US Diplomatic Cable, *Iran: UK Expects a Fourth UNSC Will Be* Necessary (10 June 2008) posted on *The Telegraph* (4 February 2011 www.telegraph.co.uk/news/wikileaks-files/london-wikileaks/8305089/IRAN-UK-EXPECTS-A-FOURTH-UNSCR-WILL-BE-NECESSARY.html (website accessed 21 October 2011).

62 Ibid. The EU agreed to push back the designation date of Bank Melli to mid-or late June in order to avoid disrupting the delivery of the package and Iran's response to it. Disclosed US Diplomatic Cable, *Ref ID: 08LONDON1396, Iran: EU Bank Melli Designation Pushed to Mid/Late June; Date Will Hinge on Tehran's Response to P5 + 1 Package* (19 May 2008) posted on *The Telegraph* (4 February 2011) www.telegraph.co.uk/news/wikileaks-files/london-wikileaks/8305057/IRAN-EU-BANK-MELLI-DESIGNATION-PUSHED-TO-MIDLATE-JUNE-DATE-WILL-HINGE-ON-TEHRAN-RESPONSE-TO-P51-PACKAGE.html (website accessed 1 November 2011).

63 The fact that the British government wanted to coordinate its policies towards Iran with the US government rather than the EU during this period is particularly highlighted in the extradition case of former Iranian Ambassador to the UK, Nosratollah Tajik. In April 2008, a British court ruled that Nosratollah Tajik should be extradited to the United States in connection with charges that he conspired to illegally export night-vision weapons sights and military night-vision goggles from the United States to Iran. Tajik was Iran's Ambassador to Jordan from 1999 to 2003 and at the time was an honorary fellow at the University of Durham. While the FCO wanted to go ahead with the extradition to the United States, there was concern over a 'series of veiled threats' from the Iranian Foreign Ministry to the British Embassy. Conscious of a 'clear pattern of retribution against UK diplomatic personnel', the FCO asked for a low-key handling of the extradition case. Disclosed US Diplomatic Cable, *Iran: UK Intends to Go Forward on Tajik Extradition but Concerned about Safety of its Tehran Embassy*, posted on *The Telegraph* (4 February 2011) www.telegraph.co.uk/news/wikileaks-files/london-wikileaks/8305087/IRAN-UK-INTENDS-TO-GO-FORWARD-ON-TAJIK-EXTRADITION-BUT-CONCERNED-ABOUT-SAFETY-OF-ITS-TEHRAN-EMBASSY.html (website accessed 1 November 2011). FCO officials told the US Embassy in London that

although the European Court might at some point require some form of compensation from HMG if the court, eventually, were to find Tajik's extradition to have been improper, actually preventing the extradition is no longer a remedy Tajik has in the European Court … the UK is bound by its 2003 extradition statute and must deliver Tajik to USG authorities by June 11.

(Disclosed US Diplomatic Cable, *Ex-Ambassador Tajik: UK May Extradite As Soon As June 11* (2 June 2008) posted on *The Telegraph* (4 February 2011) www.telegraph.co.uk/news/wikileaks-files/london-wikileaks/8305076/IRANS-EX-AMBASSADOR-TAJIK-UK-MAY-EXTRADITE-AS-SOON-AS-JUNE-11.html) (website accessed 1 November 2011).

64 The British Treasury felt 'legally hamstrung' until sanctions against Melli and Saderat were in place. The US government appreciated that while some senior officials within the British government considered the measures as 'heavy-handed at times', both governmental agencies and private banks had started to engage in practices that limited the ability of Iranian banks to do business. Disclosed US Diplomatic Cable, *UK Measure to Stem Bank Melli's Asset Flight* (10 June 2008) posted on *The Telegraph* (4 February 2011) www.telegraph.co.uk/news/wikileaks-files/london-wikileaks/8299150/S-UK-MEASURES-TO-STEM-BANK-MELLIS-ASSET-FLIGHT.html (website accessed 1 November 2011).

65 MENAS, *Iran Strategic Focus* 4, 7 (July 2008), p. 4.

66 E'temad (28 July 2008), BBC Monitoring.

67 See Siyasat-e Ruz (16 October 2008); Fars News Agency (21 October 2008), BBC Monitoring.

68 For a copy of the non-paper see www.armscontrol.org/system/files/Iran_None_Paper_20080719.pdf.

69 Ibid.

70 Ibid.

71 Alan Cowell and William J. Broad, 'Iran reports missile test, drawing rebuke', *New York Times* (10 July 2008), www.nytimes.com/2008/07/10/world/asia/10iran.html (website accessed 10 July 2012); MENAS, *Iran Strategic Focus* 4, 7 (July 2008), pp. 1–2.

72 Ibid.

73 Peter Crail, 'Iran not receptive to revised nuclear proposal', *Arms Control Association* (September 2008), www.armscontrol.org/act/2008_09/IranProposal (website accessed 12 January 2012).

74 According to the hardline daily *Iran*:

America's readiness to take part in the negotiations and send one of its high-ranking officials to Geneva proves that America badly needs the success of these talks for domestic use and particularly in the run up to the presidential election. Burn's presence in the meetings cannot be seen as a tactical change, because America is forced to cross its red lines and enter direct talks with Iran and in a way has paved the way for a change of strategy in its relations with Iran.

(*Iran* (20 July 2008), BBC Monitoring)

See also Keyhan (21 July, 2008), BBC Monitoring.

75 MENAS, *Iran Strategic Focus* 4, 10 (October, 2008), pp. 2–3. Responding to a letter from the US Congress, Ali Larijani stated that the *Majlis* was scrutinizing the letters and an appropriate response because 'we need to know on which axis the talks are going to be held'; IRNA (1 December 2008), BBC Monitoring.

76 IAEA Board of Governors, 'Implementation of the NPT Safeguards Agreement and relevant provisions of Security Council resolutions 1737 (2006), 1747 (2007) and 1803 (2008) in the Islamic Republic of Iran – Report by the Director General', *GOV/2008/38* (15 September 2008).

77 Vision of the Islamic Republic of Iran, Network 1 (9 September 2008), BBC Monitoring.
78 MENAS, *Iran Strategic Focus* 4, 9 (September, 2008), p. 1.
79 In another speech in the same month, Khamenei stated that Muslim nations 'are among those condemned to following the West for ever and remaining their apprentices indefinitely'; Fars News Agency (29 September 2008), BBC Monitoring.
80 Mehr News Agency (30 November 2008). Reflecting the overall mindset among policymakers, Vice President Parviz Davudi felt vindicated that the continuation of enrichment only strengthened Iran's position. In his speech he said:

> some [foreign powers] had claimed that if Iran activates twenty centrifuges it would face a military attack. But today, although more than 5,000 centrifuges have been activated, there is no sign of attack and they have to recognize Iran together with the nuclear technology. Although the ill-wishers of the Iranian nation and government have tried very much to prevent Iran from acquiring the nuclear knowledge and technology, but they have failed thanks to God's grace.
>
> (Fars News Agency (30 November 2008), BBC Monitoring)

81 David Albright, Jacqueline Shire and Paul Brannan, 'IAEA report on Iran: enriched uranium output steady; centrifuge numbers expected to increase dramatically; Arak reactor verification blocked', *ISIS Issue Brief* (19 November 2008).
82 MENAS, *Iran Strategic Focus* 4, 9 (September, 2008), p. 1.
83 Saeed Barzin, 'Analysis: Iran dismisses UN nuclear resolution with little sense of triumph' (29 September 2008), BBC Monitoring.
84 Text of Jalili's letter to Solana regarding nuclear talks with Iran (October 11, 2008), www.iranreview.org/content/Documents/Text_of_Jalili_s_Letter_to_Solana_Regarding_Nuclear_Talks_with_Iran.htm (website accessed 5 February 2013).
85 Ibid.
86 MENAS, *Iran Strategic Focus*, 4, 10 (October 2008), p. 1.
87 Disclosed US Diplomatic Cable, *Ref ID: 08LONDON2702, UK Will Not Participate in Iran's Nuclear Conference, Will Discourage Others From Attending* (27 October 2008) posted on *The Telegraph* (4 February 2011) www.telegraph.co.uk/news/wikileaks-files/london-wikileaks/8304777/UK-WILL-NOT-PARTICIPATE-IN-IRANS-NUCLEAR-CONFERENCE-WILL-DISCOURAGE-OTHERS-FROM-ATTENDING.html (website accessed 1 November 2011).
88 Mehr News Agency (30 November 2008), BBC Monitoring.
89 See editorial in *Iran* (11 December 2008), BBC Monitoring.
90 MENAS, *Iran Strategic Focus* 4, 12 (December 2008), pp. 3–4.
91 See 2 December meeting at the *Majlis* entitled '30 years of legislation and supervision', MENAS, *Iran Strategic Focus* 4, 12 (December, 2008), pp. 1–3.
92 Disclosed US Diplomatic Cable, *Iran: UK's Informal Comments on EU Dynamics and Iran Sanctions Prospects* (9 September 2008) posted on *The Telegraph* (4 February 2011) www.telegraph.co.uk/news/wikileaks-files/london-wikileaks/8304741/IRAN-UKS-INFORMAL-COMMENTS-ON-EU-DYNAMICS-AND-IRAN-SANCTIONS-PROSPECTS.html (website accessed 1 November 2011).
93 By December 2008, the US Mission to the IAEA said that El Baradei's position was that any 'confession' would have to be grandfathered as part of a political package as he believed that Iran would not get anything out of confessing now. With no prospect of further UNSC sanctions, his assessment was that Iran would seek to maintain the status quo until a better deal was offered. Disclosed US Diplomatic Cable, *Ref ID: IAEA: DG Discusses Syria and Iran with Acting U/S*, Origin: UNVIE (United Nations) (10 December 2008) posted on *Aftenposten* (25 August 2011) www.aftenposten.no/spesial/wikileaksdokumenter/10122008-DG-DISCUSSES-SYRIA-AND-IRAN-WITH-ACTING-US-ROOD-6284886.html (website accessed 1 December 2011).

94 On the Georgian factor, the US Embassy in London expected that tensions with Russia might be raised by the very serious matter of Georgia, but because Russia had a vested stake in preventing Iran from acquiring a nuclear weapon, it was believed that it was unlikely that Moscow would abandon the multilateral front against the Iranian government. See Disclosed US Diplomatic Cable, *Iran: Chinese Embassy Asks Whether Georgia Crisis Affects P5 + 1 Iran Posture* (22 August 2008) posted on *The Telegraph* (4 February 2011) www.telegraph.co.uk/news/ wikileaks-files/london-wikileaks/8304728/IRAN-CHINESE-EMBASSY-ASKS-WHETHER-GEORGIA-CRISIS-AFFECTS-P51S-IRAN-POSTURE.html (website accessed 1 November 2011).

95 Heinrich Böll Stiftung, *Iran Report Nr.9* (2008), p. 18; Iranian MP Mostafa Kavakebian urged the government to take advantage of the new emerging Cold War between Russia and the United States; Aftab-e Yazd (24 August, 2008), BBC Monitoring.

96 The German government reportedly insisted on agreement among all twenty-seven EU government but also among a significant number of non-Western governments. These prerequisites, according to the FCO Iran Coordination Group Multilateral Team Leader, effectively nullified the point of the 'E-4/Coalition of the Willing' exercise. Disclosed US Diplomatic Cable, *Iran: UK Current Posture – FCO Formal And Informal Views* (14 October 2008) posted on *The Telegraph* (4 February 2011) www.telegraph.co.uk/news/wikileaks-files/london-wikileaks/8304765/IRAN-UK-CURRENT-POSTURE-FCO-FORMAL-AND-INFORMAL-VIEWS.html (website accessed 1 November 2011).

97 To the FCO, German hesitation on supporting further measures was due to 'commercial interests, infighting within German ministries and a fundamental unwillingness to use the institutions of the EU in a forward-leaning way'. Disclosed US Diplomatic Cable, *Iran: UK's Informal Comments on EU Dynamics and Iran Sanctions Prospects* (9 September 2008) posted on *The Telegraph* (4 February 2011) www.telegraph.co.uk/news/wikileaks-files/london-wikileaks/8304741/IRAN-UKS-INFORMAL-COMMENTS-ON-EU-DYNAMICS-AND-IRAN-SANCTIONS-PROSPECTS.html (website accessed 1 November 2011).

98 Ibid. Chancellor Merkel expected the US, under the new leadership, to commit itself to more multilateralism; see Severin Weiland, 'Merkel Ersehnt Ende der US–Alleingänge', *Spiegel Online* (5 November 2011), www.spiegel.de/politik/deutschland/0,1518,588673,00.html (website accessed 10 January 2012).

99 Disclosed US Diplomatic Cable, *P3 Consultations on Non-Proliferation and Disarmament in Paris* (21 November 2008) posted on *The Telegraph* (4 February 2011) www.telegraph.co.uk/news/wikileaks-files/iran-wikileaks/8299119/ P3-CONSULTATIONS-ON-NONPROLIFERATION-AND-DISARMAMENT-IN-PARIS.html (website accessed 1 November 2011).

100 Disclosed US Diplomatic Cable, *Turkey: Babacan Discusses Iran, Iraq with UK FS Miliband* (13 November 2008) posted on *The Telegraph* (4 February 2011) www.telegraph.co.uk/news/wikileaks-files/london-wikileaks/8304856/TURKEY-BABACAN-DISCUSSES-IRAN-IRAQ-WITH-UK-FS-MILIBAND.html (website accessed 1 November 2011).

101 Ibid.

5 Engagement with Iran the Obama Years (2009–2012)

1 Scott Peterson, 'For Iran, WikiLeaks cables validate its skepticism of Obama's sincerity', *The Christian Science Monitor* (30 November 2010) www.csmonitor.com/ World/Middle-East/2010/1130/For-Iran-WikiLeaks-cables-validate-its-skepticism-of-Obama-s-sincerity (website accessed 28 December 2011); Bernd Kaussler and Anthony Newkirk, 'Diplomacy in bad faith – American Iranian relations today', pp. 369–370.

2 White House, Office of the Press Secretary, 'The President's message to the Iranian people' (20 March, 2009), www.whitehouse.gov/video/The-Presidents-Message-to-the-Iranian-People#transcript (website accessed 1 February 2009).
3 'Obama renews sanctions on Iran', BBC News (13 March 2009), http://news.bbc.co.uk/2/hi/americas/7941031.stm (website accessed 1 February 2011).
4 Islamic Republic of Iran News Network (21 March, 2009), BBC Monitoring. For a transcript of Khamenei's speech, see Al-Alam TV (21 March 2009), BBC Monitoring. See also Farideh Farhi, 'Iran–US: deal with the elephant in the room!' Inter Press Service (7 April 2009), www.ipsnews.net/news.asp?idnews=46422 (10 December 2009).
5 For a statement by Iran's Deputy Oil Minister for International Affairs on the impact of sanctions and much-needed US investments in Iran's oil industry, see Stanley Reed, 'Iran diary: a thawing with the US?' (13 April 2009), www.businessweek.com/globalbiz/content/apr2009/gb20090413_335347.htm (2 February 2010).
6 *Keyhan* website (7 June 2009), BBC Monitoring.
7 See several editorials in Iranian newspapers, for example Quds website (28 February 2009), BBC Monitoring. The Supreme Leader's unofficial media mouthpiece, *Keyhan*, called Ross 'a Zionist lobbyist in the US administration' and a former member of the Iranian delegation negotiating the nuclear file', Kaveh Afrasiabi said that 'Iranians have serious misgivings about Dennis Ross because of his close ties to the pro-Israel lobby … not to mention Ross's recent writings that push for tough actions against Iran while de-prioritizing the Israel–Palestinian issue'; Hadi Nili, 'Iranians' hope for US policy shift dims', *Washington Times* (11 January 2009), www.washingtontimes.com/news/2009/jan/11/iranians-short-on-hope-for-change/print/ (website accessed 12 February 2012).
8 Disclosed US Diplomatic Cable, *Ehud Barak Sets Deadline to Resolve Iran Nuclear Ambition* (1 June 2009) posted on *The Guardian* (28 December 2010) www.guardian.co.uk/world/us-embassy-cables-documents/209599 (website accessed 16 December 2011).
9 See US Diplomatic Cable, *HMG Shares US Strategy and Concerns Regarding IAEA Reports on Iran and Syria*, Origin: Embassy London (25 February 2009) posted on *The Telegraph* (4 February 2011) www.telegraph.co.uk/news/wikileaks-files/london-wikileaks/8305166/HMG-SHARES-U.S.-STRATEGY-AND-CONCERNS-REGARDING-IAEA-REPORTS-ON-IRAN-AND-SYRIA.html (website accessed 27 November 2011).
10 Disclosed US Diplomatic Cable, *IAEA/Iran: P5 + 1 Experts Meeting Useful Mechanism for Technical Dialogue* (29 April 2009), posted on the *Guardian* website, www.guardian.co.uk/world/us-embassy-cables-documents/204636 (website accessed 12 January 2012).
11 Ibid.
12 Julian Borger, 'Wikileaks cables: Iran had cleared major hurdle to nuclear weapons' *Guardian* (20 January 2011), www.guardian.co.uk/world/2011/jan/20/iran-highly-enriched-uranium-wikileaks (website accessed 12 February 2012).
13 Hilary Leila Krieger, 'AIPAC set to push Iran legislation at major conference', *The Jerusalem Post* (3 May 2009), www.jpost.com/IranianThreat/News/Article.aspx?id=140827 (website accessed 15 February 2011).
14 Disclosed US Diplomatic Cable, *Ref ID: TEL AVIV 001060, US Embassy Cables: Israel 'Can't Afford to be Wrong about Iran'*, Origin: Embassy Tel Aviv (13 May 2009), Classification: Secret; www.guardian.co.uk/world/us-embassy-cables-documents/206775?intcmp=239 (website accessed 15 February 2009).
15 Disclosed US Diplomatic Cable posted on *The Telegraph* (4 February 2011); Disclosed US Diplomatic Cable, *Ref ID: 09LONDON566 Iran: Khamenei Said to Consider Rahim Safavi and to Write Off Qalibaf, Velayati May Have Key Adviser Role* (3 March 2009); at the same time, a British MP was purportedly planning to travel to Iran to meet with Velayati in order to establish a channel of communication to the

146 *Notes*

US government. According to the MP, Khamenei, not Ahmadinejad, was 'the correct return address for' engagement. Ibid. www.telegraph.co.uk/news/wikileaks-files/london-wikileaks/8305177/IRAN-KHAMENEI-SAID-TO-CONSIDER-RAHIM-SAFAVI-AND-TO-WRITE-OFF-QALIBAF-VELAYATI-MAY-HAVE-KEY-ADVISORY-ROLE.html (website accessed 13 November 2011).

16 Disclosed US Diplomatic Cable, *O 181750Z JUN 09 SIPDIS E.O. 12958: DECL 'Iran: Salman Safavi Says Election Precluded by "Political Coup", Urges USG to Focus on Human Rights and Political Support for Protestors'* (18 June 2009), posted on www.enduringamerica.com/home/2011/9/16/wikileaks-iran-special-june-2009-brother-of-supreme-leaders.html (website accessed 16 February 2012).

17 Ibid. Also see Disclosed US Diplomatic Cable, *Ref ID: P 281409Z AUG 09, Iran: A XXXXX Contact Shares Views from a Rafsanjani Business Ally on Khamenei's Cancer and Rafsanjani's Next Steps*, posted on website www.enduringamerica.com/home/2010/11/29/wikileaks-iran-document-dubious-intelligence-election-fraud.html (website accessed 15 February 2012).

18 Alireza Nader and Joya Laha, *Iran's Balancing Act in Afghanistan: Occasional Paper Series* (Santa Monica: RAND Corporation, 2011).

19 Senior Policy Advisor to the Afghan Ministry of Foreign Affairs, email message to author (29 December 2009).

20 Bernd Kaussler and Anthony Newkirk, 'Diplomacy in bad faith: American–Iranian relations today' *Diplomacy & Statecraft* 23, 2 (2012), p. 353. In a 2007 US State Department cable, US Under Secretary of Defence for Policy Eric Edelman warned 'that Iranian support for Afghan insurgents was getting increasingly lethal' and alluded to reports that 'the Iranians are supplying insurgents in Afghanistan with deadly explosively formed projectile weapons and shoulder-launched surface to air missiles'. While Edelman appreciated that Afghanistan wanted to avoid a 'two-front' war, he warned President Karzai that if Iranians actions were not checked 'it will result in a two-front war in any event'. To that end, the US envoy considered the pending new sanctions against the IRGC Quds Force as an effective means to end Iran's assistance to insurgents. See Disclosed US Diplomatic Cable, *Ref ID: EO 12958 DECL, Iran 'Busy' Trying to Undermine the US in Afghanistan*, Origin: Embassy Kabul (10 November 2007), posted on www.guardian.co.uk/world/us-embassy-cables-documents/129626?intcmp=239 (website accessed 17 February 2012).

21 Bernd Kaussler and Anthony Newkirk, 'Diplomacy in bad faith: American–Iranian relations today', pp. 351–354.

22 Disclosed US Diplomatic Cable, *Ayatollah Tells Negroponte: US Must Stay Until the Job is Done*, Origin: Embassy Baghdad (11 October 2008) published on website http://dazzlepod.com/cable/08BAGHDAD3288/ (website accessed 1 January 2012).

23 Disclosed US Diplomatic Cable, *British Ambassador to Iran: Iran Sees US as its Biggest Strategic Issue* (30 November 2007) published on website http://wikileaks.org/cable/2007/11/07BAGHDAD3903.html (website accessed 15 December 2011).

24 US intelligence analysts warned that the insurgency was partly underwritten by weapons and explosives from Iran. Intelligence reports also claimed that the IRGC's Quds Force was involved in sniper training, targeted assassinations and kidnapping plots against Iraqi officials and US military personnel. The disclosed intelligence documents are posted at the *New York Times* website, www.nytimes.com/interactive/world/iraq-war-logs.html (website accessed 15 February 2012).

25 For military operations in Basra see Institute for the Study of War, *Operation Knight's Charge (Saulat Al-Fursian)* www.understandingwar.org/operation/operation-knights-charge-saulat-al-fursan (website accessed 12 June 2012).

26 Disclosed US Diplomatic Cable, *British Ambassador to Iran: Iran Sees US as its Biggest Strategic Issue*.

27 Disclosed US Diplomatic Cable, *Iran's Efforts in Iraqi Electoral Politics*, Origin:

Embassy Baghdad (13 November 2009) posted on *The Guardian* (4 December 2010) www.guardian.co.uk/world/us-embassy-cables-documents/234583 (website accessed 15 September 2011).

28 Ibid.

29 Following the Geneva talks in 2009, the Grand Mufti of Saudi Arabia, Sheikh Abdulaziz al-Sheikh, accused Tehran of 'collusion in sin and aggression'. Ian Black, 'Middle East's regional and sectarian rivalries escalate Yemen conflict', *Guardian* (23 November, 2009), www.guardian.co.uk/world/2009/nov/23/yemen-conflict-saudi-arabia-iran (25 November 2009). Yemeni President Ali Abdullah Saleh has accused both Iran and Iraq of supporting the al Houthis rebels; *Ahram Weekly*, www.weeklyahram.org.eg/2009/963/re4htm (1 December 2009).

30 Bernd Kaussler and Anthony Newkirk, 'Diplomacy in bad faith: American–Iranian relations today', p. 359; see Ian Black, 'Arabs scorn "evil" Iran', US Embassy Cables (28 November 2010), www.guardian.co.uk/world/2010/nov/28/arab-states-scorn-iranian-evil? (accessed 29 November 2010); To that end, a diplomatic cable quotes Deputy Commander of the UAE armed forces Sheikh Mohammed bin Zayed al-Nahyan referring to Iran as an 'existential threat' and expressing concern about 'getting caught in the crossfire if Iran is provoked by the US or Israel'. Equally, in 2009, Mohammed bin Zayed, a crown prince of UAE's Abu Dhabi, called Iranian President Ahmadinejad 'Hitler' and cautioned the US government against 'appeasement'. During a meeting at the US State Department in 2008, the Saudi ambassador to the US reportedly 'recalled the King's frequent exhortations to the US to attack Iran and so put an end to its nuclear weapons program'; Ali Gharib and Jim Lobe, 'Wikileaks reveals treacherous terrain for Iran policy' (29 November 2010), http://ipsnews.net/news.asp?idnews=53704 (accessed 30 November 2010).

31 Bernd Kaussler and Anthony Newkirk, 'Diplomacy in bad faith: American–Iranian relations today', p. 361.

32 Disclosed US Diplomatic Cable, *The Great Game in Mesopotamia: Iraq and its Neighbors Part I* (24 September 2009) posted on www.nytimes.com/inter-active/2010/11/28/world/20101128-cables-viewer.html#report/iraq-09BAGHDAD 2562 (website accessed 12 February 2012).

33 In true realist fashion, the Iranian government continues to frame Gulf security as a zero-sum game, and while advocating a collective security pact of regional states, Iran's Foreign Minister continues to insist on the 'indigenization of security'. To Mottaki this meant 'the removal of extra-regional forces and their interference with the aim of creating an unhealthy rivalry among the countries and undermining their relations'. See Iranian Foreign Minister Manouchehr Mottaki's speech to the Regional Security Summit in Manama, *Tehran Times* (5 December 2010), www.tehrantimes.com/index_View.asp?code=231542 (website accessed 31 December 2010); IRNA (1 August 2010), BBC Monitoring.

34 Disclosed US Diplomatic Cable, *Iran, Analyst XXXXXXXXXXXX Argues For: Broadening Engagement on Nuclear Issue; Nuanced Human Rights Advocacy; Iran Outreach Opportunity Generated By Gaza* (23 January 2009) posted on *The Telegraph* (4 February 2011) www.telegraph.co.uk/news/wikileaks-files/london-wikileaks/8305124/IRAN-ANALYST-XXXXXXXXXXXX-ARGUES-FOR-BROADENING-ENGAGEMENT-ON-NUCLEAR-ISSUE-NUANCED-HUMAN-RIGHTS-ADVOCACY-IRAN-OUTREACH-OPPORTUNITY-GENERATED-BY-GAZA-LONDON-00000207-001.2-OF-005.html   (website accessed 1 November 2011).

35 In a conversation between a senior US official and an Iranian interlocutor at the US Embassy, the Iranian urged the US government to engagement with Iran as agreed on past proposals but 'wryly noted no one [inside Iran] knows what is really in these documents'. Disclosed US Diplomatic Cable, *Iranian Academic XXXXXXXXXXXX*

Argues Time is Ripe for West to Make An Offer (12 October 2007) posted on *The Telegraph*, www.telegraph.co.uk/news/wikileaks-files/london-wikileaks/8304921/ IRANIAN-ACADEMIC-XXXXXXXXXXXX-ARGUES-TIME-IS-RIPE-FOR-WEST-TO-MAKE-AN-OFFER.html (website accessed 1 November 2011).

36 Public Points for Qom Disclosure Key Points, posted on www.politico.com/static/PPM41_public_points_for_qom_disclosure.html39 (website accessed 15 January 2012).

37 IAEA, 'Implementation of the NPT Safeguards Agreement and relevant provisions of Security Council Resolutions 1737 (2006), 1747 (2007), 1803 (2008) and 1835 (2008) in the Islamic Republic of Iran, Report by the Director General', *GOV/2009/74* (16 November 2009), p. 3.

38 David E. Sanger and William J. Broad, 'US and allies warn Iran over nuclear deception' (25 September 2009), *New York Times*, www.nytimes.com/2009/09/26/world/middleeast/26nuke.html?pagewanted=all (website accessed 16 February 2012).

39 Public Points for Qom Disclosure Key Points, posted on www.politico.com/static/PPM41_public_points_for_qom_disclosure.html39 (website accessed 15 January 2012). At the same time, Iraqi Prime Minister Maliki informed US Ambassador Hill that five members of the Sadrist-affiliated Promise Day Brigade had been arrested for attempting to smuggle Strela (SA-7B) shoulder-fired anti-aircraft missiles. The prime minister claimed that the weapons came from Syria and Iran. AP (3 February 2011) www.cbsnews.com/2100–501713_162–7313744.html (website accessed 3 November 2012).

40 Disclosed US Diplomatic Cable, *Saudis Assure China on Oil Supply* (27 January 2010), posted on *New York Times* website, www.nytimes.com/interactive/2010/11/28/world/20101128-cables-viewer.html#report/iran-10RIYADH123; Bernd Kaussler, 'From Geneva with love: breakthrough in US–Iranian relations?' *Foreign Policy in Focus* (30 October 2009), www.fpif.org/articles/from_geneva_with_love_breakthrough_in_us-iranian_relations (website accessed 15 February 2012); Gary Sick, 'Wikileaks, Iran and war' (29 November 2010), http://garysick.tumblr.com/post/1729417211/wikileaks-iran-and-war (website accessed 16 February 2012).

41 Elise Labott, *US Plans Serious Sanctions If Diplomacy Fails*, www.cnn.com/2009/POLITICS/10/06/us.iran.sanctions/ (website accessed 30 November 2011).

42 Declaring the referral to the UN Security Council and sanctions illegal, former negotiator Hassan Rowhani reminded the P5+1 about Iran's on-going compliance with the IAEA inspections regime and the NPT at large, citing thirteen unannounced inspection visits by IAEA teams in months prior to the Geneva talks. See E'temad (5 November 2009), BBC Monitoring; Bernd Kaussler and Anthony Newkirk, 'Diplomacy in bad faith: American–Iranian relations today', p. 360.

43 Disclosed US Diplomatic Cable, *U/S to EU: Need to Increase the Pressure on Iran* (20 November 2009) published on website www.cablegatesearch.net/cable.php?id=09BRUSSELS1562 (website accessed 16 December 2011).

44 Peter Crail, 'History of official proposals on the Iranian nuclear issue', *Arms Control Association*, www.armscontrol.org/factsheets/Iran_Nuclear_Proposals (website accessed 16 February 2012). The French Permanent Representative to the IAEA stated that Iran also pledged to give access to the Qom enrichment facility within 'two weeks'; AFP News Agency (Paris) (1 October 2009), BBC Monitoring. Following the meeting, Ali Shirzadi, the spokesperson for the IAEA, stated that Iran needed 200 kg of 20 per cent enriched uranium for its reactor, for which it would exchange the same amount of its 3.5 per cent enriched uranium; ISNA (10 October 2010), BBC Monitoring.

45 Peter Crail, 'Iranian response to LEU fuel deal unclear', *Arms Control Association* (November 2009), www.armscontrol.org/print/3936 (website accessed 14 November 2009).

46 Gary Sick, 'Real progress with Iran', *The Daily Beast* (2 October 2009), www. thedailybeast.com/articles/2009/10/02/real-progress-with-iran.html (29 December 2011).

47 Bericht des Österreichischen Botschafters (29 November) on www.oe24.at/oesterreich/chronik/Bericht-des-oesterreichischen-Botschafters/11412235 (website accessed 12 October 2011).

48 See Gareth Porter, 'Obama's Iranian discontent', *Agence Global* (9 December 2009).

49 E'temad (5 November 2009), BBC Monitoring.

50 IRNA (29 October 2009), BBC Monitoring.

51 For Jalili's statement, see http://news.gooya.com/politics/archives/2009/10/094475. php (5 January, 2010).

52 Peter Crail, 'Iranian response to LEU fuel deal unclear'. Most MPs questioned whether one could trust the Russians and dismissed the deal as contrary to Iranian interests. See Aftab-e Yazd (27 October 2009), BBC Monitoring.

53 Cited from Disclosed US Diplomatic Cable, *Tehran Nuclear Fuel Deal Drawing Domestic Political Fire* (26 October 2009) published on website www.cablegatesearch.net/cable.php?id=09RPODUBAI459 (website accessed 19 September 2011).

54 Ibid. Mehr News Agency (29 December 2009); Vision of the Islamic Republic of Iran Network 1 (9 January 2010); Press TV website (11 January 2010); Press TV website (12 December 2009), BBC.

55 Bericht des Österreichischen Botschafters (29 November) on www.oe24.at/oesterreich/chronik/Bericht-des-oesterreichischen-Botschafters/11412235 (website accessed 12 October 2011).

56 Ibid.

57 Bernd Kaussler and Anthony Newkirk, 'Diplomacy in bad faith: American–Iranian relations today', p. 367.

58 *The Guardian*, 'US embassy cables: US fails to dissuade Turkey from Iran "meddling"' (28 November 2010) www.guardian.co.uk/world/us-embassy-cables-documents/235183 (website accessed 12 November 2011).

59 Ibid.

60 Disclosed US Diplomatic Cable, *U/S to EU: Need to Increased the Pressure on Iran* (20 November 2009) published on website www.cablegatesearch.net/cable. php?id=09BRUSSELS1562 (website accessed 18 November 2011).

61 IAEA, 'Implementation of the NPT safeguards agreement and relevant provisions of Security Council Resolutions 1737 (2006),1747 (2007), 1803 (2008) and 1835 (2008) in the Islamic Republic of Iran, Resolution adopted by the Board of Governors on 27 November 2009', *GOV/2009/82*, p. 2.

62 Bericht des Österreichischen Botschafters (29 November) on www.oe24.at/oesterreich/chronik/Bericht-des-oesterreichischen-Botschafters/11412235 (website accessed 12 October 2011).

63 Disclosed US Diplomatic Cable, *IAEA/Iran: Technical Briefing Largely Focuses on Qom* (20 November 2009) published on website www.cablegatesearch.net/cable. php?id=09UNVIEVIENNA530 (website accessed 20 December 2011).

64 Ibid.

65 'Iran nukes latest offer despite initial hope', *Jane's Intelligence Weekly* (26 January 2010), http://articles.janes.com/articles/Janes-Intelligence-Weekly-2010/Iran-nukes-latest-offer-despite-initial-hope.html (website accessed 18 February 2012).

66 Disclosed US Diplomatic Cable, *Iran Ups Its Nuclear Ante to 20 Percent*, Origin: UNVIE (8 February 2010) published on website www.cablegatesearch.net/cable.php ?id=10UNVIEVIENNA43&version=1314919461 (website accessed 21 December 2011).

67 Ibid.

68 Ibid.

69 Ibid.
70 Disclosed US Diplomatic Cable, *IAEA/Board/Iran: Russia's Toughening Stance; PRC Plays to Type*, (February 2010) published on website www.cablegatesearch. net/cable.php?id=10UNVIEVIENNA76 (website accessed 23 December 2011).
71 Ibid.
72 Ibid.
73 Vision of the Islamic Republic of Iran Network 1 (11 February 2010) BBC Monitoring; Parisa Hafezi, 'Iran says nuclear fuel production goes "very well" ', Reuters (11 February 2010); for the EU statement see Statement by Robert Cooper following the EU-3+3 meeting on Iran in Brussels (20 November 2009) www.consil-ium.europa. eu/uedocs/cms_data/docs/.../111386.pdf (website accessed 16 February 2012); Disclosed US Diplomatic Cable, *UK Views on Iran Sanctions: UN, EU and US* (15 January 2010) posted on *The Telegraph*, www.telegraph.co.uk/news/wikileaks-files/ london-wikileaks/8304866/UK-VIEWS-ON-IRAN-SANCTIONS-UN-EU-AND-U.S.html (website accessed 10 January 2012). Disclosed US Diplomatic Cable, *Demarche Delivered: UK Wants to Use UPR to Pressure Iran on Human Rights* (28 January 2010) posted on *The Telegraph* (4 February 2011) www.telegraph.co.uk/ news/wikileaks-files/london-wikileaks/8304882/C-DEMARCHE-DELIVERED-UK-WANTS-TO-USE-UPR-TO-PRESSURE-IRAN-ON-HUMAN-RIGHTS.html; www. reuters.com/article/idUSTRE61A4AS 20100211 (15 March 2010) (website accessed 13 November 2011). Disclosed US Diplomatic Cable, *Outreach for Iran, Universal Periodic Review Session* (25 January 2010) published on website www.cablegate-search.net/cable.php?id=10SOFIA89 l (website accessed 13 November 2011).
74 Peter Crail, 'History of official proposals on the Iranian nuclear issue', *Arms Control Association*, www.armscontrol.org/factsheets/Iran_Nuclear_Proposals.
75 Jon Leyne, 'Iran hit by fresh UN nuclear sanctions threat', BBC News (19 May 2010), www.bbc.co.uk/news/10124238 (website accessed 1 January 2012).
76 Bernd Kaussler and Anthony Newkirk, 'Diplomacy in bad faith: American–Iranian relations today', p. 367.
77 *The Guardian*, 'US embassy cables: US fails to dissuade Turkey from Iran "meddling" ' (28 November 2010) www.guardian.co.uk/world/us-embassy-cables-documents/235183 (website accessed 17 November 2011).
78 See Disclosed US Diplomatic Cable, *Ref ID: 10ANKARA87 What Lies Beneath Ankara's New Foreign Policy* (20 January 2010) published on website http://wikile-aks.ch/cable/2010/01/10ANKARA87.html (website accessed 19 November 2011).
79 'Germany, EU react with caution to Iran nuclear deal', *Deutsche Welle* (17 May 2011), www.dw-world.de/dw/article/0,,5580253,00.html (website accessed 12 February 2012).
80 A cable from the US Embassy in Brazil in December 2009 described Brazil's foreign policy towards Iran to be working against US interests. Assessing Brazil's new assertive position in international relations, the cable stated:

> Brazil's own military and civilian nuclear programs have made it more difficult to work with them on non-proliferation, and have led to the GOB's refusal to sign an Additional Protocol and lop-sided advocacy of Iran's rights to civilian nuclear technology. Even further from Brazil's historical interests, high-level exchanges of visits with Iran and increasingly intense engagement in the Middle East peace process are among recent high-profile forays into new areas of global import.
>
> (Disclosed US Diplomatic Cable, *Brazil, Scenesetter for the December 13–14 Visit of WHA Assistant Secretary Arthuro Valenzuela*, Origin: Embassy Brasilia (10 December 2009) published on website www.cablegatesearch.net/cable. php?id=09BRASILIA1129) (website accessed 12 November 2011).

81 Cited in Disclosed US Diplomatic Cable, *Iran's Uranium Program, EU Sanctions and IRISL Activities in Port of Antwerp* (26 February 2010) published on website

www.cablegatesearch.net/cable.php?id=10BRUSSELS233 (website accessed 12 November 2011).

82 The US Permanent Representative wrote in February 2010:

> The report is sharper in tone and more clinical than those produced during former IAEA DG El Baradei's tenure. As the first such report of the Amano era, it creates a positive precedent for how he intends to run safeguards investigations.
> (Disclosed US Diplomatic Cable, *IAEA/Iran: DG Amano Gives Failing Grade to Tehran in His First Report* (19 February 2012) published on website www. cablegatesearch.net/cable.php?id=10UNVIEVIENNA66)
> (website accessed 1 November 2011).

83 Ibid.
84 See Michael Adler 'Why the Istanbul talks failed', *USIP – The Iran Primer* (23 January 2011), http://iranprimer.usip.org/blog/2011/jan/23/why-istanbul-talks-failed (website accessed 5 September 2011).
85 Scott Lucas, 'Iran nuke talks follow-up: so why did the Istanbul discussion collapse?' (24 January 2011), www.enduringamerica.com/home/2011/1/24/iran-nuke-talks-follow-up-so-why-did-the-istanbul-discussion.html.
86 President Mahmoud Ahmadinejad's answer to a question on the Istanbul talks during a TV interview aired on Vision of the Islamic Republic of Iran (19 January 2011), BBC Monitoring.
87 AFP (22 January 2011), BBC Monitoring.
88 See *Deutscher Bundestag Drucksache 17/8843 17*, Wahlperiode (29 February 2012), Antwort der Bundesregierung, http://dipbt.bundestag.de/dip21/btd/17/088/1708843. pdf, pp. 8–9 (website accessed 27 November 2012).
89 Seyed Hossein Mousavian, 'How to engage Iran – what went wrong last time and how to fix it', *Foreign Affairs* (9 February 2012), www.foreignaffairs.com/ARTICLES/137095/hossein-mousavian/how-to-engage-iran?page=show (website accessed 15 February 2012).
90 Agence France-Presse, 'No snap checks of atomic units: Iran nuclear chief', *Khaleej Times* (6 September 2011), www.khaleejtimes.com/displayarticle.asp?xfile=data/middleeast/2011/September/middleeast_September102. xml&section=middleeast&col= (20 September 2011).
91 Bernd Kaussler and Anthony Newkirk, 'Diplomacy in bad faith: American–Iranian relations today', pp. 367–368.
92 Remarks by Ambassador Susan E. Rice, US Permanent Representative to the United Nations, at a Security Council Briefing on Iran and Resolution 1737, 21 December 2011, http://usun.state.gov/briefing/statements/2011/179300.htm (website accessed 29 December 2011); 'Implementation of the NPT Safeguards Agreement and relevant provisions of Security Council resolutions in the Islamic Republic of Iran Report by the Director General', IAEA, *GOV/2011/65* (8 November, 2011), p. 8.
93 Scott Peterson, 'Iran nuclear report: why it may not be a game-changer after all', *Christian Science Monitor* (10 November 2011), www.csmonitor.com/World/Middle-East/2011/1109/Iran-nuclear-report-Why-it-may-not-be-a-game-changer-after-all (29 December 2011).
94 Ariel Zirulnick, 'Israel says Bangkok, Delhi, and Tbilisi attacks all linked – to Iran' *Christian Science Monitor* (15 February 2012), www.csmonitor.com/World/terrorism-security/2012/0215/Israel-says-Bangkok-Delhi-and-Tbilisi-attacks-all-linked-to-Iran (website accessed 12 October 2012).
95 Farideh Farhi, 'Narrowing the options on the table', *Middle East Research and Information Project* (8 December 2011), www.merip.org/mero/mero120811 (website

accessed 29 December 2011). see also Bernd Kaussler and Anthony Newkirk, 'Diplomacy in bad faith: American–Iranian relations today', p. 368.

96 Bernd Kaussler and Anthony Newkirk, 'Diplomacy in bad faith: American–Iranian relations today'.

97 During a testimony before the Select Committee on the European Union of the House of Lords, Alistair Burt, MP, Parliamentary Under-Secretary of State, Foreign and Commonwealth Office, stated on the workings of sanctions:

> It was noticeable that a further round of sanctions in 2010, and the squeeze there, took the Iranians back to the table for the Istanbul talks at the beginning of 2011. They were not effective, but they came and the door was kept open. Then I would argue that the further rounds of sanctions in 2011 has now produced, after many months, a response to the letter from Catherine Ashton ... in October to the Iranians for a further opportunity for talks, which has just been responded to a few weeks ago by the Iranians and has now been responded to by Baroness Ashton saying that we are looking for those talks.
>
> (House of Lords, transcript of evidence taken before the Select Committee on the European Union Foreign Affairs, Defence and Development Policy (Sub-Committee C) Inquiry on the EU and Iran, *Evidence Session No. 1. Heard in Public. Questions 1–41* (15 March 2012), www.parliament.uk/documents/lords-committees/eu-sub-com-c/c150312Burt.pdf (website accessed 25 November 2012))

In previous replies to Ashton, the Iranian government agreed to talk about areas where all parties agreed and which did not actually include the nuclear programme; see *Deutscher Bundestag* 17. Wahlperiode, *Drucksache17/8857* (29 February 2012), p. 17.

98 Howard LaFranchi, 'Iran nuclear talks: what world powers are offering, Iran isn't buying. Yet', *Christian Science Monitor* (24 May 2012), www.csmonitor.com/USA/Foreign-Policy/2012/0524/Iran-nuclear-talks-What-world-powers-are-offering-Iran-isn-t-buying.-Yet (website accessed 23 November 2012).

99 By Kelsey Davenport, Daryl G. Kimball and Greg Thielmann, 'The November 2012 IAEA report on Iran and its implications', *Arms Control Now* (16 November 2012), http://armscontrolnow.org/2012/11/16/the-november-2012-iaea-report-on-iran-and-its-implications-2/ (website accessed 26 November 2012).

100 Christopher de Bellaigue, 'Sanctions have crippled Iran's economy, but they're not working', *The Free Republic* (12 November 2012), www.tnr.com/print/article/politics/109971/the-sanctions-have-crippled-irans-economy-theyre-not-working (website accessed 16 November 2012).

101 Matthew M. Reed, 'Iranian oil survey: autumn update', *Tehran Bureau – PBS* (21 September 2012), www.pbs.org/wgbh/pages/frontline/tehranbureau/2012/09/business-2012-iranian-oil-survey-autumn-update.html (website accessed 16 November 2012).

102 Farideh Farhi, 'On the politics of how well sanctions are working' (19 October 2012), www.lobelog.com/on-the-politics-of-how-well-sanctions-are-working/ (website accessed 16 November 2012).

103 Ibid.

104 In his memoirs, El Baradei claims that President Ahmadinejad sent a message in 2009, through him offering Obama a grand bargain which would have covered a myriad of strategic interests, including Iranian support in Afghanistan. El Baradei claims that the Obama administration never responded to this initiative. See Mohamed El Baradei, *The Age of Deception: Nuclear Diplomacy in Treacherous Times* (New York: Metropolitan Books, 2011), pp. 191–214.

105 In a cable from the US Secretary of State, diplomatic posts were given the official deadline to report their efforts by 25 November 2009. In the cable it says that

President Obama, Secretary Clinton, and others have identified the end of the year as a key period for assessing Iran's responsiveness. If Iran continues to refuse to take meaningful steps to meet its international obligations, the international community must be prepared to take strong collective action on the pressure track.

(Disclosed US Diplomatic Cable, *US Posture on Iran's Nuclear Program and Next Steps*, Origin: Secretary of State (21 November 2009) published on website http://wikileaks.org/cable/2009/11/09STATE120288.html) (website accessed 16 October 2011).

106 Disclosed US Diplomatic Cable, *Turkey/Iran Nuclear: Turkey Still Trying TRR Deal, Urges Patience* (15 November 2009) published on website http://wikileaks. org/cable/2009/11/09ANKARA1704.html (website accessed 4 January 2012).

107 Disclosed US Diplomatic Cable, *Under Secretary December 9, 2009 Conversation with Chinese Foreign Minister*, Origin: Embassy Beijing (11 December 2009) published on website www.cablegatesearch.net/cable.php?id=09BEIJING3312 (website accessed 5 January 2012).

108 Disclosed US Diplomatic Cable, *Ref ID: 09LONDON707, PM Brown Presses for Sage Nuclear Power, Compliant Iran, and Progress on Global Disarmament*, posted on *The Telegraph* (4 December 2010) www.telegraph.co.uk/news/wikileaks-files/london-wikileaks/8305197/PM-BROWN-PRESSES-FOR-SAFE-NUCLEAR-POWER-COMPLIANT-IRAN-AND-PROGRESS-ON-GLOBAL-DISARMAMENT. html (website accessed 6 December 2011).

109 Disclosed US Diplomatic Cable, *O 181750Z JUN 09 SIPDIS E.O. 12958: DECL: Iran: Salman Safavi Says Election Precluded by 'Political Coup', Urges USG to Focus on Human Rights and Political Support for Protestors* (18 June 2009), posted on www.enduringamerica.com/home/2011/9/16/wikileaks-iran-special-june-2009-brother-of-supreme-leaders.html.

110 Disclosed US Diplomatic Cable, *Iran Analyst XXXXXXXXXXXX Argues for: Broadening Engagement on Nuclear Issue; Nuanced Human Rights Advocacy; Iran Outreach Opportunity Generated by Gaza London*, posted on *The Telegraph* (23 January 2009) www.telegraph.co.uk/news/wikileaks-files/london-wikileaks/8305124/ IRAN-ANALYST-XXXXXXXXXXXX-ARGUES-FOR-BROADENING-ENGAGEMENT-ON-NUCLEAR-ISSUE-NUANCED-HUMAN-RIGHTS-ADVOCACY-IRAN-OUTREACH-OPPORTUNITY-GENERATED-BY-GAZA-LONDON-00000207–001.2-OF-005.html (website accessed 12 November 2012).

111 Reza Marashi, 'Dealing with Iran', *The Cairo Review of Global Affairs* (November 2012), www.aucegypt.edu/gapp/cairoreview/Pages/default.aspx (website accessed 25 November 2012).

6 Not one iota of retreat: EU, US and Iranian Diplomacy

1 Walter Posch, 'Iran and the European Union', *The Iran Primer – USIP*, http://iranprimer. usip.org/resource/iran-and-european-union (website accessed 12 November 2012).

2 See Bernd Kaussler, 'British–Iranian relations, *The Satanic Verses* and the fatwa: a case of two-level game diplomacy', *British Journal of Middle Eastern Studies* 38, 2 (1 August 2011), pp. 203–225.

3 See Bernd Kaussler, 'European Union constructive engagement with Iran – an exercise in conditional human rights diplomacy', *Iranian Studies* 41, 3 (2008), pp. 269–295.

4 Walter Posch, 'Iran and the European Union', *The Iran Primer – USIP*.

5 European Commission, Brussels European Council (12 December 2003) *Presidency Conclusions Reference Doc/03/5*, http://europa.eu/rapid/press-release_DOC-03-5_en. htm?locale=en (website accessed 12 November 2012).

6 Cited from briefing of Prime Minister Berlusconi by US officials, Disclosed US

Diplomatic, *Winning Italy Over on Iraq – Corrected Version Technical* (23 September 2002) published on website http://dazzlepod.com/cable/02ROME4484/?rss=1 (website accessed 19 November 2011).

7 Disclosed US Diplomatic Cable, *Italy's EU Presidency Has Uneven Success but Delivers on US Security Interests*, Origin: Embassy Rome (29 December 2003) published on website www.cablegatesearch.net/cable.php?id=03ROME5665 (website accessed 13 November 2011).

8 Disclosed US Diplomatic Cable, *IAEA/Iran: Dutch MFA Nonpro Chief on Elbaradei Report* (13 November 2003) published on website www.cablegatesearch.net/cable.php?id=03THEHAGUE2846 (website accessed 13 November 2011).

9 Disclosed US Diplomatic Cable, *EU–Iran: Solana's January Trip to Tehran, Origin* (11 December 2003).

10 See Nuclear Threat Initiaitve, *EU Drafts Iran Security Council Referral Resolution* (18 January 2006) www.nti.org/gsn/article/eu-drafts-iran-security-council-referral-resolution/ (website accessed 12 April 2013).

11 See Walther Posch, 'Iran and the European Union', *The Iran Primer* (United States Institute of Peace); Stephan Bierling, *No More 'Sondwerg': German Foreign Policy Under Chancellor Merkel*, Kondrad Adenauer Stiftung (15 September 2006) www.kas.de/wf/doc/kas_9114-1522-2-30.pdf?060916131555 (website accessed 12 September 2012).

12 Disclosed US Diplomatic Cable, *IAEA/Iran: UK and France Look Forward, DG to Meet Miliband.*

13 Walter Posch, 'Iran and the European Union', *The Iran Primer – USIP.*

14 Bericht des Österreichischen Botschafters (29 November) published on website www.oe24.at/oesterreich/chronik/Bericht-des-oesterreichischen-Botschafters/11412235 (website accessed 12 October 2011).

15 Peter Crail, 'IAEA details Iran's alleged warhead work', *Arms Control Today* (October 2011), www.armscontrol.org/act/2011_10/IAEA_to_Detail_Iran_Alleged_Warhead_Work (website accessed 12 November).

16 Meghan L. O'Sullivan, *Shrewd Sanctions: Statecraft and State Sponsors of Terrorism* (Washington, DC: Brookings, 2003), p. 55; *Bulletin of the European Union EU-4–1996* (1.4.82) Council conclusions on the Helms–Burton Act; *Bulletin of the European Union 7/8–1996* (1.4.14), EU Rapid Press Release, 'Irish Presidency and Commission protested to the US Administration against the Iran Libya Sanctions Act', *Rapid Reference IP/96/793* (9 August 1996).

17 A main concern to the US government was the fact that the process of initiating EU-wide sanctions was the political decision-making process involving twenty-seven member states and subsequent legal challenges in respective courts as well as the European Court of Justice. See Disclosed US Diplomatic Cable, *US-EU Sanctions Informal* (25 February 2010); Disclosed US Diplomatic Cable, *The EU and Sanctions (Introducing the EU, Part VIII).*

18 For a good comparison of EU and US perception of diplomacy towards Iran, see Curtis H. Martin, ' "Good cop/bad cop" as a model for non-proliferation policy toward North Korea and Iran', *The Non Proliferation Review* 14, 1 (2007), pp. 61–88.

19 Disclosed US Diplomatic Cable, *The EU and Sanctions.*

20 Disclosed US Diplomatic Cable, *Germany Deputy NSA Believes Timing Could Undermine MD Efforts at NATO Summit*, Origin: Embassy Berlin (26 February 2010) published on website www.cablegatesearch.net/cable.php?id=10BERLIN218 (website accessed 15 November 2011).

21 Disclosed US Diplomatic Cable, *German MFA Hope Iran Sanctions Target Leaders Not Masses* (21 January 2010) published on website http://wikileaks.org/cable/2010/01/10BERLIN81.html (website accessed 15 November 2011).

22 Disclosed US Diplomatic Cable, *Iran's Uranium Program, EU Sanctions and IRISL Activities in Port of Antwerp* (26 February 2010) published on website www.cable-

gatesearch.net/cable.php?id=10BRUSSELS233 (website accessed 15 November 2011).

23 Cited in Paul Mutter, 'Treasury touts economic unrest in Iran as policy success; UANI urges "economic blockade" ', *LobeLog Foreign Policy* (5 October 2012) www.lobelog.com/treasury-touts-economic-unrest-in-iran-as-policy-success-uani-urges-economic-blockade/ (website accessed 18 November 2012).

24 Djavad Salehi-Isfahani, *Should the United States Rethink Sanctions Against Iran? Opinion* (6 August 2012), Brookings, www.brookings.edu/research/opinions/2012/08/sanctions-iran-salehi-isfahani (website accessed 12 November 2012).

25 See key demands by the P5 + 1 during 2012 talks, *History of Official Proposals on the Iranian Nuclear Issue*, www.armscontrol.org/factsheets/Iran_Nuclear_Proposals (website accessed 12 November 2012).

26 Cited from Council of the European Union, Brussels (23 April 2012) 5555/3/12 REV 3 Presse 15 Updated Version, Factsheet, *The European Union and Iran*, http://consilium.europa.eu/uedocs/cms_data/docs/pressdata/EN/foraff/127511.pdf; see also *Official Journal of the European Union*, 'Council decisions 2012/35/CFSP of 23 January 2012 amending Decision 2010/413/CFSP concerning restrictive measures against Iran', http://eur-, lex.europa.eu/LexUriServ/LexUriServ.do?uri=OJ:L:2012:019:0022:0030:EN:PDF; *Official Journal of the European Union*, 'Council decisions 2011/235/CFSP of 12 April 2011 concerning restrictive measures directed against certain persons and entities in view of the situation in Iran', http://eur-lex.europa.eu/LexUriServ/LexUriServ.do?uri=OJ:L:2011:100:0051:0057:EN:PDF; 'European Union restrictive measures (sanctions) in force (Regulations based on Article 215 TFEU and Decisions adopted in the framework of the Common Foreign and Security Policy' (updated 10 January 2012), www.eeas.europa.eu/cfsp/sanctions/docs/measures_en.pdf.

27 See Bernd Kaussler, 'From engagement to containment: EU–Iran relations and the nuclear programme: 1992–2011', *Journal of Balkan and Near Eastern Studies* 14, 1 (2012), pp. 53–76.

28 http://muse.jhu.edu/journals/international_security/v033/33.4.pressman.html.

29 Jeremy Pressman, 'Power without influence: the Bush administration's foreign policy failures in the Middle East', *International Security* 33, 4 (Spring 2009), p. 166.

30 Ibid.

31 See Arshin Adib-Moghaddam, 'Manufacturing war: Iran in the neo-conservative imagination', *Third World Quarterly* 28, 3 (April 2007), pp. 635–653.

32 See Dafna Linzer, 'Russia won't block US on Iran', *Washington Post* (12 January 2006) www.washingtonpost.com/wp-dyn/content/article/2006/01/11/AR2006011102124.html (website accessed 12 December 2012).

33 See US State Department, *United States Increases Sanctions Against the Government of Iran and its Proliferation Networks; Treasury and State Department Actions Target More Than 50 Entities Tied to Iran's Procurement, Petroleum, and Shipping Networks* (12 July 2012) www.state.gov/r/pa/prs/ps/2012/07/194923.htm (website accessed 1 December 2012).

34 Disclosed US Diplomatic Cable, *U/S Burns' Moscow Meetings* (22 January 2010) published on website www.cablegatesearch.net/cable.php?id=10MOSCOW144 (website accessed 15 November 2011).

35 Cited in Jeffrey Goldberg, 'Obama's crystal clear promise to stop Iran from getting a nuclear weapon', *The Atlantic* (2 October 2012), www.theatlantic.com/international/archive/2012/10/obamas-crystal-clear-promise-to-stop-iran-from-getting-a-nuclear-weapon/262951/ (website accessed 19 November 2012).

36 Ben Armbruster, 'Senate passes measure rejecting containment of a "nuclear weapons capable" Iran', *Think Progress* (22 September 2012), http://thinkprogress.org/security/2012/09/22/893771/senate-resolution-iran-nuclear-weapons-capable/ (website accessed 19 November 2012).

37 Paul D. Miller, 'Five pillars of American grand strategy', *Survival: Global Politics and Strategy* 54, 5 (2012), pp. 15–16.
38 Andrew Butfoy, 'American exceptionalism and President Obama's call for abolition of nuclear weapons', *Contemporary Security Policy*, DOI:10.1080/13523260.2012.72 7680 (2012), pp. 11–13.
39 Ibid, p. 12.
40 For Obama's speech on a nuclear-free world, see Ian Tranor, 'Barrack Obama launches doctrine for nuclear free world', *The Guardian* (5 April 2009) www. guardian.co.uk/world/2009/apr/05/nuclear-weapons-barack-obama (website accessed 10 November 2012); U.S. Department of State, *Strengthening the Nuclear Nonproliferation Regime: A Blueprint for Progress* (12 August 2009) www.state.gov/t/isn/rls/ rm/127886.htm (website accessed 10 November 2012); U.S. Department of State, *Priorities for Arms Control Negotiations Post-New Start* (1 February 2013) www. state.gov/t/us/205051.htm; Report of the Defense Science Board Task Force on Nuclear Deterrence Skills (September 2008) www.defense.gov/npr/docs/dsb%20 nuclear%20deterrence%20skills%20chiles.pdf (website accessed 10 November 2012); see Steven Hildreth and Carl Ek (Congressional Research Service), *Long-Range Ballistic Missile Defense in Europe* (23 September 2009), p. 5.
41 See Anthony Newkirk, 'Tracking the Saudi Arms Deal', *FPIF* (1 July 2001) www. fpif.org/articles/tracking_the_saudi_arms_deal (website accessed 1 December 2012).
42 Yair Evron, 'Extended deterrence in the Middle East', *The Nonproliferation Review* 19, 3 (2012), p. 379.
43 *IBN Live*, 'Wikileaks cablegate: Pakistan's obsession with India', (1 December 2010) http://ibnlive.in.com/news/wikileaks-cablegate-pakistans-obsession-with-india/136078–53. html (website accessed 1 January 2012).
44 Kayhan Barzegar, 'The Arab Spring and the balance of power in the Middle East', Institute for Middle East Strategic Studies (30 October 2012), http://en.merc.ir/ default.aspx?tabid=98&ArticleId=468 (website accessed 20 November 2012).
45 See statement by President Shimon Perez on Iran's alleged escalation of the conflict in Gaza, Nicole Gaouette, 'Israeli attacks in Gaza also serve as a warning to Iran', *Bloomberg News* (20 November 2012), www.businessweek.com/news/2012–11–20/ israeli-attacks-in-gaza-also-serve-as-a-warning-to-iran.
46 US Department of the Treasury, 'An overview of OFAC regulations involving sanctions against Iran', www.treasury.gov/resource-center/sanctions/Programs/Documents/iran.pdf (website accessed 21 November 2012).
47 Christina Sinha and Nasrina Bargzie, Asian Law Caucus (eds), 'Unintended victims: the impact of the Iran sanctions on Iranian Americans – November 2012', prepared by the Asian Law Caucus, the Iranian American Bar Association, the National Iranian American Council and the Public Affairs Alliance of Iranian Americans, www.asianlawcaucus.org/wp-content/uploads/Unintended-Victims_Nov-2012_FINAL-Report. pdf (website accessed 21 November 2012); see also NIAC, 'Sanctions – stand with the Iranian people', www.niacouncil.org/site/PageServer?pagename=Policy_iran_ sanctions (website accessed 19 November 2012).
48 Trita Parsi and Reza Marashi, 'How Obama can succeed on Iran', (7 November 2012), *Huffington Post*, www.huffingtonpost.com/trita-parsi/obama-iran-second-term_b_2085937.html (website accessed 15 November 2012).
49 David E. Sanger, 'Iran offers plan, dismissed by US, on nuclear crisis', *New York Times* (4 October 2012), www.nytimes.com/2012/10/05/world/middleeast/iranians-offer-9-step-plan-to-end-nuclear-crisis.html (website accessed 19 November 2012); Adrian Blomfield, 'US rejects Iran nuclear offer', *The Telegraph* (5 October 2012), www.telegraph.co.uk/news/worldnews/middleeast/iran/9590493/US-rejects-Iran-nuclear-offer.html (website accessed 19 November 2012).
50 Malou Innocent, 'The limits of coercive diplomacy with Iran, debate: should the US rethink sanctions against Iran?' (16 July 2012), Federation of American Scientists,

www.fas.org/policy/debates/20120801_iran.html#_edn1   (website   accessed   21 November 2012).

51 Yousaf Butt, 'By not lifting sanctions, West and Obama are helping Iran enrich uranium', *Christian Science Monitor* (25 May 2012), www.csmonitor.com/Commentary/Opinion/2012/0525/By-not-lifting-sanctions-West-and-Obama-are-helping-Iran-enrich-uranium (website accessed 21 November 2012).

52 As recalled by US officials in Disclosed US Diplomatic Cable, *Ref ID: 09UNVI-ENNA538, IAEA/Iran: Board of Governors Criticize Failures on Code 3.1 While Adopting a Resolution Censuring Iran*, Origin: UNVIE (United Nations) (2 December 2009), Classification: Confidential/Noforn.

53 Xenia Dormandy, 'Is India or will it be a responsible stakeholder?' *The Washington Quarterly* 30, 2 (2007), p. 122; The White House, Office of the Press Secretary (18 July 2005), 'Joint statement between President George W. Bush and Prime Minister Manmohan   Singh',   http://georgewbushwhitehouse.archives.gov/news/releases/2005/07/20050718–6.html (website accessed 19 November 2012).

54 Andrew B. Kennedy, 'India's nuclear odyssey: implicit umbrellas, diplomatic disappointments, and the bomb', *International Security* 36, 2 (Fall 2011), p. 153.

55 C. Christine Fair, 'India and Iran: a balancing act', *The Washington Quarterly* 30, 3 (2007), p. 146. India has faced severe criticism from the Non-Aligned Movement for having abandoned its historic neutrality, with many Indian politicians calling it a 'client state of the US'; see Disclosed US Diplomatic Cable, *Ref ID: 05NEW DELHI7493, Indian Government Aggressively Defending Its Vote on Iran*, Origin: Embassy New Delhi (26 September 2005), Classification: Confidential.

56 See Disclosed US Diplomatic Cable, *UN/Germany: State Secretary on Iran, Latin America and UN Reform*, (23 March 2006) published on website http://wikileaks.org/cable/2006/03/06USUNNEWYORK581.html (website accessed 12 September 2012).

57 Graham Allison, 'Red lines in the sand – Israel's credibility problem on Iran', *Foreign Policy* (12 October 2012), www.foreignpolicy.com/articles/2012/10/11/red_lines_in_the_sand (website accessed 19 November 2012).

58 'Is Israel's Gaza campaign laying the groundwork for an attack on Iran?' *The Atlantic* (21 November 2012), www.theatlantic.com/international/archive/2012/11/on-to-iran-is-israels-gaza-campaign-the-groundwork-for-an-attack-on-iran/265513/   (website accessed 5 February 2013).

59 Trita Parsi, 'Israel's diplomatic scare game', (8 August 2012) www.salon.com/2012/08/08/israels_diplomatic_scare_game/ (website accessed 19 November 2012).

60 For a good analysis on Chinese and Russian perception of the West's stewardship of the nuclear file, see Graham E. Fuller, 'Adult supervision from Moscow and Beijing', (11 February 2012) www.conflictsforum.org/2012/adult-supervision-from-moscow-and-beijing/ (website accessed 1 December 2012).

61 Laura Rozen, 'Ex-Obama official warns: take Israel Iran threat very seriously', *Al Monitor* (14 August 2012), www.al-monitor.com/pulse/originals/2012/al-monitor/israel-threats-against-iran-are.html (website accessed 20 November 2012).

62 See for example Harriet Sherwood, 'Israeli PM says time is running out to stop Iran's nuclear program', *The Guardian* (1 August 2012) www.guardian.co.uk/world/2012/aug/01/israeli-pm-iran-nuclear-programme (website accessed 1 December 2012); 'Benjamin Netanyahu: Israel wants "crippling sanctions" against Iran', (27 August 2009)   www.telegraph.co.uk/news/worldnews/middleeast/israel/6099784/Benjamin-Netanyahu-Israel-wants-crippling-sanctions-against-Iran.html (website accessed 10 July 2011).

63 Disclosed US Diplomatic Cable, *McCain's Meeting with Prime Minister Netanyahu* (27   January   2010)   published   on   website   www.cablegatesearch.net/cable.php?id=10TELAVIV180 (website accessed 12 November 2012).

64 AIPAC, 'Back tougher Iran sanctions', www.aipac.org/legislative-agenda/agenda-

display?agendaid={50658C91–75FD-4EAC-956F-2041719CF4F3} (website accessed 19 November 2012).

65 For example see Laura Rozen, 'Netanyahu aimed to provoke confrontation amid 2010 US peace push', *Al Monitor* (7 November 2012), http://backchannel.al-monitor.com/index.php/2012/11/3098/netanyahu-intended-to-provoke-us-iran-confrontation-amid-2010-us-peace-push/ (website accessed 20 November 2012).

66 Seymour Hersh, 'Our men in Iran', *The New Yorker* (6 April 2012), www.newyorker.com/online/blogs/newsdesk/2012/04/mek.html#ixzz2CwpFQ0bo (website accessed 19 November 2012).

67 Julian Borger, 'Who is responsible for the Iran nuclear scientist attacks?' *Guardian* (12 January 2012), www.guardian.co.uk/world/2012/jan/12/iran-nuclear-scientists-attacks (website accessed 20 November 2012).

68 Associated Press, 'Iranians "confess" to nuclear scientist murders on state television', *Guardian* (6 August 2012), www.guardian.co.uk/world/2012/aug/06/iranians-confess-nuclear-scientist-murders (website accessed 5 February 2013).

69 'US enters new phase of hostility towards Iran by delisting MKO', IRNA (1 October 2012), http://old.irna.ir/News/Politic/US-enters-new-phase-of-hostility-towards-Iran-by-delisting-MKO/80349352 (website accessed 21 November 2012); Jim Lobe and Jasmin Ramsey, 'US to take Iran anti-regime group off terrorism list', IPS (22 September 2012), www.ipsnews.net/2012/09/u-s-to-take-iran-anti-regime-group-off-terrorism-list/ (website accessed 12 November 2012).

70 James P. Farwell and Rafal Rohozinski, 'The new reality of cyber war', *Survival: Global Politics and Strategy* 54, 4 (June–July 2012), p. 111.

71 Ibid.

72 James P. Farwell and Rafal Rohozinski, 'Stuxnet and the future of cyber war', *Survival: Global Politics and Strategy* 53, 1 (2011), p. 29.

73 Sean Collins and Stephen McCombie, 'Stuxnet: the emergence of a new cyber weapon and its implications', *Journal of Policing, Intelligence and Counter Terrorism* 7, 1 (2012), p. 88.

74 Thomas Schelling uses the term 'compelling threat' to describe a situation in which A threatens B intending to keep him from starting something rather than intending to make B do something. The threat that compels rather than deters, therefore, often takes the form of not administering the punishment *until* the other acts, rather than administering it *if* he acts. See Philip M. Barnett, 'Rational behaviour in bargaining situations', *Noûs* 17, 4 (November 1983), pp. 623–624; for Baldwin's critique on 'complement threats' see David A. Baldwin, 'Thinking about threats', *The Journal of Conflict Resolution* 15, 1 (March 1971), pp. 71–78.

75 R. K. Ramazani, 'Iran's foreign policy: independence, freedom and the Islamic Republic', in Anoushiravan Ehteshami and Mahjoob Zweeir (eds), *Iran's Foreign Policy: From Khatami to Ahmadinejad* (Reading: Ithaca Press, 2011), p. 2.

76 Disclosed US Diplomatic Cable, *The Iranian MFA's Think-Tank Director on Iran and Regional Security* (19 May 2008) published on website www.cablegatesearch.net/cable.php?id=08ISTANBUL287 (website accessed 12 November 2012).

77 Cited in R. K. Ramazani, 'Iran must make a move to save diplomacy', *Middle East Online* (7 March, 2012), www.middle-east-online.com/english/?id=51062 (website accessed 21 November 2012).

78 Disclosed US Diplomatic Cable, *The Iranian MFA's Think-Tank Director on Iran and Regional Security*.

79 Seyed Hossein Mousavian, 'Iran, the US and weapons of mass destruction', *Survival: Global Politics and Strategy* 54, 5 (2012), p. 189.

80 Paul K. Kerr, 'Iran's nuclear program: Tehran's compliance with international obligations', Congressional Research Service (18 September 2012), p. 10.

81 Ibid.

82 David Albright, Christina Walrond and Andrea Stricker, *ISIS Analysis of IAEA Iran*

Safeguards Report, Rev. 1 (16 November 2012), http://isis-online.org/uploads/isis-reports/documents/ISIS_Analysis_IAEA_safeguards_Report_November_16_2012-final.pdf (website accessed 20 November 2012).

83 IAEA, Board of Governors, 'Implementation of the NPT Safeguards Agreement and relevant provisions of Security Council resolutions in the Islamic Republic of Iran. Report by the Director General', *Gov/2012/37* (30 August 2012), www.iaea.org/Publications/Documents/Board/2012/gov2012–37.pdf (website accessed 23 November 2012).

84 David Albright, Christina Walrond and Andrea Stricker, *ISIS Analysis of IAEA Iran Safeguards Report, Rev. 1.*

85 IAEA, *Implementation of the NPT Safeguards Agreement and Relevant Provisions of Security Council Resolutions 1737 (2006), 1747 (2007), 1803 (2008) and 1835 (2008) in the Islamic Republic of Iran Report by the Director General* GOV/2010/28 (31 May 2010); IAEA, *Implementation of the NPT Safeguards Agreement and Relevant Provisions of Security Council Resolutions in the Islamic Republic of Iran Report by the Director General GOV/2013/6* (21 February 2013).

86 David Albright, Christina Walrond and Andrea Stricker, *ISIS Analysis of IAEA Iran Safeguards Report, Rev. 1.*

87 Office of the Iranian President, 'Government will not retreat even one iota from their rights' (19 July 2012), http://president.ir/en/39706 (website accessed 21 November 2012).

88 Bernd Kaussler and Anthony Newkirk, 'Diplomacy in bad faith: American–Iranian relations today', p. 349.

89 For more on the resignation of Larijani and Saeedi, see Meir Javedanfar, 'Another Iranian nuclear negotiator resigns', *Real Clear World* (15 December 2009) http://realclearworld.com/blog/2009/12/another_iranian_nuclear_negotiator_resigns.html (website accessed 1 January 2013).

90 Cited in Farideh Farhi, 'Iran's national security and nuclear diplomacy: an insider's take' (7 August 2012), *LobeLog Foreign Policy* www.lobelog.com/irans-national-security-and-nuclear-diplomacy-an-insiders-take/ (website accessed 28 September 2012).

91 The AIOC threatened the six major Western oil companies with a law suit should they purchase any Iranian oil. This resulted in a complete boycott of oil tankers at Iranian ports and had profound economic consequences for Iran. See Mary Ann Heiss, *Empire and Nationhood: The United States, Great Britain, and Iranian Oil, 1950–1954* (New York: Columbia University Press, 1997), p. 78; Ali M. Ansari, *Modern Iran since 1921: The Pahlavis and After* (London: Longman Pearson, 2003), p. 117.

92 See Stephen Kinzer, *All the Shah's Men: An American Coup and the Roots of Middle East Terror* (New Jersey: John Wiley & Sons, 2003), pp. 167–192; for a speech by Rafsanjani on the perils of not learning from history, see Voice of Islamic Republic of Iran (23 March 2007), BBC Monitoring.

93 In the Persian Gulf, the GCC member states felt less threatened by Iran's conventional forces, which consist mainly of ageing military hardware. Iranian air power constitutes no real threat to the modern air forces of Saudi Arabia and UAE. Rather, IISS argues that the main threat to the GCC is Iran's navy, which is following irregular, asymmetric warfare. IISS, 'Chapter Seven: The Middle East and North Africa', *The Military Balance* 112, 1 (2012), p. 307.

94 See Rafael D. Frankel, 'Keeping Hamas and Hezbollah out of a war with Iran', *The Washington Quarterly* 35, 4 (2012), pp. 53–65.

Conclusion

1 See Nicholas J. Wheeler and Dani Nedal, 'Iranian nuclear negotiations: a long way from trust', *RUSI Newsbrief* 32, 4 (31 July 2012).

2 Ronald J. Fischer, 'Prenegotiation problem-solving discussions: enhancing the potential for successful negotiation', in Robert Matthews and Charles Pentland (eds), 'Getting to the table: processes of international prenegotiation', *International Journal* XLIV, 2 (Spring 1989), p. 442.

3 www.parliament.uk/documents/lords-committees/eu-sub-com-c/c150312Burt.pdf (website accessed 5 February 2013).

4 Literature on reciprocity tells us that state A must show how state B stands to gain from the new creation, without hiding the fact that it too will benefit; too great a gain for state B will arouse suspicion, whereas too great a gain for state A will not attract the other party. See I. William Zartman and Maureen R. Berman, *The Practical Negotiator* (New Haven, CT: Yale University Press, 1982), p. 72.

5 G. R. Berridge, *Diplomacy: Theory and Practice* (London: Palgrave, 2002), p. 30.

6 The conditions put forward have been articulated by Richard Haas and are cited in David W. Ziegler, *War, Peace and International Politics* (New York: Longman, 2000), p. 247.

7 I. William Zartman, 'Prenegotiation: phases and functions', in Robert Matthews and Charles Pentland (eds), 'Getting to the table: processes of international prenegotiation', *International Journal* XLIV, 2 (Spring 1989), p. 244.

8 Ibid.

9 Robert D. Putnam, 'Diplomacy and domestic politics: the logic of two-level games', *International Organization* 42, 3 (Summer, 1988), p. 434; see also James Fearon, 'Domestic political audiences and the escalation of international disputes', *American Political Science Review* 88, 3 (September, 1994), pp. 577–592.

10 Despite warnings by the White House that more punitive measures would 'undercut' talks with Iran, Congress has already indicated that it is seeking more sanctions against Iran; Trita Parsi, 'Three worries about the next Iran talks', *Al Monitor* (10 December 2012), www.al-monitor.com/pulse/originals/2012/al-monitor/three-worries-about-the-next-ira.html?utm_source=dlvr.it&utm_medium=twitter#ixzz2EiT7BijI (website accessed 14 December 2012).

11 Harold Nicholson, *The Evolution of Diplomatic Method* (London: Constable, 1954), p. 180.

12 USC US-China Institute, *US Embassy, 'PRC/Iran: Scholar Suggests U.S. Negotiate Secretly with Iran'* (28 December 2010) posted on website http://china.usc.edu/ (S(pw5zoy55llay4d555ee4lb55)A(MFpNga3jzQEkAAAAODI4ZDU1MmYtMTljYi 00Y2YxLWE0YWQtODgwZWRjODE3NjczVnqnww-MPhLTFZT3PLaty3aozcw1))/ ShowArticle.aspx?articleID=2305&AspxAutoDetectCookieSupport=1   (website accessed 12 December 2012).

13 Ibid.

14 Dominic Tierney, 'Prepare for war: "The insane plan to outlaw diplomacy with Iran"', *The Atlantic* (6 December 2011), www.theatlantic.com/international/archive/2011/12/prepare-for-war-the-insane-plan-to-outlaw-diplomacy-with-iran/249478/.

15 Mathieu von Rohr, 'US-Botschaftskabel:Schweiz Schweiz drängte sich USA als Iran-Vermittler', *Der Spiegel* (12 December 2010) aufwww.spiegel.de/politik/ausland/us-botschaftskabel-schweiz-draengte-sich-usa-als-iran-vermittler-auf-a-734057.html (website accessed 28 December 2012).

16 I. William Zartman, 'Prenegotiation: phases and functions', p. 248.

17 Disclosed US Diplomatic Cable, *Ref ID: 09BEIJING2438 PRC/Iran: Scholar Suggests US Negotiate Secretly with Iran*, Origin: Embassy Beijing (25 August, 2009), Classification: Confidential; see also Disclosed US Diplomatic Cable, *Ref ID:*

07BEIJING6638, Chinese Iran Expert Says PRC Seeking Opportunities for Mediating Role in Nuclear Crisis, Origin: Embassy Beijing (12 October 2007), Classification: Confidential.

18 Robert Jervis, 'Realism, game theory, and cooperation', *World Politics* 40, 3 (April 1988), p. 317.

19 Robert Axelrod, *The Evolution of Cooperation* (New York: Basic Books, 1984), p. 46. Homan argues that the exchange of rewards tends towards stability and continued interaction, while the exchange of punishments tends towards instability and the eventual failure of interaction in escape and avoidance; George C. Homans, *Social Behaviour: Its Elementary Forms* (New York: Harcourt, Brace and World, 1961), p. 57.

Select Bibliography

Ansari, Ali *Confronting Iran – The Failure of American Foreign Policy and the Roots of Mistrust* (London: Hurst 2006)

Arms Control Association, *History of Official Proposals on the Iranian Nuclear Issue* http://www.armscontrol.org/factsheets/Iran_Nuclear_Proposals

Axelrod, Robert, *The Evolution of Cooperation* (New York: Basic Books, 1984)

Barash, David P. (ed.) *Approaches to Peace – A Reader in Peace Studies* (Oxford: Oxford University Press, 2000)

Berridge, G.R., *Diplomacy – Theory and Practice* (London:Palgrave, 2002)

Berridge, G.R., Keens-Soper Maurice, Otte T.G., *Diplomatic Theory From Machiavelli to Kissinger* (Houndsmills, Palgrave, 2001)

Cohen, Raymond *Negotiating across cultures – International Communication in an Interdependent World*, (Washington D.C.: United States Institute of Peace Press, 2000)

Cortright, David (ed.), *The Price of Peace – Incentives and International Conflict Prevention* (New York: Rowman and Littlefield, 1997)

Coker, Christopher *The United States and South Africa 1968- 1985: Constructive Engagement and its Critics,* (Durham: Duke University Press, 1986)

Der Spiegel "Wikileaks Diplomatic Cables" http://www.spiegel.de/international/topic/wikileaks_diplomatic_cables/

Diplomatic Cables from the U.S. State Department available on http://cablegatesearch.net/

ElBaradei, Mohamed *The Age of Deception: Nuclear Diplomacy in Treacherous Times* (New York: Metropolitan Books, 2011)

Ehteshami, Anoushiravan and Zweeir, Mahjoob (eds), *Iran's Foreign Policy: From Khatami to Ahmadinejad* (Reading: Ithaca Press, 2011)

European Commission – External Action Service: Documents on EU-Iran Relations http://eeas.europa.eu/iran/index_en.htm

George, Alexander *Bridging the Gap: Theory and Practice in Foreign Policy* (Washington, DC: United States Institute for Peace, 1993)

George, Alexander and Craig, Gordon A. *Force and Statecraft – Diplomatic Problems of our Time* (Oxford: Oxford University Press, 2006)

The Guardian: "The US Embassy Cables" Database http://www.guardian.co.uk/world/interactive/2010/nov/28/us-embassy-cables-wikileaks

Haas, Richard N. *Transatlantic Tensions: The US, Europe and Problem Countries* (Washington DC: Brookings Institution, 1999)

Haas, Richard N. and. O ́Sullivan, Meghan L *Honey and Vinegar – Incentives, Sanctions and Foreign Policy*, (Washington, D.C.:Brookings Institution, 2000)

Hinnebusch, Raymond *The International Politics of the Middle East* (Manchester University Press, 2003)

House of Commons, Foreign Affairs Select Committee – Reports, Oral and Written Evidence http://www.publications.parliament.uk/pa/cm/cmfaff.htm

Hufbauer, Gary C., Schott, Jeffrey J. Elliott, Kimberly Ann. *Economic Sanctions Reconsidered- History and Current Policy* (Washington, DC, Institute for International Economics, 1990)

Kissinger, Henry, *A World Restored* (New York: Grosset & Dunalp, 1964)

Kissinger, Henry, *Diplomacy* (New York: Simon & Schuster, 1994)

International Atomic Energy Agency: Documents on IAEA and Iran http://eeas.europa.eu/iran/index_en.htm

Limbert, John W. *Negotiating With Iran – Wrestling the Ghosts of History* (Washington, DC, United States Institute of Peace Press, 2009)

Long, William, *Economic Incentives and Bilateral Cooperation* (Ann Arbor: University of Michigan Press, 1996)

Miall, Hugh, Ramsbotham, Oliver, Woodhouse, Tom, *Contemporary Conflict Resolution* (Cambridge: Polity Press, 1999)

Miyagwa, Makio *Do Economic Sanctions Work?* (London: Macmillan Press, 1992)

Mousavian, Seyed Hossein *The Iranian Nuclear Crisis – A Memoir* (Washington, DC: Carnegie Endowment for International Peace, 2012)

New York Times, "Wikileaks" www.nytimes.com/interactive/world/statessecrets.html

Nicholson, Harold *Diplomacy* (Georgetown: Institute for the Study of Diplomacy, 1988)

Nicholson, Harold *The Evolution of Diplomatic Method* (London: Constable, 1954)

Iran Primer, United States Institute for Peace http://iranprimer.usip.org/

Richmond, Oliver, Mediating in Cyprus: The Cypriot Communities and the United Nations (London: Frank Cass, 1988)

Richmond, Oliver *Maintaining Order, Making Peace*, (New York: Palgrave 2002)

Rubin J.Z. and Pruitt, D.G *Social Conflict: Escalation, Stalemate and Settlement* (New York:McGraw, 1994)

Tenet, George, *At the Center of the Storm – The CIA During America's Time of Crisis*, (New York: Haper, 2007)

Oye, Keenth A., *Cooperation Under Anarchy* (Princeton: Princeton University Press1986)

Zartman, William (ed), *Peacemaking in International Conflict: Methods and Techniques* (Washington, DC: United States Institute of Peace, 2007)

Zartman, William and Berman, Maureen R., *The Practical Negotiator* (New Haven: Yale University Press, 1983)

Ziegler, David W. *War, Peace and International Politics*, (New York: Longman, 2000)

Index